Hermann Lehner

A Formal Definition of JML in Coq

Hermann Lehner

A Formal Definition of JML in Coq
and its Application to Runtime Assertion Checking

Südwestdeutscher Verlag für Hochschulschriften

Impressum/Imprint (nur für Deutschland/only for Germany)
Bibliografische Information der Deutschen Nationalbibliothek: Die Deutsche Nationalbibliothek verzeichnet diese Publikation in der Deutschen Nationalbibliografie; detaillierte bibliografische Daten sind im Internet über http://dnb.d-nb.de abrufbar.
Alle in diesem Buch genannten Marken und Produktnamen unterliegen warenzeichen-, marken- oder patentrechtlichem Schutz bzw. sind Warenzeichen oder eingetragene Warenzeichen der jeweiligen Inhaber. Die Wiedergabe von Marken, Produktnamen, Gebrauchsnamen, Handelsnamen, Warenbezeichnungen u.s.w. in diesem Werk berechtigt auch ohne besondere Kennzeichnung nicht zu der Annahme, dass solche Namen im Sinne der Warenzeichen- und Markenschutzgesetzgebung als frei zu betrachten wären und daher von jedermann benutzt werden dürften.

Coverbild: www.ingimage.com

Verlag: Südwestdeutscher Verlag für Hochschulschriften GmbH & Co. KG
Heinrich-Böcking-Str. 6-8, 66121 Saarbrücken, Deutschland
Telefon +49 681 37 20 271-1, Telefax +49 681 37 20 271-0
Email: info@svh-verlag.de

Approved by: Zürich, ETH, Diss., 2011

Herstellung in Deutschland:
Schaltungsdienst Lange o.H.G., Berlin
Books on Demand GmbH, Norderstedt
Reha GmbH, Saarbrücken
Amazon Distribution GmbH, Leipzig
ISBN: 978-3-8381-3064-4

Imprint (only for USA, GB)
Bibliographic information published by the Deutsche Nationalbibliothek: The Deutsche Nationalbibliothek lists this publication in the Deutsche Nationalbibliografie; detailed bibliographic data are available in the Internet at http://dnb.d-nb.de.
Any brand names and product names mentioned in this book are subject to trademark, brand or patent protection and are trademarks or registered trademarks of their respective holders. The use of brand names, product names, common names, trade names, product descriptions etc. even without a particular marking in this works is in no way to be construed to mean that such names may be regarded as unrestricted in respect of trademark and brand protection legislation and could thus be used by anyone.

Cover image: www.ingimage.com

Publisher: Südwestdeutscher Verlag für Hochschulschriften GmbH & Co. KG
Heinrich-Böcking-Str. 6-8, 66121 Saarbrücken, Germany
Phone +49 681 37 20 271-1, Fax +49 681 37 20 271-0
Email: info@svh-verlag.de

Printed in the U.S.A.
Printed in the U.K. by (see last page)
ISBN: 978-3-8381-3064-4

Copyright © 2012 by the author and Südwestdeutscher Verlag für Hochschulschriften GmbH & Co. KG and licensors
All rights reserved. Saarbrücken 2012

Abstract

The Java Modeling Language (JML) is a very rich specification language for Java, which many applications use to describe the desired behavior of a program. The meaning of JML is described in a reference manual using natural language. The richness of JML, and the inherent ambiguity of natural language leads to many different interpretations of the same specification constructs in different applications.

We present a formalization of a large subset of JML in the theorem prover Coq. A formally defined semantics of JML provides an exact, unambiguous meaning for JML constructs. By formalizing the language in a theorem prover, we not only give a mathematically precise definition of the language but enable formal meta-reasoning about the language itself, its applications, and proposed extensions. Furthermore, the formalization can serve as JML front-end of a verification environment.

Frame conditions are expressed in JML by the `assignable` clause, which states the locations that can be updated by the method. For abstraction, the clause can mention dynamic data groups, which represent a set of heap locations. This set depends on the program state and may contain a large number of locations.

We present the first algorithm that checks `assignable` clauses in the presence of dynamic data groups. The algorithm performs very well on realistic and large data structures by lazily computing the set of locations in data groups and by caching already-computed results. We implemented the algorithm in OpenJML.

As an important contribution to runtime assertion checking, and as an interesting application of our formalization of JML in Coq, we proved in Coq that our algorithm behaves equivalently to the formalized JML semantics. This shows not only soundness and completeness of our algorithm to check `assignable` clauses, but also the usefulness and expressiveness of our JML formalization.

Online Resources

The Coq sources of our formalization of JML and the proof of the runtime assertion checker are too big to be printed as an Appendix. We refer the interested reader to the web-presence of this work. Beside the thesis and the formalization in Coq, we provide examples and the OpenJML implementation of our algorithm on this page.

<code>http://jmlcoq.info/</code>

Contents

1 **Introduction**   1
    1.1 Motivation 1
    1.2 Goals 4
          A Formal Definition of JML in Coq 4
          An Efficient RAC for Assignable Clauses 5
          A Machine Checkable Proof of the RAC 5
    1.3 Approach 6
    1.4 Scientific Contributions 7
    1.5 Related Work 7
    1.6 Overview 12
    1.7 Conventions 13
          Coq Source Text 13
          Coq Proofs 15
          JML Source Code 15
    1.8 Preliminaries 17
        1.8.1 Coq 17
              Inductive Definitions 17
              The Curry-Howard Isomorphism 18
              Short Introduction to Other Constructs 20
        1.8.2 JML 21
              Overview 21
              Method Specifications 22
              Frame Conditions 23

2 **A JML Formalization in Coq**   27
    2.1 Approach 27
    2.2 Architecture 28
        2.2.1 Basis of the Formalization 30
        2.2.2 Axiomatizations in Coq 31
    2.3 Language Coverage 31
    2.4 Definition of JML Syntax Constructs 33
        2.4.1 Basic Syntax Constructs 36

v

		JML Programs	36
		Classes and Interfaces	37
		Fields	40
		Methods	42
		Statements and Blocks	45
		Expressions	47
	2.4.2	Syntactic Rewritings	48
	2.4.3	Notations	50
2.5	A Domain for Java Programs in Coq		53
	2.5.1	The Program State	53
		State	54
		Frame	56
		Additions	57
		Notations	58
	2.5.2	Domain constructs	59
		A General Purpose Dictionary	59
		The Heap Model	61
		Basic Data Types	62
2.6	A Formal Semantics of JML in Coq		65
	2.6.1	An Interface to JML Specifications	65
		The Annotation Table Interface	67
		The Interface for Frame Conditions	68
	2.6.2	The Definition of the JML Semantics	69
		Additions to the Program State	70
		Definition of the Initial State	72
		Definition of New Frames	72
		Implementation of the Annotation Table Interface	73
		Evaluation of JML Expressions	79
		Implementation of the Frame Conditions Interface	91
		Evaluation of Assignable Locations	92
2.7	Summary		96

3 An Efficient RAC for Assignable Clauses 97

3.1	Approach		98
3.2	Running Example		99
3.3	Checking Assignable Clauses with Static Data Groups		102
	3.3.1	Data Structures	102
		Field Identifiers	103
		Assignable Locations	103
		Fresh Locations	104
		Static Data Groups	104

		3.3.2	Code Instrumentation	104

                        Method Invocation 105
                        Field Update 105
                        Object Creation 106
                        Method Return 106

   3.4   Checking Assignable Clauses with Dynamic Data Groups 107
          3.4.1   Data Structures 109
                  Dynamic Data Groups 109
                  Stack of Assignable Maps and Fresh Locations 110
                  Stack of Updated Pivots 111
          3.4.2   Code Instrumentation 111
                  Method Invocation 111
                  Field Update 111

   3.5   Optimizations 116
   3.6   Implementation and Evaluation 118
   3.7   Theoretical Results 121
   3.8   Summary 122

4   Correctness Proof of the RAC for Assignable Clauses   123
   4.1   Approach 124
   4.2   The Main Theorem 125
   4.3   An Operational Semantics for Java 127
   4.4   Proof of Determinism 132
   4.5   First Refinement 134
          4.5.1   Additions to the Program State 134
          4.5.2   The Implementation of a Stack Data Type in Coq 135
          4.5.3   The Bisimulation Relation 139
          4.5.4   Implementation of the Frame Conditions Interface 141
          4.5.5   Proof of the First Refinement 142
                  Correctness Proof of the Frame Condition Implementation 143
                  Proof of the Bisimulation Property 147
   4.6   Second Refinement 152
          4.6.1   Additions to the Program State 152
          4.6.2   Dealing with Excluded Pivots 152
                  Data Group Unfolding and Membership 152
                  Facts about Data Group Unfolding and Membership 154
          4.6.3   Lazy Unfolding of Data Groups 160
          4.6.4   Equivalence Relation on Assignable Clauses 163
          4.6.5   The Bisimulation Relation 165
          4.6.6   Implementation of the Frame Conditions Interface 166
          4.6.7   Proof of the Second Refinement 167

		Proof of Preservation of Equivalent Assignable Clauses	168

                Proof of Preservation of Equivalent Assignable Clauses 168
                Correctness Proof of the Frame Condition Implementation 169
                Proof of the Bisimulation Property 174
    4.7   Third Refinement 174
        4.7.1   Additions to the Program State 175
        4.7.2   Implementation of Data Group Relations 177
        4.7.3   Operations on Back-Links 180
        4.7.4   A Tree of Back-Links 183
        4.7.5   Implementation of FieldInDg 192
        4.7.6   Implementation of Lazy Unfolding Operations 198
        4.7.7   The Bisimulation Relation 199
        4.7.8   Implementation of the Frame Conditions Interface 200
        4.7.9   Proof of the Third Refinement 201
                Correctness Proof of the Frame Condition Implementation 201
                Proof of the Bisimulation Property 202
    4.8   Proof of the Main Theorem 203
    4.9   Summary 204

5   Conclusion   205
    5.1   Achievements 205
    5.2   Experience 206
    5.3   Future Work 209

List of Coq Tutorials

1 Conventions 16
2 Inductive and Abstract Data Types 33
3 Modules and Name Conflicts 38
4 Inductive Predicates 39
5 Syntactic Sugar for Pattern Matching 41
6 Mutually Dependent Types 47
7 Notations 52
8 Implementation of a Data Type 55
9 Pattern Matching on Several Variables 74
10 Sections 76
11 Axiomatized Functions 84
12 Dealing with Mutual Induction in Proofs 128
13 Avoiding Undecidability in Implementations 136
14 Creating Custom Induction Principle 184

Chapter 1

Introduction

1.1 Motivation

In 1969, flying to the moon required just some ten thousand lines of assembler code [4] and even though the landing was a success, it didn't happen without a serious software problem during the descent [3]. Since this early computer era, software systems have become several magnitudes larger and more complex, and have found their way into nearly every sector of our daily lives. And still, software is most often the failing component in a system; be it the ATM that is out of order, the mobile phone that randomly reboots, or the car's board computer that refuses to start the engine for some spurious reason. We have got used to the fact that software is unreliable [43] and often treat software quality as nice to have but not indispensable. However, with the ever-growing dependency on software, its quality needs to be a central concern of software producers. The fact that cyber crime, which most often exploits software vulnerabilities, has become a real threat [31, 23] supports the call for better-quality assurance for software.

We can ensure and increase software quality by different quality control techniques, that is, by testing (unit tests, integration tests, system tests, etc.), static analyses (code-style check, dead code analysis, etc.), or formal verification (proven correct behavior of code). [1, 82]. However, the immense complexity and size of today's software makes quality control an inherently difficult and expensive task.

Today's most common quality control technique is testing [8, 56]. While testing is a very good means to ensure the quality requirements of hardware (e.g., testing the strength of a metal beam), it is less successful in ensuring the quality of software. Testing means that we run (parts of) the software for some set of inputs and compare the computed results to expected results. By cleverly choosing the inputs, we can be reasonably sure that the software behaves as expected in the anticipated situations. However, we can never guarantee the complete absence of errors by testing. As the input space of a program is normally infinite or at least unfeasibly large, we always test only a tiny fraction of possible inputs and have to hope that all other inputs are treated correctly by the software as well.

Our vision is that tomorrow's most common quality control techniques are based on formal specifications of the behavior of the software. The idea has been introduced as "Design by Contract" [57] by Meyer. The code is equipped with human- *and* machine-readable specifications that describe the desired behavior of the software. While contracts are a built-in concept in Eiffel[58], specification languages have been introduced for many other object oriented languages such as Larch for C++ [45], Spec# for C# [5] and the Java Modeling Language (JML) for Java [46].

Such specifications can be used for a great variety of tools and applications [10, 47]. For instance, we can automatically generate unit tests from specifications [59, 84], introduce runtime assertion checks [58, 14], perform static analyses [78, 32, 33], or do formal verification [5, 79, 2, 62]. As opposed to contracts in Eiffel, theses specification languages not only use a side effect free subset of expressions from their respective language, but feature powerful additional constructs in order to be more expressive. For instance, it's possible to quantify over variables of any type, define frame conditions using abstraction [54], or specify a program by defining a model [49, chapter 15].

A specification language like JML, which is the focus of this thesis, is extremely feature-rich. Furthermore, there are a large number of tools that support some subset of the language to perform different kinds of verification. While the semantic meaning of certain JML constructs often depends on the tool, it is the reference manual [49] that defines the baseline. The manual is a draft of 200 pages written in natural language that explains the language constructs in greater or lesser detail, depending roughly on their popularity and the general understanding of the intended meaning. Quite often, the natural language description is not precise enough to clearly and unambiguously describe the language constructs. In these situations, a formally defined semantics for the specification language in a mathematical language helps to ensure that all tools and applications implement the same understanding of the language constructs.

As the specification language is defined on top of the underlying programming language and adds another layer of constructs, defining a formal semantics for a specification language is a challenging task. If this work is done on paper like in Bruns' thesis [9], it provides a good and unambiguous understanding of the semantics of JML constructs. However, the semantics cannot directly be used by an application, and checking the consistency of the semantics can only be done by manual inspection. Therefore, we believe that it is well-advised to use a proof system to formalize a semantics of such a complex language as we can use the proof system to perform validations of the formalization. Furthermore, a formalization in a theorem prover can be used by a great number of applications. In a technical report [48], Leavens et al. describe a preliminary definition of a core subset of JML in PVS[22]. Their main goal is to unambiguously define a core part of JML. However, our main motivation is to use the formalization for meta-reasoning on JML but also as part of a program verification environment. By "meta-reasoning", we understand to prove properties of the JML language or to show that a JML based verification technique is correct.

We want to show the usefulness of our formalization by an application that is not only a challenge to formalize but also an important contribution on its own. We develop the first algorithm to check frame conditions in the presence of data abstraction at runtime [50] and formally prove the correctness of the algorithm with respect to our formalization of JML.

Frame conditions define which heap locations a method may modify, and, more importantly, that everything else in the heap stays unchanged. To verify interesting program properties, it is important to know the side effects of a method, which are specified by the frame conditions. In JML, a method specification expresses such frame conditions by the use of the assignable clause. This clause declares the heap locations that may be updated during method execution.

To achieve information hiding, an assignable clause can mention *data groups* to abstract away from concrete locations [52, 51]. For any field of an object, we can specify which data group(s) it belongs to. That is, a data group defines a set of concrete locations. A data group is *static* if it only contains fields of the same object. Otherwise, the data group is *dynamic*. Dynamic data groups are crucial to specify frame properties for aggregate or recursive data structures, but make reasoning about assignable clauses an inherently non-modular and difficult task.

JML's semantics for checking frame conditions is to determine upon method invocation the set of locations in the data groups mentioned in the assignable clause. The number of locations in a dynamic data group is unknown at compile time and can grow as fast as the heap itself. Therefore, a naïve implementation of the semantics would lead to a large memory and time overhead.

Our algorithm differs significantly from this naïve implementation. It can check assignable clauses efficiently at runtime. The motivation for such checks is twofold: first, we can use a runtime assertion checker (RAC) to check a program's validity with little effort and small annotation overhead before starting to prove its correctness in an interactive theorem prover. In this way, we find bugs early and reduce the risk of getting stuck in an expensive manual proof. Second, if we use an automatic verification tool, we often get spurious error messages because of under-specification or deficiencies of the prover. In this case, we can use runtime assertion checks to see if the program really violates the specification for the input values from the counter example.

Many static verification tools [2, 12, 32, 55, 78, 79] support assignable clauses to some extent; some partly support static data groups, but no static verification tool currently handles dynamic data groups. To precisely reason about dynamic data groups, a verification environment produces proof obligations that have to be discharged manually, as checking the containment in a dynamic data group is essentially a reachability problem, which is not handled well by SMT solvers. Existing static analyses can only provide an over-approximation that is too imprecise to be useful. The situation for runtime assertion checkers is similar: the RAC for JML presented in Cheon's dissertation [14] does not provide checks for `assignable` clauses. Ye [83] adds limited support for static data groups only.

In these tools, `assignable` clauses are interpreted quite differently. Some tools allow a method to assign to locations that are not mentioned in `assignable` clauses as long as the original value is written back before the method terminates, other tools do not check `assignable` clause if the method does not terminate. Again other tools ignore aliasing. Tools that perform static analyses typically do not allow to call a method whose `assignable` clauses contains locations that are not assignable in the caller.

The quite heterogenous interpretations of `assignable` clauses in existing tools, as well as the fact that our algorithm differs a lot from a naïve implementation of the semantics are a strong motivation for formally proving the equivalence between the runtime assertion checker and the semantics. Moreover, the proof is an interesting and challenging application of our formalization.

1.2 Goals

A Formal Definition of JML in Coq

We want to formally define an interesting and realistic subset of the specification language JML in a state of the art theorem prover. The subset covers all constructs that are needed to provide interesting program specifications, including preconditions, normal and exceptional postconditions, frame conditions, object invariants, and local assertions, just to mention the most important ones. We define the exact subset in section 2.3.

Enable Meta-Reasoning as well as Program Verification Our formalization shall serve several purposes. Beside the obvious goal of having a formal and therefore unambiguous semantics for JML, we want to be able to do meta-reasoning on the specification language itself. Furthermore, we want to be able to integrate the formalization into a program verification environment like the Mobius PVE [62].

To integrate the formalization in a verification environment, we want to provide an interface to JML specifications that can be used by the verification environment to generate proof obligations. Furthermore, it's necessary to formalize JML such that it's possible to conveniently embed JML annotated Java programs in Coq.

Emphasis on the Relevant Software Qualities In order to be useful, our formalization needs to fulfill the following three software qualities:
Readability Only if the formal definition of JML is readable and understandable by people working in the formal verification area, will it be used for different applications as described above.

Maintainability As the formalization only covers a subset of JML, it is important to ensure maintainability of the formalization. Enlarging the supported subset means that some existing need to be changed in order to support the new constructs. Furthermore, one might want to actually change the semantics of certain constructs. For instance, besides the semantics for object invariants defined in the reference manual, there exist several proposals of different semantics that allow modular reasoning. The formalization is maintainable if the design of the formalization allows such changes in a clear and straightforward way. Part of maintainability is also a decent documentation of the semantics, which should be provided in this thesis.

Usability In the previous goal, we already emphasized that the formalization should not only provide an unambiguous definition of JML, but also provide a basis for a variety of applications. The design needs to embrace these different use cases and allow easy integration in other systems.

An Efficient RAC for Assignable Clauses

We want to develop an efficient way of checking JML's `assignable` clauses at runtime in the presence of dynamic data groups. The code instrumentations by our algorithm should exactly enforce the semantics of `assignable` clauses. Most notably, the checks should be performed independently of if and how a method terminates (as opposed to the implementation of most tools). Furthermore, the algorithm should not enforce that the `assignable` clause of a callee contains only locations that are also assignable in the caller (which is a significant over-approximation).

Manage to Check a Non-Modular Property at Runtime Dynamic data groups lead to non-modular reasoning because their size is only bounded by the size of the heap. Our goal is to develop an algorithm that can deal well with the introduced non-modularity.

Minimize Time Overhead at Reasonable Costs We want to focus on minimizing time overhead while keeping the memory footprint reasonable. As we see the runtime assertion checker as a means to quickly check if a program behaves as expected, time is more of an issue than memory, especially as the latter is normally available in these days. In the average case, the algorithm should not tear down the performance significantly. In the worst case, it should still be possible to run an annotated program for fairly large data structures. It would not be much of a runtime assertion checker, if it couldn't handle realistic data structures.

A Machine Checkable Proof of the RAC

We want to create a machine checkable proof of correctness of the algorithm to check `assignable` clauses at runtime. Our goal is to show that such proofs are scientifically interesting, because for certain language constructs, a runtime assertion checker instruments the code in a way that cannot obviously be mapped to the semantics of the respective JML construct. Our check of `assignable` clauses is a good example for a non-trivial connection between the runtime assertion checker implementation and the intended semantics.

Prove Soundness and Completeness We want to show that our runtime assertion checker is sound an complete. That is, the checker does not allow an assignment to a heap location if the semantics forbids it (soundness), but also that it does allow assignment to any heap location which is assignable according to the semantics (completeness). While the soundness criterion is not debatable, the second is, as it prevents the algorithm to perform any kind of over-approximation.

Showcase the Usefulness of the JML Formalization Beside the direct result of having a proof, that is, the certainty that our algorithm is correct, we also want to show that our formalization of JML can be used to perform challenging meta-reasoning on the language and its tools. Therefore, the proof should be well documented (in this thesis) and its structure should be an elegant application of the formal definition of JML. To achieve this best, we also want this proof to have the same software qualities as the formalization.

1.3 Approach

In this section we give a short high-level summary of the approach. Each subsequent technical chapter contains a more detailed section on the approach.

A Formal Definition of JML in Coq We provide a formalization of JML in the theorem prover Coq [19], which has been used to reason about programming languages on several occasions. We base our work on an existing formalization of the Java Virtual Machine [70]. Therefore, we can reuse the formalization of underlying language concepts like the object model. In order to improve readability and usability, we make heavy use of *notations*, which are additional directives for the parser and pretty printer of Coq. Throughout the formalization, we apply the concept of separation of concerns: we encapsulate different parts of the formalization in modules, such that individual parts of the formalization can be exchanged without influencing everything else. This greatly improves the maintainability of the formalization and also has a positive impact on usability. For instance, we can easily exchange one part of the formalization and formally show equivalence between the original and the exchanged part.

An Efficient RAC for Assignable Clauses We overcome the non-modularity of dynamic data groups by applying lazy evaluation techniques that we base on observation of typical uses of dynamic data groups. Instead of evaluating the content of assignable data groups upon method invocation, we determine upon field assignment if the field location is contained in an assignable data group. Furthermore, we introduce data structures for representing data groups and `assignable` clauses that allow to compute static data group membership in constant time. Finally, we avoid performing the same computation multiple times by introducing caches that store all intermediate results during a method execution.

A Machine Checkable Proof of the RAC We prove soundness and completeness of the runtime assertion checker by showing that the semantics and the runtime assertion checker are bisimilar [69, 61], that is, they are equivalent. We apply a refinement strategy that uses the semantics as the abstract model and concretize the model in each refinement step to end up in a model that describes the runtime assertion checker. The modular nature of the formalization allows us to elegantly define the different models and plug them into the formalization in order to prove the equivalence of the refinements.

1.4 Scientific Contributions

- We provide the first formal definition of a rich specification language like JML with a useful subset that is tailored towards both program verification and meta-reasoning. The formalization is written in a successful and popular theorem prover and embraces changes and extensions. Thus, we make sure that our work can be used as a solid foundation for future work in the area.

- We present the first algorithm that faithfully checks `assignable` clauses with dynamic data groups. Our work closes a gap in the runtime assertion checker for JML. Our algorithm can be adapted to check similar currently unsupported constructs such as the `accessible` clause.

- We perform the first proof of correctness and completeness of a runtime assertion checker for a specification language construct. Even though checking `assignable` clauses is a difficult task where the code instrumentation significantly differs from the semantics description, we can show that it's possible to exactly define the effect of the instrumentation and prove that the runtime assertion checker enforce the semantics without over-approximation.

1.5 Related Work

We split our discussion of related work into several areas. Fig. 1.1 visualizes the related work in four overlapping ellipses that represent the different research areas. On the upper left, we have related work that concentrates on describing the JML semantics in a formal way. On the upper right, we have tools that we compare to our work. On the lower right, we discuss work that explicitly concentrates on `assignable` clauses, and on the lower left, we discuss work that formalizes languages in a theorem prover.

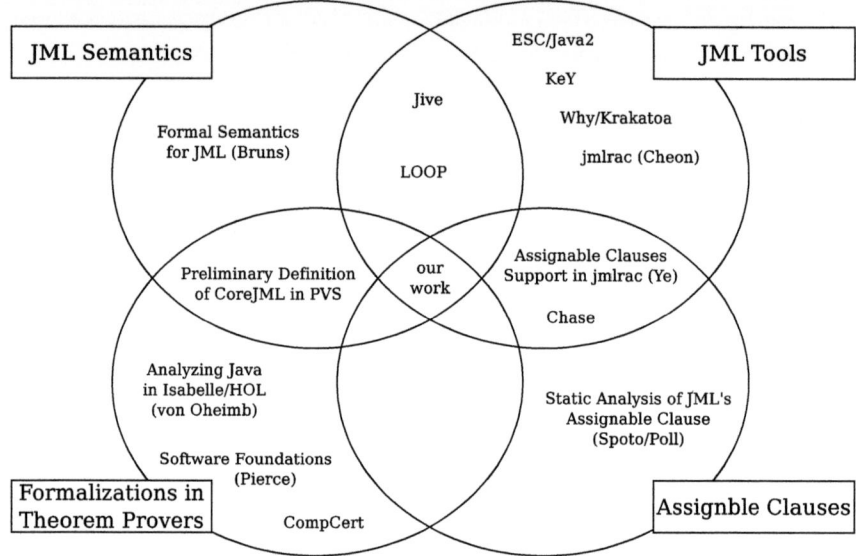

Figure 1.1: The most relevant related work, arranged by research fields.

Formal Semantics of JML In the field of formal semantics for JML, we have the work by Bruns and the preliminary definition of core JML by Leavens et al., which define a formal semantics independently from an application. In the case of the JML tools JIVE and LOOP, a formal semantics of JML is discussed on paper. Beside explaining the overall approach of the related work, we emphasize the handling of the `assignable` clause for JML semantics and tools, as it's interesting to see how differently this clause is treated.

Bruns describes in his diploma thesis [9] a formal semantics for JML on paper. It is a very thoroughly and nicely written semantics that helps to understand the exact meaning of JML constructs, that can help to agree on a common understanding of JML specifications. Their semantics differs in certain points to ours where either the reference manual is not specific or where one of us deliberately changed the semantics from the one presented in the reference manual. One difference is how the semantics handles side effects in specifications. While expressions in Bruns' semantics not only yield a value but also a post-state which corresponds to the solution presented by Darvas and Müller [26], expressions in specifications do not change the state in our formalization of the semantics. While the former is more accurate, the latter is simpler. Therefore, we cannot handle object creations in specifications properly. However, our modular formalization of the semantics would allow to implement a different handling of specification expressions without problems. Another interesting difference is the handling of `assignable` clauses. While a method does not have to respect its `assignable` clause if it does not terminate, our semantics states that `assignable` clauses need to be respected in any case, no matter if the method terminates or not.

The preliminary definition of Core JML [48] in PVS by Leavens, Naumann, and Rosenberg was the first work that formalized JML in a theorem prover. As the title suggests, only the very core parts of JML are formalized in this work. This mainly covers many aspects of behavioral subtyping. While it covers these aspects in detail, the formalization doesn't contain the definition of any other part of JML. Thus, we cannot really compare the work to our approach.

The LOOP tool by van den Berg, Jacobs, Poll et al. [79] generates PVS or Isabelle[66] proof obligations for a given JML annotated Java program. The tool automatically translates JML annotated Java programs into their special purpose logic, which is described by Jacobs and Poll in [39] and extended in [80]. The LOOP tool is mainly used to prove non-trivial properties of JavaCard [13] applications. As opposed to our approach, their logic is designed to serve one specific purpose, that is, being used in the verification tool. The logic is based on standard Hoare logic [37] and extends the Hoare triples with JML specific constructs and can handle abrupt termination. The actual verification is done in PVS or Isabelle, using tailor-made proof strategies to simplify the process. The Logic used in the LOOP tool covers `modifies` clauses that behave differently than `assignable` clauses. It only guarantees that the values of all heap locations not mentioned in the `modifies` clause are the same in the pre- and post-state. Means of data abstraction like data groups are not handled in the LOOP tool.

Similar to the LOOP tool, the JIVE system [60] is an interactive verification environment that produces proof obligations in a Hoare style logic for PVS for JML annotated JavaCard code. For this system, Darvas and Müller define a formalized subset of JML in [27]. JIVE implements the universe type system [30, 63] to enable modular verification of invariants and `assignable` clauses. However, their semantics of `assignable` clauses allows to temporarily change the value of non-assignable locations, as long as the original value is restored upon method termination. The issue is discussed but not addressed, as the underlying logic does not provide a way of checking such properties throughout method execution.

Related JML Tools ESC/Java2, the KeY approach, Krakatoa, and JML's runtime assertion checker are interesting tools that choose quite different approaches to JML based program verification. These projects do not provide a formal semantics of JML but implement it as part of the tool in form of translations from JML to proof obligations for some kind of prover or as code instrumentations.

ESC/Java2 [32] is a powerful static checker for JML. It provides various checks for a large subset of JML. The latest version is integrated in the Mobius Program Verification Environment [62]. Its main goal is to find common programming errors quickly without full functional verification. That is, it neither needs or wants to be sound nor complete. The tool creates proof obligations that may or may not be discharged by an automated theorem prover like Simplify [29] or more recently Z3 [28]. ESC/Java2 is the only tool that can deal with `assignable` clauses and dynamic data groups. However, ESC/Java2 can only check an over-approximation of the semantics due to the dynamic nature of data groups. The checker does not allow to call a method whose `assignable` clause contains locations that are not assignable in the current method. Therefore, it requires the user to exactly specify the `assignable` clause of all methods in the program, as a left out `assignable` clause is interpreted as `assignable \everything`.

The KeY program verification tool by Beckert, Hähnle, Schmitt et al. [6, 2] does not rely on a general purpose theorem prover but translates JML (or OCL) specifications into proof obligations in dynamic logic [72]. Dynamic logic features rules for each Java language construct. Verifying a program means to symbolically execute the dynamic logic program by applying the correct rules, and to use induction for recursive calls and loops. While the LOOP and similar tools provide a set of proof strategies (tactics) to simplify proofs in the underlying theorem prover, KeY introduces a concept called *taclets*. A taclet is basically a sequent calculus rule equipped with the information when to apply it. As JML constructs are not embedded in the underlying dynamic logic, the generated proof obligations do not directly resemble the JML specifications. For `assignable` clauses, the translation from JML to dynamic logic introduces in the generated proof obligations that state that all heap locations except for the ones mentioned in the `assignable` clause stay unchanged when calling this method. This corresponds to the `modifies` semantics that we explained for the LOOP tool. To introduce a means of abstraction to `assignable` clauses, Schmitt, Ulbrich, and Weiß introduce the concept of dynamic frames[44] in dynamic logic [76] as an interesting alternative to dynamic data groups.

Krakatoa [55] is a verification tool for Java that generates proof obligations in Coq to be discharged manually using the Why front-end[34]. The tool nicely relates the generated proof obligations by highlighting the part of the JML specifications that led to the current proof obligation. The specification language of Krakatoa is similar to JML and contains an *assigns* clause to specify a list of locations that can be assigned. However, it is not possible to apply any kind of abstraction in the description of assignable locations. The translation of JML to proof obligations in Coq is not formally defined.

Cheon's runtime assertion checker for JML [14] instrument Java source code to enforce the JML specifications. While they present the runtime checks in detail and discuss their approach to check many JML constructs thoroughly, they do not formally prove that the code instrumentations actually enforce the semantics, or even stronger that the runtime checks lead to equivalent behavior to the semantics. Cheon's runtime assertion checker provides data structures to represent `assignable` clauses and data groups but does not generate checks for it. Ye uses these data structures in his thesis [83] to implement an `assignable` clause checker in the presence of static datagroups only. The checks have a time overhead linear in the size of the set of locations from the `assignable` clause, whereas our algorithm for static datagroups works in constant time.

Work on Assignable Clauses There are two interesting projects that specifically concentrate on JML's `assignable` clause. The ChAsE tool that performs static checks for `assignable` clauses and Spoto's and Poll's static analysis to reason about `assignable` clauses.

The ChAsE tool by Cataño and Huisman [12] is a static analysis tool for `assignable` clauses. The tool provides a simple means to discover common specification mistakes, but is not designed to be sound. It performs a purely syntactic check on `assignable` clauses, ignores aliasing, and does not support data groups. At the time when ChAsE was written, ESC/Java did not check `assignable` clauses yet, which means that ChAsE filled a big gap in the static checking of JML specifications. Today, as described above, ESC/Java2 checks `assignable` clauses, which makes the use of this tool obsolete.

Spoto and Poll [78] formalized a trace semantics for a sound reasoning on `assignable` clauses. Their approach takes aliasing into account, but data groups are not supported. They conclude that JML's `assignable` clause may be unsuitable for a precise and correct static analysis, with which we agree.

Language Formalizations in Theorem Provers Our work is the first to formally define the semantics and runtime checks of `assignable` clauses in a theorem prover, therefore, no other work is in the overlapping area of the two research fields.

There exist many formalizations of (imperative) languages in theorem provers. Beside the already discussed formalization of core JML in PVS, we want to relate our work to von Oheimbs Java formalization in Isabelle/HOL and to two textbook implementations of language formalizations in Coq.

Von Oheimb presents in [81] a formalization of Java^{light}, which is similar to JavaCard, in Isabelle/HOL. They present the formalization of syntax, type system and wellformedness properties and an operational semantics of Java^{light}. As applications of their formalization, they show type safety of the formalized type system and introduce an axiomatic semantics in form of a Hoare logic and prove soundness and completeness w.r.t. the operational semantics. Their work is in many aspects similar to our formalization. However, their aim is clearly meta-reasoning on the language, which results in a quite smaller formalization, as they do not have to provide an implementation of the abstract data types to embed actual Java programs in the theorem prover.

"Software Foundations" is a great book by Pierce et al. [71] entirely generated from Coq sources. It is a textbook suited for a one semester course on formal semantics in

Coq. If this book had been available at the time we started our formalization of JML, we would have spent less effort to formalize JML, as it covers many interesting aspects of language formalizations in Coq in great detail. Beside many other topics, the book formalized a very simple imperative language (IMP) with the usual language constructs, that is, variable declarations, assignments and simple control structures. It formalizes this simple language very carefully and puts a great emphasize on how this task is done most elegantly in Coq, which is natural for a textbook on Coq. In addition to the operational semantics of the language, a Hoare style logic is developed to perform reasoning over IMP programs. Furthermore, the book introduces the formalization of interesting type systems in Coq, including records and subtyping. By choosing a simple toy language, they avoid many problems that arose in our formalization due to the complex language that we formalized. For instance the absence of circularly dependent data types or no method calls. Similarly to our formalization, the book makes use of notations in Coq to improve understandability of the Coq source text.

The CompCert project [53] aims at creating a proven correct realistic compiler for C by completely writing the compiler in Coq. The CompCert C compiler is a nice showcase example of formalizing an imperative language in a theorem prover. The project shows that it's possible to develop large scale formalizations in Coq. The language coverage is continuously being increased. Since just recently, expressions can produce side effects, which means that method calls are now correctly formalized as expressions rather than as statements. While the whole project is quite impressive, the language formalization of the chosen C subset is naturally simpler than our formalization, as there is no dynamic method binding, inheritance, and other object oriented constructs to formalize. Other simplifications to the language is that their method bodies simply contain a statement (which might be a compound statement), and not a block of statements as we formalize it. The difficulty with blocks and statements is that the two concepts are mutually dependent, which is difficult to formalize in a theorem prover, and blocks introduce a structure of local variable scopes.

1.6 Overview

In the remainder of this chapter, we present the conventions and preliminary work. Chapter 2 presents our formalization of JML in Coq, which includes a deep embedding of the Java and JML syntax and the definition of their semantic meaning. Chapter 3 presents our algorithm to efficiently check `assignable` clauses at runtime in the presence of dynamic data groups. Chapter 4 presents a machine checkable refinement proof of our runtime assertion checker presented in chapter 3, based on the JML formalization of chapter 2. Chapter 5 concludes this thesis by summarizing our achievements, reporting on the experiences and discussing the future work.

1.7 Conventions

In this section, we present the notation, font, and styles that we use to identify different constructs throughout this thesis. We need to clearly distinguish between Coq program text, and JML source code as in many explanations, we talk about both languages at the same time, and often, both languages feature the same keywords and symbols.

Coq Source Text

Listing 1.1 shows an example Coq text, that shows all syntax features that we discuss in this paragraph. Whenever we refer to Coq source text, we use this sans serif font. Coq constructs like **Fixpoint** or **Prop** are highlighted in bold, keywords like match or intros are highlighted. We use *(* this italic font *)* for comments and "this font" for notations. We use this conventions not only in listings, but also in the text. Coq supports the use of UTF-8 symbols. Thus, we use these symbols for better readability. For example, we use the symbol ∀ instead of its ASCII counterpart forall. We also use nice arrows, for example ⇒ instead of =>. In listings, we use ellipsis points "..." to indicate omitted code. The omitted code can be just one line but may also be a huge portion of the formalization. If it helps with understanding the code, we add a comment after the ellipsis points to indicate what we omit.

Quite often, we replace certain Coq constructs with simpler mathematical notations that are intuitively understandable. For instance, we prefer to write "elem ∈ stack" instead of the original version "In elem stack". We also overload such operators and use them for different data types. For example, we use the operation ∈ not only for stacks, but also for lists, sets of any type, and other collections. By defining the appropriate notations in Coq, we can profit from a much easier to read Coq program text.

We use small numbers to refer to a certain line in a listing. Often, we put that number in front of a whole sentence, if the sentence talks about a construct mentioned on that line. The following paragraph is an example of how we usually refer to lines in listings:

> Listing 1.1 shows the implementation of the recursive function 11 truncate. The function has two parameters: n, which is the target size of the stack, and s, which is the stack that should be truncated to this size. 12 The function performs a pattern matching on the result of nat_compare n |s|. 13-17 If n is smaller than the size of s, 15 we remove the top of the stack and call truncate on the new stack. It can never occur that we have an empty stack at hand in this case, but nevertheless, 16 we need to define the behavior, as pattern matchings in Coq always need to be complete. 18 If n is not smaller than the size of the stack, the function doesn't change s.

```
1   Require Import List.
2
3   Section Stack.
4
5     Variable A: Type.
6     Definition stack := list .
7
8     Notation "e ∈ list" := (In e list) (at level 30).
9     Notation "| s |" := (length s).
10
11    Fixpoint truncate (n : nat) (s : stack A) : stack A :=
12      match nat_compare n |s| with
13      | Lt ⇒
14        match s with
15        | h :: t ⇒ truncate n t
16        | _ ⇒ nil
17        end
18      | _ ⇒ s
19      end.
20    ... (* Other definitions omitted *)
21
22    (** The size of a stack that has been truncated is exactly n. *)
23    Lemma truncate_1:
24      ∀ n (s : stack A),
25      n ≤ |s| →
26      n = |truncate n s|.
27    Proof. intros. unfold truncate in ⊢ *. ... Qed.
28
29    ... (* Other proofs omitted *)
```

Listing 1.1: An example Coq program text

Sometimes, we refer to Coq text that isn't actually part of our formalization, normally, to show an alternative way of defining a construct, wrong statements, or possible applications of the formalization. In this case, we leave away the border and the background of the listing:

(* Use this axiom if you're stuck *)
Axiom MagicalProofSimplifier:
  ∀ (x : nat),
    x = 42.

Coq Proofs

We discuss proofs mostly on a conceptual level, all details can be checked in the Coq sources. To describe a proof, we often show simplified intermediate steps of a proof. Listing 1.2 shows a proof excerpt from lemma truncate_1 in listing 1.1. Above the line, we show the 1-9 relevant hypotheses to prove the 10 goal below the line. Each hypothesis gets a name, in this case "H" and "H0". As with Coq text, we perform some additional prettifying, to make the goals and hypotheses more readable.

```
H : n ≤ |a :: s|
H0 : n <
    S
    ((fix length (l : list A) : nat :=
        match l with
        | nil ⇒ 0
        | _ :: l' ⇒ S |l'|
        end) s)
─────────────────────────
n ≤ |s|
```

Listing 1.2: Proof excerpt

JML Source Code

Listing 1.3 shows an example JML source code, which shows all relevant syntax constructs. We always use **typewriter font** for Java and JML code. Java-keywords like **class** or **this** are highlighted in bold, JML-keywords like requires or \result are highlighted. We use /* *italic font* */ for comments that are not JML contracts. Please note that although JML contracts are always within Java comments, we do not format them as comments. We use this conventions not only in listings, but also in the text. Again, we use ellipsis points "..." to indicate omitted code in listings.

We will use this code to explain certain JML constructs in the next section. Thus, the example is slightly big.

```
class Node {
  JMLDataGroup struct;
  JMLDataGroup footprint;

  private Node left; //@ in struct;
  /*@ maps left.struct \into struct; */
  /*@ maps left.footprint \into footprint; */
```

```
8
9     private Node right; //@ in struct;
10    /*@ maps right.struct \into struct; */
11    /*@ maps right.footprint \into footprint; */
12
13    Item item;
14    /*@ maps item.footprint \into footprint; */
15
16    //@ assignable this.item;
17    Node(Item i) { item = i; }
18
19    /*@ public normal_behavior
20      @   {|
21      @     requires ! this.contains(i);
22      @     assignable this.struct;
23      @   also
24      @     requires this.contains(i);
25      @     assignable \nothing;
26      @   |}
27      @   ensures this.contains(i);
28      @*/
29    void insert (Item i) { ... }
30
31    boolean /*@ pure */ contains(Item i) { ... }
32
33    private void balance() { ... }
34
35    ... // Other methods omitted.
36 }
```

Listing 1.3: Excerpt of class Node.

From time to time, when it seems fit, we introduce some Coq concepts that should help to read and understand the Coq text in this thesis in form of a Coq tutorial:

──────────────── A MADE-TO-MEASURE COQ TUTORIAL ────────────────

Part 1 Conventions

We mark these tutorials with the icon you can see at the side and use slanted font throughout the tutorial. The tutorials do not introduce new concepts and ideas, but just concentrate on explaining how something can be done in Coq.

Proof. In proofs, we use normal upright font, even within a tutorial. □

A reader with a good background in Coq can safely ignore these tutorials and continue to read after the following line that marks the end of the tutorial:

1.8 Preliminaries

In this section, we provide a short introduction of the theorem prover Coq and interesting aspects of the specification language JML. In both cases, the introduction is tailored to understand the subsequent chapters. For a more in-depth introduction to Coq, we refer to the excellent Coq Tutorial by Giménez and Castéran [35] and the introduction to JML by Leavens, Backer, and Ruby [46].

1.8.1 Coq

Coq is an interactive theorem prover that implements a calculus of inductive constructions, which is the original calculus of constructions [20] with the extension of inductive definitions [21, 35]. We can define a formalism in Coq using functional programming constructs as well as inductive definitions and prove properties of the formalization by providing a proof script which can be efficiently executed by Coq in order to check the proof.

Inductive Definitions

Inductive definitions have a name and a type and zero or more rules that define the inductive type. Each rule has an unique name called *constructor*. While it is not possible to have a recursive occurrence of the inductive type in a non positive position, Coq does not prevent the user from writing inductive definitions that do not reduce the size of the term.

Example. The following inductive definition is not allowed, as its possible to prove False with such a definition, see [35, section 3.4.1]:

Inductive paradox :=
| rule : ¬ paradox → paradox.

However the following definition is fine, even though useless, as applying the constructor rule on the term "useless" leaves us again with the premise useless, we didn't gain anything by applying the only constructor of the inductive type.

Inductive useless :=
| rule : useless → useless .

Let's look at an inductive definition of the operator $\leq$ on natural numbers in Coq:

Inductive le (n : nat) : nat → **Prop** :=
| le_n : le n n
| le_S : ∀ m : nat, le n m → le n (S m).

The (mutual) inductive definition takes one parameter n and the yields a term of type nat → **Prop** which is a function from peano numbers to the type of logical propositions in Coq. The definition consists of two rules. The first rule, le_n, states that any number n is smaller or equal than itself. The second rule, le_S, states that for any number m, if n ≤m holds then n ≤m+1 holds. The inductive definition is well-founded because of the first rule and covers all possible pairs of n and m because of the second rule.

The Curry-Howard Isomorphism

According to the Curry-Howard isomorphism [77], which applies for the calculus of constructions, a proof of a proposition in Coq is a function whose type is the proposition itself.

Because of the way the Curry-Howard isomorphism is implemented in Coq, there is no syntactic distinction between types and terms. A type is always a term of another type. In the following example, we show this on the simple type nat of peano numbers. Coq features three built-in basic types, **Set**, **Prop**, and **Type**, which we will quickly introduce in the examples. We call (only) these types *sorts*.

Example. The type of the term "3" is nat, which stands for natural numbers. The term "nat" is of sort **Set**, which is the type of other language specification constructs like list , or bool. Finally, "Set" is of sort **Type**.

The same applies to propositions. For propositions, the type–term correspondence is much less obvious, but much more interesting. A proposition is of course a term of sort **Prop**, but also a type itself. If we can prove a proposition, the prove is a term of that type and the proposition holds. If we cannot prove it, the proposition *may be* a type that is not inhabited; there might not exists a term of such a type. In this case, we do not know if the proposition holds or not. If we can prove the negation of the proposition, we know that the proposition is a non-inhabited type. We show the Curry-Howard isomorphism with a slightly larger example.

Example. Let's look at the term "0 ≤2". Its sort is **Prop**, which is the type of all logical propositions. The sort of "**Prop**" is again **Type**. Interestingly, the term "0≤2" is also a type itself. If and only if we find a term of this type, the proposition holds. So how does a term look like whose type is 0≤2?

The term "0≤2" is a notation for "le 0 2". If we look at the inductive definition of le above, it becomes clear how to build a term of this type: we start with the constructor le_n with parameter n set to 0, that is, "le_n 0". This term has type 0 ≤0. We can apply the term "le_S 0 0", which has type $0 \leq 0 \to 0 \leq 1$. Thus, the resulting type is $0 \leq 1$ and we can apply le_S again to get $0 \leq 2$: "le_S 0 1 (le_S 0 0 (le_n 0))" : $0 \leq 2$.

Of course, we do not have to build these terms manually to prove a proposition, but we can use the proof language of Coq to create these terms:

The following excerpt defines a lemma that states the proposition in question. The proof can be performed by the auto tactic, which tries to apply constructors of the involved inductive definitions up to a certain times.

Lemma zero_le_four: $0 \leq 2$.
Proof. auto. **Qed**.

We were able to prove the proposition, thus there needs to exist a term of this type. We can actually look at the term built by the proof by printing out the lemma:

Print zero_le_four .

ZeroLEFour = le_S 0 1 (le_S 0 0 (le_n 0))
: $0 \leq 2$

If we generalize our term to "$\forall$ n : nat , $0 \leq$ n", we perform a proof by induction on n and the resulting proof obligations can be discharged automatically again.

Lemma zero_le_n : $\forall$n : nat , $0 \leq$ n.
Proof. induction n;auto. **Qed**.

The term generated by the proof is actually a program that computes the deviation sequence shown above for any input n. The function nat_ind is the inductive principle of type nat, which takes ₄ the proposition to prove, ₅ the proof of the base case whose type is $0 \leq 0$ as we have seen above, ₆ the proof of the step case whose type is $\forall$ n0 : nat, $0 \leq$ n0 $\to 0 \leq$ S n0, and of course n as arguments.

```
1  zero_le_n =
2  fun n : nat ⇒
3    nat_ind
4      (fun n0 : nat ⇒ 0 ≤n0)
5      (le_n 0)
6      (fun (n0 : nat) (IHn : 0 ≤n0) ⇒ le_S 0 n0 IHn)
7      n
```

Below, we show the definition of nat_ind. It is a recursive function (₃ fix F) that performs a pattern matching on the argument n. ₅ If it is 0, the supplied proof of the base case is applied, ₆ otherwise the proof of the step case is applied and F is called recursively with n0, which is n−1.

```
1  nat_ind =
2  fun (P : nat → Prop) (f : P 0) (f0 : ∀ n : nat, P n → P (S n)) ⇒
```

```
3  fix F (n : nat) : P n :=
4    match n with
5    | 0 ⇒ f
6    | S n0 ⇒ f0 n0 (F n0)
7    end
```

Short Introduction to Other Constructs

Parameters, Variables, Axioms, and Hypotheses These four constructs declare an identifier of some term (type). If the term is of sort **Prop**, it makes more sense to use **Axiom** or **Hypothesis**, otherwise **Parameter** or **Variable** are appropriate, depending on the scope in which the identifier is declared. Semantically, the four constructs are identical.

Example. The first two identifiers are declared reasonably, whereas the latter two are in principle correct but should use a different construct for better readability.

```
(* good examples *)
Parameter n : nat.
Hypothesis H : answer = 42.
(* type−correct but bad examples *)
Variable even_or_odd : ∀ n, even n ∨ odd n.
Axiom b : bool.
```

Mind that with any of these declarations, we can introduce propositions in the proof environment that are not inhabited and thus lead to inconsistency.

Definitions and Fixpoints The constructs **Definition** and **Fixpoint** are used to define non-recursive and recursive functions, respectively. Coq enforces that recursive functions are defined such that one parameter of the function always structurally decreases, which ensures termination on a syntactic level.

Example. The following recursive function is structurally decreasing on the first argument as we remove the head of the list upon each recursive call. Therefore, it is syntactically ensured that the function terminates eventually. It computes the sum of all numbers in a list. The function performs a syntactic pattern matching on parameter l in order to either deal with the empty list or to split the list into head and tail.

```
Fixpoint sum (l : list nat) : nat :=
match l with
| nil ⇒ 0
| h :: t ⇒ h + sum t
end.
```

Functions in Coq are always total. For every possible term in the domain, the function needs to define a term in the range of the function. However, we can simulate partial functions by yielding a term of type option A, where A is the desired return type of the function. The option type has two constructors, None and Some A.

Example. In this example, we define a function that returns the maximum of a list if the list is not empty. The function relies on a standard library function ₇ max: nat → nat → nat that yields the bigger of the two provided numbers. If ₃ the list is empty, the function yields None with which we indicate that the function is not defined in this case. If ₄ the list is not empty, we call Max on the tail and perform a pattern matching on that result. If ₆ the tail is empty and thus Max t yielded None, the maximum is obviously the value of the head. Otherwise, ₇ the call to Max t yielded a number n in which case the function yields the maximum of h and n.

```
Fixpoint Max(l : list nat) : option nat :=
  match l with
  | nil ⇒ None
  | h :: t ⇒
    match Max t with
    | None ⇒ Some h
    | Some n ⇒ Some (max h n)
    end
  end.
```

We conclude the preliminary chapter on Coq at this point. Further information about more concrete aspects of Coq are available in the Coq tutorials that are spread over the chapters 2 and 4.

1.8.2 JML

In this section, we provide a short introduction to the aspects of JML that are relevant for this thesis and a more in-depth discussion of method specifications and the JML constructs needed to specify method frame conditions.

Overview

JML provides a great variety of means to specify many different aspects of Java programs. The most common constructs are the `requires` and `ensures` clauses to specify the pre- and post-conditions of a method, the `signals` clause to specify exceptional behavior of a method, object and static invariants that specify the consistent state of an object and a type, respectively, as well as the `assignable` clause to specify the frame condition of a method.

Invariants have to hold in all visible states. In short, the visible state semantics requires all invariants to hold in the pre- and post-state of methods, with certain exceptions. For instance, the invariants of an object do not need to hold (and can not be assumed to hold) in the pre-state of a constructor of that object. The visible state semantics allows to break any invariant between visible states, as long as they are re-established in the upcoming visible state. We refer to the section 8.2 of the reference manual [49] for a detailed discussion.

Beside type- and method-specifications, JML features the statements `assert` and `assume` to specify local assertions and assumptions in method bodies and the `maintaining` clauses to specify loop invariants. All these clauses and statements contain an expression that evaluates to a boolean value.

In order to express interesting properties in specifications, JML adds *primary* expressions to the side effect free subset of Java expressions. The most relevant JML primaries are the \old(*expr*) expression, which can occur in annotation statements and specification clauses that are evaluated in the post-state of the method and which evaluates the supplied expression *expr* in the pre-state of the method, the \result expression, which can occur in ensures clauses to refer to the value returned by the method, the $\backslash\text{fresh}(l_1,\ldots,l_n)$ expression, which asserts that the supplied locations are fresh, that is, their object have not been allocated in the pre-state of the current method.

Beside these common constructs, JML features a large number of constructs that are more specialized but at the same time less supported by tools. This is why JML defines language levels '0' to '3', as well as 'C' for concurrency related constructs and 'X' for experimental features. Level '0' constructs should be supported by all tools. The higher the number of the level, the less common the constructs are and thus less support is available [49, section 2.9].

Method Specifications

Method specifications like the `requires`, `ensures`, `signals`, as well as the `assignable` clauses are organized in specification cases. The `requires` clause(s) defines in which situations the specification case applies. A method can have an arbitrary number of specification cases and cases from overwritten methods are inherited. A specification case can be *lightweight* or *heavyweight*. The specification of the constructor 17 `Node` in listing 1.3 shows an example of a lightweight specification case. It only contains a single `assignable` clause, everything else is omitted. The specification is visible wherever the method is visible. The method 29 `insert` contains a heavyweight specification case. The difference is that heavyweight specification cases contain a visibility modifier and they are marked as *behavior*, *normal behavior*, or *exceptional behavior*. Normal behavior cases implicitly add the clause "`signals (java.lang.Exception) false`", which means that the method must not terminate exceptionally. Analogously, exceptional behavior cases implicitly add the clause "`ensures false`", which means that the method must not terminate normally if the case applies. Furthermore, heavyweight specification cases can contain *nested* specification cases. In the specification case of `insert`, we see one heavyweight specification case that contains two nested specification cases and an `ensures` clause.

All of the mentioned forms of specification cases can be syntactically desugared into flat (non-nested) behavior specification cases. We want to show this intuitively with the specification of `insert`.

Example. Let's first understand exactly what the specification of method `insert` expresses. [21,22] If the method `contains` yields `false`, that is, if the item `i` is not contained in the tree with the current node as root, then `this.struct` is assignable (we will see later what this means exactly). [24,25] if item `i` is already contained in the tree, nothing is assignable in the method. In both cases [27], we want to ensure that the item `i` is contained in the tree in the post-state of the method. We also know that the method must not terminate exceptionally, as the *normal* behavior specification always applies, because either of the two `requires` clauses holds.

By flattening the nested cases and adding the signals clauses as described above, we can desugar the specification of `insert` into the following specification cases:

```
/*@ public behavior
  @   requires ! this.contains(i);
  @   assignable this.struct;
  @   ensures this.contains(i);
  @   signals (java.lang.Exception) false;
  @ also
  @ public behavior
  @   requires this.contains(i);
  @   assignable \nothing;
  @   ensures this.contains(i);
  @   signals (java.lang.Exception) false;
  @*/
```

Frame Conditions

We can specify frame conditions in JML using the `assignable` clause and data groups. We introduce both concepts in detail as we concentrate on frame conditions in the chapters 3 and 4.

Before we present the two concepts, we need to agree on the following notation that we will use in this section and in chapter 3:

- At runtime, a field of an object is called a *location*. For convenience, we define a function $obj(\cdot)$ that yields the object of a location. For example, $obj(o.f)$ yields o.

- We introduce the binary relation $m_1 \hookrightarrow m_2$ which states that method m_2 is called by m_1 at runtime. We also introduce the reflexive transitive closure: $m_1 \hookrightarrow^* m_2$, meaning, m_1 is m_2 or m_1 is a direct or transitive caller of m_2.

Assignable Clauses We can specify the frame of a method using the clause `assignable` $l_1,\ldots,l_n$;, where l_i has the form `o.f` to refer to a field of an object. JML provides several other forms to specify assignable locations which we will introduce in section 2.4.1, but it's sufficient to stick to this one form to explain the concept.

The semantics of an `assignable` clauses is defined as follows. The fields mentioned in the clause are evaluated to a set of locations. This evaluation is performed in the pre-state of the method, that is, upon method invocation. The `assignable` clause only restricts assignment to locations that already existed in the pre-state of the method.

Let $\mathcal{A}_m$ be the set of locations from the `assignable` clause of method m. Furthermore, let $\mathcal{F}_m^\triangleleft$ be the set of locations that have been freshly allocated *during* the execution of m. The little triangle $\triangleleft$ indicates that this set contains the locations that have been freshly allocated in m and all methods directly or transitively called by m.

Let's assume a method m that is called by m' (i.e., $m' \hookrightarrow m$). According to the JML semantics, a location is assignable in m if it is either freshly allocated or it is in the set of locations evaluated from the `assignable` clause of m and it was already assignable in m'. We can write this condition as follows:

$$\mathcal{A}_m^{\text{effective}} = \mathcal{F}_m^\triangleleft \cup (\mathcal{A}_m \cap \mathcal{A}_{m'}^{\text{effective}}).$$

We call $\mathcal{A}_m^{\text{effective}}$ the set of locations that are effectively assignable in m. An important consequence of JML's semantics is that it is permitted to call a method whose `assignable` clause contains locations that are not assignable in the caller, as the set of effectively assignable locations contains the intersection of the assignable locations of the two methods.

Example. Let's assume that we are calling the method `balance` (see ₃₃ listing 1.3) in method `insert`. The method `balance` does not contain a specification, as it is intended for internal use only and the programmer did not bother to specify it. We treat an omitted `assignable` clause as "`assignable \everything`". That is, the method can assign to any location on the heap.

Even though this assignable clause clearly allows assignment to locations that are not assignable in `insert`, the call is permitted. However, during the execution of the method `balance`, only the locations specified in the `assignable` clause of `insert` can be updated.

Data Groups Data groups are sets of locations. Every field of a program defines its own data group that initially contains only the field itself.

1.8. PRELIMINARIES

If we are not interested in the value of the field but only its data group, JML provides a special type JMLDataGroup to indicate that the field just serves as a declaration of the corresponding data group.

To add all locations in the data group of a location $o.f$ to a data group of the same object o, JML uses the in clause at the field declaration.

Example. In the class Node in listing 1.3, the two fields left and right are declared to be in the data group of the field struct. We declare struct of type JMLDataGroup, since we are interested in its data group, but not its value. By this declaration, the data group of field struct contains the three locations this.struct, this.left, and this.right.

To add all locations in the data group of a location $o.f$ to a data group of another object, JML uses the maps ... \into clause. Adding locations from other objects makes a data group *dynamic*; the set of locations in the data group now depends on the program state.

Example. For instance in class Node, we add the data groups left.struct and right.struct to the data group of field struct. The fields left and right are called *pivot fields*, as an update of one of these fields changes the contents of data group struct. Since left.struct and right.struct also have a data group themselves, we essentially nest data groups in our example.

Upon evaluation of an assignable clause in method m, the semantics states that each data group mentioned in the assignable clause is evaluated to a set of locations. We call this process *unfolding* of the data group. Data groups that contain nested data groups do not evaluate to nested sets of locations, but result in one single set of locations which is added to the set $\mathcal{A}_m$.

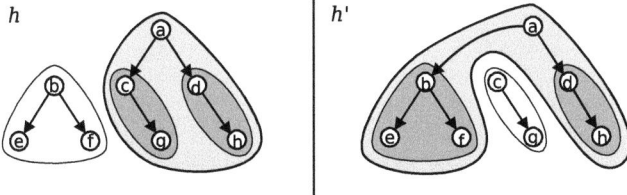

Figure 1.2: A set of Node objects. Shapes depict the struct data groups. Objects within the shape contain fields that the data group contains. Arrows depict references. Left: The situation in the pre-state. Right: The state after assigning b to a.left.

Example. Fig. 1.2 shows the dynamic data group of a.struct in light gray. One can see that a.struct also contains all locations that are mentioned in nested data groups, depicted by a darker gray. The left picture shows the initial state where the pivot field `a.left` points to node `c`, the right picture depicts the data group of `a.struct` after executing the statement `a.left = b`. White shapes depict data groups that are not in `a.struct`. This example illustrates that dynamic data groups may contain different locations in different program states.

Chapter 2
A JML Formalization in Coq

In this chapter, we introduce a deep embedding of a large subset of JML in Coq. That is, we define the syntax of all JML language constructs as data types in Coq and provide a semantic meaning for the interesting aspects of JML. In order to describe the semantics of these constructs, we also provide an embedding of the domain for JML annotated Java source code, that is, we formalize an execution state, based on a deterministic heap model for reference types and a model for Java primitive types.

Overview. Section 2.1 introduces the approach that we have chosen to formalize JML in Coq. Section 2.2 presents an architectural overview of the formalization and section 2.3 describes the language subset that we formalized. The following three sections present the highlights of the actual formalization in Coq: section 2.4 introduces the data types in Coq that define the syntax elements of JML and section 2.5 presents the domain on which the semantics presented in 2.6 operates.

2.1 Approach

As discussed in the introduction, one of the goals of our work is to provide a formalization that has a wide variety of applications. We achieve this by separating the semantics of JML specifications from the operational semantics, and providing a direct interface to JML annotations. This gives us the freedom to use the formalization not only as part of a verification environment, but also in other applications, for instance to prove properties of the JML language itself, or, as we do in chapter 4, to formalize and prove the correctness of a JML tool such as the runtime assertion checker.

In order to properly separate these two concerns (the semantics of JML constructs and the operational semantics), we distinguish between the data structures in the program state used by Java and the data structures added for JML. The Java data structures, such as the current heap or local variables, are visible to an application of the JML semantics, whereas the JML data structures, such as the pre-heap or the set of assignable locations, are additions to the program state that are only visible within the definition of the JML semantics.

The approach of providing a direct interface to JML specifications instead of "baking" the JML semantics into a verification environment comes at a price: we cannot enforce that the interface is used correctly. For instance, a verification environment could request the precondition of a method but then use it as postcondition. Therefore, it is important to provide a clear and simple interface together with a precise description of how to use it. The interface contains two parts to access JML specifications: an *annotation table* and a *frame conditions interface*. The following two paragraphs introduce both parts.

Most JML constructs express a property that holds at a given point in the program. For instance, an ensures clause describes a proposition that holds upon normal termination of a method, in its post-state. Some constructs are associated with several points in the program, for instance object invariants, which hold at all visible states of a program execution. For these constructs, our interface to JML annotations provides a so called *annotation table*. For any program point, this table provides access to a proposition that combines the properties stemming from all JML constructs associated with this program point.

There are a few JML constructs whose semantics cannot be described in terms of properties at certain program points, but which rather describe properties that need to be valid throughout execution of a program. The most prominent such construct is the assignable clause, which defines the heap locations that may be updated during the execution of a method. Other examples are the accessible clause, which declares the read effects of a method, or the working_space clause, which declares the maximum memory consumption for a method (however, these two constructs are very uncommon). In order to faithfully define the semantics of such constructs, we need to identify the situations that either influence the property defined by the construct, or may break it. For these situations, our interface needs to provide functions that either update some JML data structures in the program state that reflect the property, or express a predicate that needs to hold in the current situation. The assignable clause is the only construct supported by our formalization that requires such special treatment. The *frame conditions interface* contains all functions that are necessary to deal with all aspects of assignable clauses.

In section 2.6.1, we present the JML specifications interface in detail, including a precise description of the situations in which the individual functions from the interface need to be applied.

2.2 Architecture

Figure 2.1 gives an overview of our JML formalization in Coq. The different parts of the formalization are depicted by boxes. Usually, such a box corresponds to one

Module in Coq. The figure also depicts the dependencies between modules: modules can use functionality from modules below them. For instance, JML Program State depends on JML Semantics Interface, that itself indirectly depends on Java Program State, and so JML Program State has access to the Java Program State.

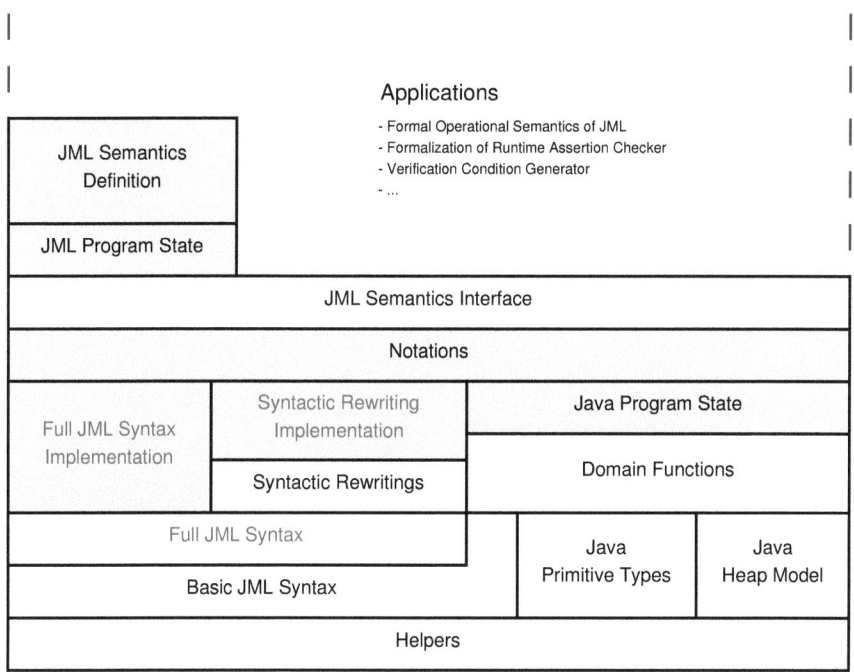

Figure 2.1: Overview of the JML formalization. Gray boxes depict implemented (constructively defined) modules as boxes, whereas white boxes depict modules that contain axiomatized definitions (see section 2.2.2). Modules with grayed out text are not discussed in this thesis, but available in the Coq formalization.

Syntax We split the definition of the JML syntax into two parts. The Basic JML Syntax defines a syntactic subset, to which the Full JML Syntax can be reduced by applying Syntactic Rewritings. In this thesis, we present the basic syntax in section 2.4 and briefly explain the rewriting steps in section 2.4.2, but omit the definition of the Full JML Syntax. We use axiomatized abstract data types to define the syntax constructs. The upside of this decision is that the data types are relatively small and readable. **Parameter**s declare the function signatures and **Axiom**s describe the desired behavior. The downside is that the axioms could potentially lead to inconsistencies, furthermore, we cannot represent a concrete instance of a JML program without actually implementing the axiomatized data types. Therefore, our formalization also provides an implementation of the axiomatized JML syntax constructs: we define functions that match the signature and prove the axiomatized properties as lemmas. However, this part of our implementation is not important to understand the formalization of JML and we completely omit it in this thesis.

Domain With the formalization of Java Primitive Types as well as the Java Heap Model, we define the domain of the JML semantics. In Domain Functions, we define a set of functions that help to operate on these constructs, for example functions for casting primitive types, or functions to determine if a value has the right type to be assigned to a field. As part of the domain, we also define a data type for the Java Program State so that it can be extended with JML constructs later on.

JML Semantics As explained in the last section, the JML Semantics Interface provides access to JML specifications. Beside the already-mentioned signatures of the annotation table and the frame condition interface, it defines the signatures of functions to create an initial program state, and a new frame for a given method. The JML Semantics Definition provides an implementation of the interface that reflects the JML Semantics as described in [49]. The semantics operates on the JML Program State, which is an extension of the Java Program State. Section 2.6.2 presents the definition of the JML semantics and the necessary additions to the program state.

Figure 2.1 suggests that there could also be different implementations of the interface. As a matter of fact, in the process of defining a correct runtime assertion checker for assignable clauses, we will add different implementations of the same interface.

2.2.1 Basis of the Formalization

We base our development on the Bicolano Java bytecode formalization [70], adapted to Java source code. Many aspects of the formalization do not differ between source code and bytecode. The Java Heap Model and the formalization of numbers in Java Primitive Types originate in Bicolano. We also reuse the Bicolano formalization of Java syntax down to method bodies, with minor changes to integrate the JML extensions into the language. On several occasions, we stick to the Bicolano formalization, even when there is another way of specifying a construct.

The reasons for this are two-fold. From a software engineering point of view, reusing a component comes with many advantages. We can rely on a carefully written formalization of the Java language and concentrate on the formalization of JML, instead of spending effort on defining basic Java language features. Furthermore, common theorem prover development environments do not offer any refactoring assistance. On the other hand, keeping our formalization close to Bicolano minimizes the effort of relating the two worlds.

For instance, it facilitates the formalization a sound translation from JML to its bytecode counterpart, BML [11, 16] as another application of the JML semantics.

2.2.2 Axiomatizations in Coq

As depicted in the figure by the white boxes, we allow to use axiomatized definitions in several parts of the formalization. However, axiomatizations comes with the risk of introducing inconsistencies into the formalization. Therefore, we need to identify the situations in which an axiomatization can be considered to be safe:

- The axiomatization describes a model that is backed up by an implementation of the model in another module. That is, we show the consistency of the axiomatized model by providing a concrete instantiation. For example, the Full JML Syntax Implementation provides a concrete implementation of the abstract data types axiomatized in Basic JML Syntax.

- The axiomatization describes the behavior of a function as a predicate, and is accompanied by a proof that for all possible input parameters of the function in question, the predicate holds for exactly one result value. We will discuss axiomatized functions in detail in tutorial 11 later on.

- The consistency of the axiomatization is shown as a result of related work. For example, we use an axiomatized heap model which has been proven to be consistent in [73]

- The axiomatization is straight-forward and not a central part of the formalization of JML. A good example is the axiomatized dictionary presented in section 2.5.2. In such cases, we do not to prove the consistency of the formalization.

2.3 Language Coverage

Table 2.1 gives an overview of the scope of our project. We split the coverage into syntax and semantics definitions. Often, a construct is defined on a syntactic level without a semantic meaning. That is, we define the abstract data type to represent a syntactic construct, but we do not provide a semantic interpretation for the given construct.

Java Version Although quite some effort has been spent in the JML community to port JML from Java 1.4 to Java 5 and 6, we decided to stick to Java 1.4 constructs only. The main reason is that the JML constructs for Java 1.4 are pretty stable, whereas JML support for newer constructs, such as generics or enums, is still a moving target. Most notably, none of these new constructs are discussed in the JML reference manual, which is the basis for our formalization.

Constructs	Syntax Coverage	Semantics Coverage
Java 1.4	Full support except for long integers, string literals, floating point numbers, concurrency, and inner classes.	Operational semantics for the most interesting constructs, including method calls, field updates, and object creation.
JML Level 0	Full support	Full support
JML Level 1	Full support except for the constructs \implies_that, \for_example, set-comprehension, and safe math extensions.	Support for interesting constructs such as the pure modifier, dynamic data groups, and generalized quantifiers.
JML Level 2	Full support except for safe math extensions.	–
JML Level 3	Full support.	–
JML Level C	Full support except for the lock-set ordering operators.	–
JML Level X	The \readonly modifier.	–

Table 2.1: Coverage of our formalization

Syntax Coverage We cover most syntax constructs of Java and JML. However, we completely ignore certain aspects of the language. Firstly, we do not add a formalization of floating point numbers and big integers to Bicolano, as we see these issues as a mere distraction for our work. Secondly, we do not reason about concurrency as part of this work. The other constructs that we omit in this work are either not suitable for a formalization in Coq, not well defined at the time when this formalization was started (such as the safe math extension) or were left away to simplify the formalization without making the result significantly less interesting.

Semantics Coverage We aim at defining the semantics for all level 0 JML constructs and interesting level 1 concepts. On level 1, we focus on the most useful constructs as well as constructs that lead to interesting aspects of the formalization. Among others, we concentrate on dynamic data groups (which are crucial to facilitate the definition of non-trivial frame properties), the modifier pure, and generalized quantifiers, which are satisfactory use-cases for defining non trivial JML expressions formally.

It is not our goal to come up with as complete as possible an operational semantics for Java. This would blow up the scope of this project. We define a subset that is necessary to perform the correctness proof of our runtime assertion checker for assignable clauses, see chapter 4.

2.4 Definition of JML Syntax Constructs

In this section we give an overview of the JML syntax definition. We highlight only the interesting aspects and parts that we need in the following chapters, and leave out many constructs that look similar to what we've already shown.

We aim to facilitate the representation of any well-formed program in our formalization. However, we do not impede that an ill-formed program can be represented. For instance, it's possible to represent the assignment 5 = a; in our data types. For certain applications of the formalization, one might need to add a well-formedness predicate that restricts the inputs to only valid and type correct programs. We believe that it is beneficial for the formalization to separate the two concerns, as the data types that represent JML constructs become much simpler.

Outline. In the so-called "Basic JML Syntax" presented in subsection 2.4.1, we define JML constructs in their simplest form. In subsection 2.4.2, we briefly describe a syntactic rewriting in Coq that desugars JML constructs into this basic form. Subsection 2.4.3 introduces additional rules for the Coq parser: so called **Notation**s to dramatically improve the readability of embedded JML constructs in Coq.

Before we go ahead, we have a look at the different possibilities there are for defining the syntax of a language in Coq.

--- A MADE-TO-MEASURE COQ TUTORIAL ---

Part 2 Inductive and Abstract Data Types

To define syntax constructs in Coq, we either introduce inductive or abstract data types, depending on their purpose and complexity.

Listing 2.1 shows an example of an inductive definition that merely describes an enumeration. The data type Visibility *is of sort* **Set** *and contains the elements* Package, Protected, Private, Public, Spec_Public, *and* Spec_Protected. *We can perform pattern matching on the inductive data type. However, Coq doesn't allow partial pattern matching, all cases need to be addressed. This ensures that we need to deal with all possibilities for a given type. However, it's possible to apply a single action to several matchings, and to use the wildcard "_" that matches with all constructors that have not been addressed already. The definition* isJMLVisibility *shows both concepts in action.*

```
Inductive Visibility : Set :=
  | Package | Protected | Private | Public
  | Spec_Public | Spec_Protected.

Definition isJMLVisibility (v : Visibility) : bool :=
  match v with
```

```
7  | Spec_Public | Spec_Protected ⇒ true
8  | _ ⇒ false
9  end.
```

Listing 2.1: An example for a simple inductive definition and pattern matching on it

We also use inductive definitions to define simple record types. In listing 2.2, we define the type Literal of sort Set to express integer and boolean Java literals, using the predefined sorts bool and Z for booleans and integer numbers, respectively. We can use pattern matching to extract the data from the record type as shown in definition Literal2Z that yields 0 for false, 1 for true, and z for the integer literal z.

```
1  Inductive Literal : Set :=
2  | BoolLiteral (b : bool)
3  | IntLiteral (z : Z).
4
5  Definition Literal2Z (l : Literal) : Z :=
6  match l with
7  | BoolLiteral b ⇒ if b then 1 else 0
8  | IntLiteral z ⇒ z
9  end.
```

Listing 2.2: An example for a inductive definition carrying additional data

For more complex data types, we choose to define abstract data types using the Coq module system. We introduce a **Module Type** that features a **Parameter** t, which will be the type of our abstract data type and functions that operate on t. The example in listing 2.3 shows a possible definition of local variable signatures. In the module type VARSIG_TYPE We declare parameter t of sort **Type** to be the type for variable signatures. The module type declares two functions over t: the function name, which yields the name of the parameter, the function type, which yields the static type of the parameter, and an axiom eq_dec that states equality to be decidable for type t.

To use the abstract data type, we can implement a module that adheres to the signature of the module type VARSIG_TYPE. To achieve this, we need to define (we also say "implement") type t as well as the two functions name and type. We also need to prove the proposition eq_dec as a lemma. Alternatively, [12] we can just declare such a module without providing a definition. However, that way we do not get any guarantees that such a module can really be constructed and that the axioms are consistent. [15,16] At the end of the listing, we show how we can access identifiers from a module using fully qualified names.

```
1  Parameter VarName : Set.
```

```
2  Inductive StaticType : Set :=
3    (* omitted *)
4
5  Module Type VARSIG_TYPE.
6    Parameter t        : Type.
7    Parameter name  : t → VarName.
8    Parameter type   : t → StaticType.
9    Axiom       eq_dec : ∀ v1 v2 : t , {v1=v2}+{¬v1=v2}.
10 End VARSIG_TYPE.
11
12 Declare Module VARSIG : VARSIG_TYPE.
13
14 (** Example: Declare a variable signature *)
15 Parameter vsig : VARSIG.t.
16
17 (** Example: Check the type of function 'name' applied to 'vsig' *)
18 Check VARSIG.name vsig.
```

Listing 2.3: An example for a definition of local variable signatures as an abstract data type, using Coq's module system.

In our development, we often declare the type of an abstract data type outside the module-type, and give it an unambiguous name. In listing 2.4, we again define local variable signatures; this time we declare VarSig of sort **Type** outside VARSIG_TYPE, and change the affected signatures accordingly.

```
1  Parameter VarSig : Type.
2
3  Module Type VARSIG_TYPE.
4    Parameter name  : VarSig → VarName.
5    Parameter type   : VarSig → StaticType.
6    Axiom       eq_dec : ∀ v1 v2 : VarSig , {v1=v2}+{¬v1=v2}.
7  End VARSIG_TYPE.
```

Listing 2.4: The same definition as in listing 2.3. This time, we use parameter VarSig as the type for the abstract data type

2.4.1 Basic Syntax Constructs

In JML, some syntax constructs come in different flavors. For instance, and most notably, there are many different kinds of method specifications in JML: lightweight, normal behavior, exceptional behavior, nested, or even just omitted specification cases. There can be specification cases with multiple occurrences of the same kind of method specification clause, or omitted clauses.

In the basic syntax, we define the JML syntax constructs in their simplest form, as long as a transformation from the more complex can be performed in a straight-forward way in a syntactic rewriting. That is, the supported subset is identical to the full syntax as described in section 2.3, but in a simpler form.

In the case of method specifications, the basic syntax only defines behavior specification cases in which each clause appears exactly once. In section 2.4.2, we present the simplifications in the basic syntax together with the rewriting steps from the full syntax.

In the following paragraphs, we present interesting or relevant constructs from the basic syntax, starting with the abstract data type **Program**.

JML Programs

The abstract data type for a JML program in listing 2.5 declares two functions **class** and **interface** that yield the abstract data type of a class and of an interface, respectively, for a given name. If the program doesn't contain a class or an interface with the specified name, these functions yield **None**.

The predicate defined_Class holds if and only if the program contains a given abstract data type for a class. For the defined classes of a program, no two can have the same name, and **class** must act as the inverse of **CLASS.name**. The predicate defined_Interface is defined accordingly.

```
1  Parameter Program : Type.
2
3  Module Type PROG_TYPE.
4    Parameter class     : Program →ClassName →option Class.
5    Definition defined_Class (p : Program) (cl : Class) : Prop :=
6      class p (CLASS.name cl) = Some cl.
7
8    Parameter interface : Program →InterfaceName → option Interface .
9    Definition defined_Interface (p : Program) (i : Interface ) : Prop :=
10     interface p (INTERFACE.name i) = Some i.
11 End PROG_TYPE.
```

Listing 2.5: The abstract data type for JML Programs

Classes and Interfaces

As classes and interfaces share similar properties, we define a data type TYPEDEF.t for both constructs. On the last two lines in listing 2.6 we define the two types class and interface to be synonyms for this abstract data type. Furthermore, the two types ClassName and InterfaceName are synonyms for the type TypeDefName.

The TYPEDEF module declares several functions to access the different properties of a class or interface. Again, it's not our concern to restrict the abstract data type to make it impossible to represent invalid JML constructs. For instance, if t represents an interface, the function superClass should yield None ,and several other constraints apply.

We define fields, model fields, and methods in the same way that we define classes and interfaces in programs: accessor functions retrieve the element by its name, and predicates state whether or not an element is a member of the class or interface.

```
1  Module Type TYPEDEF_TYPE.
2    Parameter t : Type.
3    Parameter name            : t → TypeDefName.
4    Parameter visibility      : t → Visibility .
5    Parameter superInterfaces : t → list t.
6    Parameter superClass      : t → option t.
7    Parameter typeSpec        : t → TypeSpec.
8    ...
9
10   Parameter field           : t → ShortFieldName →option Field .
11   Definition definedField (c : t) (f : Field) :=
12     field c (FIELDSIGNATURE.name (FIELD.signature f)) = Some f.
13
14   Parameter method          : t → ShortMethodSignature →option Method.
15   Definition definedMethod (c : t) (m : Method) :=
16     method c (METHOD.signature m) = Some m.
17   ...
18 End TYPEDEF_TYPE.
19
20 Declare Module TYPEDEF : TYPEDEF_TYPE.
21
22 Definition Class := TYPEDEF.t.
23 Definition Interface := TYPEDEF.t.
```

Listing 2.6: The abstract data type for classes and interfaces

The JML type specifications can be accessed by the function typeSpec. We show a condensed version of the abstract data type of type specifications in listing 2.7, only showing the details for invariants and omitting all other constructs. A class or interface can contain an arbitrary number of the same type declaration construct. For instance, a class can contain not just one, but several invariants, and each invariant is either a static or an instance invariant and has its own visibility modifier.

We can access the predicate defining an invariant by the function **pred**, which yields an inductive data type for a JML expression, which we will illuminate later.

```
1   Module TYPESPEC.
2     Module Type INVARIANT_TYPE.
3       Parameter t : Type.
4       Parameter pred       : t → Expression.
5       Parameter visibility : t → Visibility.
6       Parameter isStatic   : t → bool.
7       ...
8     End INVARIANT_TYPE.
9     Declare Module INVARIANT : INVARIANT_TYPE.
10
11    ...
12
13    Module Type TYPESPEC_TYPE.
14      Parameter t : Type.
15      Parameter invariant   : t → list INVARIANT.t.
16      ...
17    End TYPESPEC_TYPE.
18    Declare Module TYPESPEC : TYPESPEC_TYPE.
19  End TYPESPEC.
20  Definition TypeSpec := TYPESPEC.TYPESPEC.t.
```

Listing 2.7: The abstract data type for JML type specifications

———————— A made-to-measure Coq Tutorial ————————

Part 3   Modules and Name Conflicts

A module in Coq opens a new name space. Furthermore, modules can be nested. Within new name spaces, we can reuse existing names without generating conflicts. The module ₁₈ TYPESPEC of listing 2.7 happens to have the same name as the ₁ enclosing module. To access an element of an inner module, we need to use its fully qualified name. For instance, in the ₂₀ term which defines the type **TypeSpec** to be a synonym for the cumbersome type TYPESPEC.TYPESPEC.t.

38

If we are hiding an element from outside a module by introducing an element of the same name within module, we can still access the former from within the module by using its fully qualified name.

We define several predicates and definitions for easier handling of the abstract data type for classes and interfaces. We highlight just one predicate that we will use later on. This gives an impression of how we can work with the abstract data types that we have defined.

In listing 2.8, we define the predicate SubType sub super which holds if sub is a subtype of super or if sub and super are equal. In order to define such a predicate, we define a predicate direct_subtype that holds if either super is declared to be the super class of sub, or if it is one of the interfaces of sub. We express this in an inductive definition with two constructors. The predicate holds if one of the constructors applies.

The definition of SubType is the reflexive transitive closure over the direct_subtype. We use the predicate clos_refl_trans from the Coq standard library, parameterized by the type of the elements: TYPEDEF.t, the predicate for one step: direct_subtype, and the two types in question: sub and super.

```
Inductive direct_subtype (sub super: TYPEDEF.t) : Prop :=
  | direct_subtype_extends :
      TYPEDEF.superClass sub = Some super →
      direct_subtype sub super
  | direct_subtype_implements :
      super ∈ (TYPEDEF.superInterfaces sub) →
      direct_subtype sub super.

Definition SubType (sub super : TYPEDEF.t) : Prop :=
  clos_refl_trans  TYPEDEF.t (direct_subtype) sub super.
```

Listing 2.8: The two predicates SubType and direct_subtype

———————— A MADE-TO-MEASURE COQ TUTORIAL ————————

Part 4   Inductive Predicates

We can read inductive definitions in Coq as a set of inference rules. Each constructor of the inductive definition corresponds to one rule. For the definition of direct_subtype, we get the two inference rules:

$$\text{direct\_subtype\_extends} \frac{\text{TYPEDEF.superClass sub} = \text{Some super}}{\text{direct\_subtype sub super}}$$

$$\text{direct\_subtype\_implements} \frac{\text{super} \in (\text{TYPEDEF.superInterfaces sub})}{\text{direct\_subtype sub super}}$$

Instead of using an inductive definition, we could define the predicate direct_subtype in a more direct fashion:

Definition direct_subtype (sub super: TYPEDEF.t) : **Prop** :=
TYPEDEF.superClass sub = Some super ∨
super ∈ (TYPEDEF.superInterfaces sub).

Although this definition looks simpler, its handling in the Coq proof system is less comfortable than using the inductive definition. So, quite often even when we could write a definition, we choose to use an inductive definition to express a predicate.

Fields

Following the definitions in Bicolano, we provide two separate modules for fields and field signatures. This separation sometimes requires us to perform an additional operation to retrieve a field from a type definition.

```
1  Parameter Field : Type.
2  Parameter ShortFieldName : Set.
3  Parameter ShortFieldSignature : Set.
4  Definition FieldName       := TypeDefName * ShortFieldName.
5  Definition FieldSignature  := TypeDefName * ShortFieldSignature.
6
7  Module Type FIELDSIGNATURE_TYPE.
8    Parameter name : ShortFieldSignature  → ShortFieldName.
9    Parameter type : ShortFieldSignature  → StaticType.
10   Axiom   eq_dec : ∀ f1 f2 : ShortFieldSignature , {f1=f2}+{¬f1=f2}.
11 End FIELDSIGNATURE_TYPE.
12
13 Module Type FIELD_TYPE.
14   Parameter signature    : Field → ShortFieldSignature .
15   Parameter dataGroups   : Field → list DATA_GROUP.t.
16   ...
17 End FIELD_TYPE.
```

Listing 2.9: The abstract data types for field signatures and fields

A field in JML can be contained in several data group declarations. To that end, the function dataGroups in module FIELD yields a list of abstract data types for data groups.

Listing 2.10 shows how we define this data type.

In JML, we can either declare a field to be statically contained in a data group, using the "in" keyword, or we can declare a dynamic data group dependency between two fields using the "maps ... into" clause. If the data group relation is dynamic, we can use the function pivotTarget to access the target of the dynamic data group definition, which is either a field or "*" to represent all fields of the target object. The function isDynamic distinguishes between static and dynamic declarations. The definition of isDynamic relies on the fact that for a well-formed program, a dynamic data group declaration always specifies a pivot target.

Each data group declaration can mention one or more data groups. This is why the function dataGroups yields a list of field signatures, [14] which must be non-empty.

```
1   Inductive PivotTarget :=
2   | FieldDg ( fsig  : FieldSignature ).   (* Represents: target.fsig *)
3   | AllFieldsDg.                          (* Represents: target.*   *)
4
5   Module Type DATA_GROUP_TYPE.
6     Parameter t : Type.
7     Parameter pivotTarget  : t → option PivotTarget.
8     Parameter dataGroups   : t → list FieldSignature.
9     ...
10
11    Definition isDynamic (dg : t) : bool :=
12      if pivotTarget dg then true else false.
13
14    Axiom dataGroups_not_nil: ∀ t, dataGroups t ≠ nil.
15  End DATA_GROUP_TYPE.
```

Listing 2.10: The abstract data types for field signatures and fields

──────────────── A MADE-TO-MEASURE COQ TUTORIAL ────────────────

Part 5   *Syntactic Sugar for Pattern Matching*

We can use the term "if *opt* then x else y", as seen on line 11 of listing 2.10 to perform a case distinction on variable "*opt* : option T". If *opt* contains some element of type T then the term evaluates to x. If *opt* is equal to None, the term evaluates to y. The following pattern matching is equivalent to the term above:

```
match opt with
| Some _ ⇒ x
| None   ⇒ y
```

end.

Methods

Similarly to fields, we follow Bicolano and have separate modules for methods and method signatures. Listing 2.11 shows the two modules.

```
Module Type METHODSIGNATURE_TYPE.
  Parameter name       : ShortMethodSignature →ShortMethodName.
  Parameter parameters : ShortMethodSignature → list Param.
  Parameter result     : ShortMethodSignature →option StaticType.
  ...
End METHODSIGNATURE_TYPE.

Module Type METHOD_TYPE.
  Parameter signature : Method →ShortMethodSignature.
  Parameter specs     : Method → list SpecificationCase.
  ...
End METHOD_TYPE.
```

Listing 2.11: The abstract data types for method signatures and methods

We are mainly interested in method specifications, accessed by the function specs. In listing 2.12, we highlight two method specifications, requires clauses and assignable clauses. The other clauses are formalized similarly. In the basic syntax, a specification case is always a "full behavior case" that contains each specification construct exactly once. Thus, the functions ₂₀ requires and ₂₁ assignable yield one instance of the given construct.

```
Module METHODSPEC.

  Module Type REQUIRES_TYPE.
    Parameter t : Type.
    Parameter pred    : t → optional Expression.
    Parameter isSame  : t → bool.
  End REQUIRES_TYPE.

  Module Type ASSIGNABLE_TYPE.
    Parameter t : Type.
```

```
11      Parameter storeRefs   : t → optional  StoreRefList .
12      End ASSIGNABLE_TYPE.
13
14      ...
15
16      Module Type SPECIFICATION_CASE_TYPE.
17      Parameter t : Type.
18      Parameter visibility      : t → Visibility .
19      ...
20      Parameter requires        : t → REQUIRES.t.
21      Parameter assignable      : t → ASSIGNABLE.t.
22      ...
23      End SPECIFICATION_CASE_TYPE.
24
25   End METHODSPEC.
```

Listing 2.12: The abstract data types for method specifications

Even though all constructs need to be mentioned in a specification case, they can be declared \not_specified. To that end, we introduce the inductive type optional A which behaves pretty much like option A and can be parametrized by any type A, see listing 2.13. The reason for introducing the type optional instead of just using option lies in the readability of embedded JML specifications. If a clause is set to be NotSpecified, it is clear that the clause has explicitly been set to \not_specified, whereas the corresponding constructor None from the option type might suggest that the clause is not mentioned in the specification.

```
1   Inductive optional (A : Type) : Type :=
2   |  NotSpecified
3   |  Specified (t : A).
```

Listing 2.13: The data type optional to express \not_specified method clauses in a readable way

Each kind of method specification clause is defined as a nested module within the module METHODSPEC. Each module features a parameter t as the type of the abstract data type for the method clause, and one or several accessor functions depending on the clause. The data type for requires clauses has a function pred that either yields NotSpecified if the clause has been marked as such, or a boolean expression. The clause has another function isSame that yields true to represent the special clause requires \same. In this case, the value of pred is irrelevant.

In JML, the `assignable` clause mentions a list of *store refs*. A store ref is either the keyword \nothing, which denotes that the method doesn't have side effects, \everything, which denotes that the method may potentially change every location in the heap, or a term that identifies one or more heap locations. There are many forms of identifying heap locations, see [49, section 12.7]. In the subsequent formalization, we support the following forms:

- A static field reference.

- A path $o.f_1 \ldots f_n$, where o is either `this` or a method parameter and $f_1 \ldots f_n$ are field identifiers.

- All fields of an object: $o.f_1 \ldots f_n.*$.

In listing 2.14, we introduce the data type StoreRef.

```
Inductive StoreRefPrefix :=
  | ThisRef
  | ParamRef (param : Param)
  | PathRef (target : StoreRefPrefix) (fsig : FieldSignature).

Inductive StoreRef :=
  | StaticFieldRef (fsig : FieldSignature)
  | FieldRef (target : StoreRefPrefix) (fsig : FieldSignature)
  | AllFieldsRef (target : StoreRefPrefix).

Inductive StoreRefList :=
  | Nothing
  | Everything
  | StoreRefs (sr : list StoreRef).
```

Listing 2.14: The data types for store refs

In JML, a method has to obey not only its own specification cases, but also those inherited from its super types. For that reason, we want to be able to identify all the specification cases that are defined for a method. In listing 2.15, we show an inductively defined predicate DefinedCase c m sc; it holds if the specification case sc is declared at method m in c or a super type of c. The inductive definition reads as follows ₃: if there is a class c' such that c' = c or c is a subtype of c' and ₄ if that class c' features a method m' with a signature m and ₅ if that method m' declares the method case sc, then ₆ we define that predicate DefinedCase c m sc holds. In tutorial 4 on page 39 we explain why we sometimes choose an **Inductive** definition instead of a more direct definition.

```
1  Inductive DefinedCase (c : Class) (m : Method) (sc : SpecificationCase ) : Prop:=
2  | DefinedCase_def :  ∀ m' c ',
3     SubType c c' →
4     TYPEDEF.method c' (METHOD.signature m) = Some m' →
5     In sc (METHOD.specs m') →
6     DefinedCase c m sc.
```

Listing 2.15: Inductive Definition of a predicate DefinedCase

Statements and Blocks

A method body in Java is a block of statements that can contain nested blocks. This mutual dependency introduces a hurdle when defining the abstract data types, as we cannot use an abstract data type before it has been defined in the text. In the upcoming tutorial, we learn how Coq supports mutual dependent types, but we cannot apply this technique in the case of abstract data types. Thus, we proceed as follows to define statements and blocks.

We introduce three data types. An inductive data type representing the different kinds of statements, and two abstract data types, one for statements and one for blocks. All three constructs have mutual dependencies that we need to resolve.

Firstly, we define the inductive data type as sketched in listing 2.16 to define both Java and JML statements. As we haven't defined the abstract data types for statements and blocks yet, we add two parameters Statement and Block of sort **Type** to the inductive definition. We can now use these types to refer to statements and blocks, respectively, for instance in the argument block of constructor Compound. Other than the two parametric types, the inductive data type for statements doesn't contain any surprises.

```
1  Inductive StatementType {Statement Block: Type}: Type :=
2  (** Java statements *)
3  | Compound       (block : Block)
4  | ExprStmt       (e : Expression)
5  | WhileLoop      (anno : LoopAnnotation)
6                   (test : Expression) (body : Statement)
7  ...
8  (** JML statements *)
9  | LocalAssertion  (expr : Expression) (label : option Expression)
10                   (redundantly : bool)
11 ...
```

Listing 2.16: The inductive data type StatementType to define the different kinds of statements

Secondly, we define the module **STATEMENT**, see listing 2.17. It contains a parameter b of sort **Type**. We declare b as the type of the abstract data type for blocks. Function pc yields a "program counter" that we assign to each statement. The program counter for statements is unique within a method body. We use it to retrieve statements from blocks or methods. The function type yields a StatementType that we have just defined before. At this point, ₆ we can assign t and b to the two parameters **Statement** and **Block**.

```
1  Module Type STATEMENT_TYPE.
2    Parameter t : Type. (* ADT for Statements *)
3    Parameter b : Type. (* ADT for Blocks *)
4    Parameter label : t → option Label.
5    Parameter pc    : t → PC.
6    Parameter type : t → StatementType (Statement := t) (Block := b).
7  End STATEMENT_TYPE.
```

Listing 2.17: The abstract data type for statements

Thirdly, we define the module **BLOCK** as in listing 2.18 in which we use the previously declared type STATEMENT.b. The data type contains a list of local variables as well as several axiomatized functions to access statements in a block and to navigate through statements.

₁₀ Axiom elem_def defines the behavior of the function elem in terms of the functions statementAt and STATEMENT.pc. It states that: if function elem yields true for a given pc of a block, then there exists a statement at that program counter in the block. The statement retrieved by the function statementAt at this position contains the same pc as program counter.

₁₂ Axiom statementAt_def defines the behavior of statementAt. If the function yields a statement for a given pc, the statement's program counter is set to pc. We have omitted here further axioms defining the behavior of the functions first , last , and next.

```
1  Module Type BLOCK_TYPE.
2    Definition t := STATEMENT.b.
3    Parameter localVariables : t → list  Var.
4    Parameter elem            : t → PC →bool .
5    Parameter statementAt     : t → PC →option STATEMENT.t.
6    Parameter first           : t → option PC.
7    Parameter last            : t → option PC.
8    Parameter next            : t → PC →option PC.
9
```

```
10   Axiom elem_def : ∀ t pc, elem t pc = true →
11     ∃ s, statementAt t pc = Some s ∧STATEMENT.pc s = pc.
12   Axiom statementAt_def : ∀ t pc s,
13     statementAt t pc = Some s →STATEMENT.pc s = pc.
14   ...
15
16   End BLOCK_TYPE.
```

Listing 2.18: The abstract data type for blocks

--------- A MADE-TO-MEASURE COQ TUTORIAL ---------

Part 6   Mutually Dependent Types

We have just seen how we can deal with mutual-dependent abstract data types. For inductive data types, definitions, or fixpoints, that mutually depend on each other, Coq provides the following solution.

We can define several such constructs together, using the keyword with. In this way, all constructs are defined at the same point in the text and thus can refer to each other. An application is the definition of the inductive type StaticType, which we have already encountered on several occasions.

We define the data type StaticType to be either a primitive type or a reference type, as shown in listing 2.19. A reference type can be an array of any StaticType, which introduces a cyclic dependency. By defining the two data types together, we are allowed to keep that dependency.

```
1   Inductive StaticType : Set :=
2     | ReferenceType (rt : refType)
3     | PrimitiveType (pt : primitiveType)
4   with refType : Set :=
5     | ArrayType   (type : StaticType)  (um : utsModifier)
6     | TypeDefType (td : TypeDefName) (um : utsModifier)
7     | NullType.
```

Listing 2.19: The mutually dependent types StaticType and refType

Expressions

Listing 2.20 shows a short excerpt of the inductive data type for Java and JML expressions. As discussed earlier, it is possible to build ill-formed expressions. For instance, the optional target of fields and methods can only be an expression that evaluates to an object reference type, but this doesn't reflect in our data type, in which we can set any kind of expression as target. It is the semantics that will deal with the well-formedness of expressions.

```
1   Inductive BinaryIntOp : Set :=
2   | Addition | Multiplication
3   ...
4   | BitwiseAnd | BitwiseXor
5   ...
6
7   Inductive Expression : Type :=
8   (** Java expressions *)
9   | literal           (l : Literal )
10  | new               (t : StaticType)
11  | method            (method : MethodSignature)
12                      (target : option Expression )
13                      (params: list Expression )
14  | field             ( field : FieldSignature )
15                      (target : option Expression )
16  | UnaryBoolExpr     (op : UnaryBoolOp) (expr : Expression )
17  | BinaryIntExpr     (op : BinaryIntOp)
18                      ( left : Expression ) ( right : Expression )
19  | Assignment        ( left : Expression ) ( right : Expression )
20  ...
21
22  (** JML expressions *)
23  | Quantification    (q : Quantifier ) (var : Var) (range : Expression )
24                      (expr : Expression ).
25  ...
```

Listing 2.20: The inductive data type for expressions, along with two examples for inductive definitions of operators.

2.4.2 Syntactic Rewritings

In the basic syntax description, we provide simplified versions of three constructs: method specifications that consist of a list of full behavior specification cases, quantified expressions that feature exactly one quantified variable, and loop annotations with a field expression; a predicate which expresses the conjunction of all loop invariants. We provide a syntactic rewriting from the full forms of these constructs into their simplified forms. In our technical report on the formalization [42], we describe the extended syntax and the syntactic rewriting in detail. This thesis only presents the general idea of the rewriting. While the rewriting of quantified expressions and loop invariants is straight-forward, the desugaring of method specification cases deserves a short description.

The syntactic rewriting of method specification cases directly follows the technical report [74] by Raghavan and Leavens. The authors split up the desugaring of method specifications into eleven steps; we perform eight of these steps, the remaining three steps being unnecessary as our semantics can deal with the sugared version directly.

Desugaring Non-null for Arguments This desugaring adds an additional clause "requires p != null" to each specification case of the method for every parameter p that is implicitly or explicitly declared to be non-null. If the method doesn't feature any specification cases, these additional requires clauses are added to a new lightweight specification case.

Desugaring Non-null Results This desugaring adds an additional ensures clause "ensures \result != null" to every non-exceptional specification case if the method is declared non_null. If no specification case is defined, we add the additional ensures clause to a new lightweight specification case.

Desugaring pure This desugaring adds two clauses to every specification case of pure methods. The additional clauses are "diverges false" and, in case of a constructor "assignable this.*", otherwise "assignable \nothing". Again, if the method has no specification, the clauses are added to a new lightweight specification case.

Desugaring Empty Specifications This desugaring adds a default specification to the given method if the method features no explicit specification and the first three desugarings didn't create a lightweight specification case already. The default specification is a lightweight specification case with the clause "requires \not_specified" for any non-override method or "also requires false" for an override method.

Desugaring Nested Specifications This desugaring recursively flattens nested specification cases into a semantically equivalent list of specification cases. As opposed to the description in the underlying report, we do not have to deal with variable capturing issues when merging several definitions of quantified variables into one case, as all quantified variables introduced in specifications are globally unique already.

Desugaring Lightweight, Normal, and Exceptional Specifications This desugaring transforms lightweight, normal- and exceptional behavior specification cases into behavior specification cases. For normal behavior cases this amounts to adding a clause "signals (Exception e) `false`". For exceptional behavior cases, we add a clause "ensures `false`". For lightweight specification cases, the visibility is set to the visibility of the enclosing method and a default clause is added for every clause kind that is missing in this case.

Standardizing Signals Clauses This desugaring standardizes every signals clause "signals (ET n) P", where variable n is the declares the exception object of type ET, into a signals clause "signals (Exception e) (e `instanceof` ET) $\Rightarrow$ P'". P' denotes expression P where every occurrence of n is substituted by "(ET) e". This rewriting becomes interesting when performing the next desugaring step. We can easily merge several signals clauses into one by using one unified exception variable e.

Merging Multiple Clauses of the Same Kind This desugaring merges multiple clauses of the same kind within a specification case into a single clause. For instance, two requires clauses "requires $p1$; requires $p2$" are merged into a single requires clause "requires $p1$ && $p2$ ". Note that we build the conjunction of $p1$ and $p2$ and not the disjunction, as the clauses appear in the same specification case.

2.4.3 Notations

An implementation of the data types defined in this chapter allow us to embed JML programs in Coq. However, without using Coq notations, it's very inconvenient to read the resulting statement data type in Coq. The quite simple `if` statement in listing 2.21 results in the data type shown in listing 2.22. If we want to use our formalization as part of a program verifier, this embedding means a lot of trouble for the user as he has a hard time to understand the JML annotations and the program that he wants to verify. The whole idea of being able to embed a JML program in an interactive theorem prover is pointless if we cannot read what we want to verify.

```
1  if (i % 2 == 0) {
2    sumEven += i;
3  } else {
4    sumOdd += i;
5  }
```

Listing 2.21: A simple Java statement

```
1  STATEMENT.Build_t 5%Z None (IfStmt (RelationalExpr IntEquality
2  (BinaryIntExpr Remainder (var x) ( literal  ( IntLiteral  2)))
3  ( literal  ( IntLiteral  0))) (STATEMENT.Build_t 5%Z None (Compound
```

2.4. DEFINITION OF JML SYNTAX CONSTRUCTS

```
4  (BLOCK.Build_t [] [STATEMENT.Build_t 6%Z None (ExprStmt
5  (IntAssignmentExpr AssignmentAddition (var sumEven) (var i )))])))
6  (Some (STATEMENT.Build_t 7%Z None (Compound (BLOCK.Build_t []
7  [STATEMENT.Build_t 7%Z None (ExprStmt (IntAssignmentExpr
8  AssignmentAddition (var sumOdd) (var i )))])))))).
```

Listing 2.22: The same statement embedded in Coq

We can solve the issue by making heavy use of notations, that is, additional rules for the Coq parser and pretty printer. With clever notations in place, we manage to embed JML code in Coq while maintaining readability. Listing 2.23 shows the same data type with our notations enabled. Although there is some unavoidable noise such as the constructors var, int, and stmt, and quite a few brackets, the code remains readable. A user who wants to verify this statement is able to read and understand the code and directly map it to the original JML code.

```
1  5% :> ife ((var i) mod (int 2) == (int 0)) {: 5 :>>
2      [6 :> stmt ((var sumEven) += (var i))]
3      :} else_ {: 7 :>>
4      [7 :> stmt ((var sumOdd) += (var i))]
5      :}
```

Listing 2.23: The same statement embedded in Coq, using notations

In listings 2.24 and 2.25, we show a nested specification case in JML and its counterpart in Coq, using notations to make the code readable, respectively. Again, there is a bit of added noise, for instance, the constructors spec_case and simple_case to identify the data type, and the use of empty lists "[]" for omitted or default parts of the specification case.

```
1   normal_behaviour
2
3     requires x != null
4     {|
5       requires x.getValue() ≥ 0;
6       ensures \result == x.getValue();
7     also
8       requires x.getValue() < 0;
9       ensures \result ≥ 0;
10    |}
```

Listing 2.24: An example of a nested specification case in JML

```
1  spec_case [ public ] normal_behaviour (
2    nested_case [] []
3    [requires (: (var x) != null :)]
4    {|
5      simple_case [] []
6        [requires (: (callT (var x) getValue []) ≥ ( int 0) :)]
7        [ensures (: \result == (callT (var x) getValue []) :)]
8      ;
9      simple_case [] []
10       [requires (: (callT (var x) getValue []) < ( int 0) :)]
11       [ensures (: \result ≥ ( int 0) :)]
12   |}
13 ).
```

Listing 2.25: The same nested specification case embedded in Coq, using notations

Listing 2.25 illustrates why we add quite so many different kinds of brackets around the JML constructs in our notations. If we look at the ₃ first `requires` clause in the Coq representation, we see that the expression is surrounded by a special pair of brackets: "(: ... :)". If we look at the data type for method level specifications on page 42, we see that a requires clause isn't of type **Expression**, but **optional Expression**, as the requires clause is either `\not_specified` or an expression, which we express by using the type **optional** described on page 43. So we would write " requires (Specified ((var x) != null))".

As we need to put brackets around the **optional** type anyway, we believe it's more readable, if we add different brackets around the **optional** type, which allows us to omit the keyword **Specified** and also to omit the brackets around the expression itself.

──────────── A MADE-TO-MEASURE COQ TUTORIAL ────────────

Part 7   Notations

We give here a quick discussion of two definitions of notations in Coq. We use the notation from listing 2.26 to define a block that contains a list of statements. As a block is basically a **Compound** statement, the block needs to have a PC associated.

Coq allows us to declare an arbitrary-length list of variables of the same type in a notation using the two dots in the term "x ; .. ; y". All other special symbols, that is, brackets and punctuations, are considered as terminal symbols for the parser. All identifiers are considered variables and are treated as non-terminal symbols.

₂₋₆ The definition of the notation is now clear: we build a **Compound** statement that itself contains a block of the list of statements. To talk about an arbitrary list as declared in ₁ "x ; .. ; y", we need to use the construct ₆ "(cons x .. (cons y nil) ..) ". It defines how to build up the data type for the list and defines what to do with the last element, that is, append nil.

```
Notation "{: pc :>> x ; .. ; y :}" :=
  (STATEMENT.Build_t
    pc       (* the pc of the statement *)
    None     (* the label of the statement *)
    (Compound STATEMENT.t STATEMENT.b (BLOCK.Build_t
      (cons x .. (cons y nil) ..)))) : jml_scope.
```

Listing 2.26: The notation for an unlabeled block containing any number of statements

We can specify the level (precedence) of the notation and its associativity, if we want to. Listing 2.27 shows the example of the "+" operator in Java, which has left associativity and is set to level 50, whereas for instance multiplication has level 40. Thus, we do not need to put brackets around sub-expressions to specify the default evaluation order.

```
Notation "x + y" := (BinaryIntExpr Addition x y )
                    (at level 50, left associativity ) : jml_scope.
```

Listing 2.27: The notation for a binary operation on expressions

2.5 A Domain for Java Programs in Coq

In this section, we present the definition of the domain for Java in Coq. We introduce a program state which can be extended with auxiliary data structures on demand, an abstract data type for the heap, data structures for various elements of method frames, and a formalization for basic data types of Java source code.

2.5.1 The Program State

Our definition of the domain features an extensible formalization of the program state. In its basic form, the program state represents the state of a Java program with no support for additional data structures needed by the JML semantics. The implementation of the JML semantics can add its data structures either globally, or locally to the currently executed method.

Fig. 2.2 depicts the structure of the program state. The state only contains the frame of the currently executing method and not a whole method frame stack. This significantly simplifies the model of the program state. If, for some reason, an application of the domain

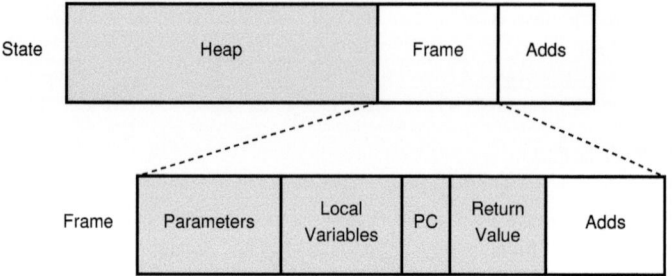

Figure 2.2: The program state, consisting of the heap, the method frame and auxiliary data structures. Gray boxes denote data structures that are implemented here, white boxes denote data structures that have to be provided by the implementation of the JML semantics, as we will see later.

needs access to the method frames of the callers, the corresponding information can be stored in the auxiliary data structures, as we will see later.

In this subsection, we present the three abstract data types **STATE**, **FRAME**, and **ADDS** (for "additions"), which define the structure of the program state and provide an implementation for accessing and updating individual elements of the state.

State

Listing 2.28 shows the complete module type **STATE**. The module type declares the two modules Adds and Frame. In other words, the module type **STATE** declares that any implementation of **STATE** has to define two modules Add and Frame that adhere to the specified module types. As opposed to most of the module types that we've seen in section 2.4.1, **STATE** already provides an implementation of all other constructs, instead of only declaring the function signatures and providing an axiomatization. As a consequence, we are able to implement a module of type **STATE** in the following way, where MyAdds is some implementation of module type **ADDS** and MyFrame is some implementation of module type **FRAME**:

Declare Module MyState : STATE
  with **Module** Adds := MyAdds
  with **Module** Frame := MyFrame.

In the last part of tutorial 2 on page 33, we presented two alternative ways to create a module of a given module type: either implement the whole module, or just declare it. There is a third, elegant way to define a module of a module type: we can implement just certain elements of the module and carry the other elements over from the existing module type. This is how we defined MyState above.

2.5. A DOMAIN FOR JAVA PROGRAMS IN COQ

The state provides access to the following constructs: the current heap h, the method frame fr, and the additions adds. We also define a function build that takes a heap, a frame, and additions, and yields a state containing these elements.

```
1  Module Type STATE.
2   (* Parametric modules, to be defined upon declaration *)
3   Declare Module Adds : ADDS.
4   Declare Module Frame : FRAME.
5
6   (* Implementation of the module *)
7   Record t : Type := make {
8     h  : Heap.t;
9     fr : Frame.t;
10    adds : Adds.t
11  }.
12
13  Definition set_h (st : t) (h : Heap.t) : t :=
14    make h (fr st) (adds st).
15  Definition set_fr (st : t) (fr : Frame.t) : t :=
16    make (h st) fr (adds st).
17  Definition set_adds (st : t) (adds : Adds.t) : t :=
18    make (h st) (fr st) adds.
19
20  Definition build := make.
21
22  End STATE.
```

Listing 2.28: The module type for a program state

_____ A made-to-measure Coq Tutorial _____

Part 8 Implementation of a Data Type

Let's take a closer look at the implementation of module STATE. 7 We define a **Record** with three fields h, fr, and adds. This defines a type t : **Type** and three functions with the following signatures:

h   : t → Heap.t.
fr   : t → Frame.t.
adds : t → Adds.t.

Using a **Record** is a very convenient way to implement an abstract data type. Beside the accessor functions that we get for free from the record definition, we provide three functions to set individual fields of the record. As there is no built-in way of changing individual fields of records, we need to implement this by creating a new record and copying over all fields from the old record except for the field we want to change, which we set to the new value.

We do not need to implement the function build, as the definition of the record generates a function make with exactly the desired behavior. We simply define build to be an alias for make. We could of course directly use the name "build" in the definition of the record, but we stick to the convention that within a data type, we use "make" to create records, while from outside, we provide a function build to build a variable of the data type. Sometimes, this involves additional computation and not just the creation of the record.

Frame

The module type FRAME, sketched in listing 2.29 is very similar to the module type STATE. The module type declares the module Adds to store local auxiliary data structures, which have to be provided upon declaration of a frame module in the same way we declared a state module:

Declare Module MyFrame : FRAME
   with **Module** Adds := MyFrameAdds.

Beside the already discussed additions and the type t as the type of a frame, we provide functions to access and update dictionaries for parameters and local variables, the current program counter, and the return value.

In addition to the fields of the record, the module provides some definitions for easier access to some frame constructs. For instance, the reference **this** is stored as parameter with the predefined name paramThis, if the method has a receiver. The definition [14] this simplifies access to the reference **this**.

The definition build is, as opposed to the one in module type STATE, not trivial. The reason is that not all information stored in the record needs to be provided, most of it can either be computed or set to default initial values. The only information that we need to build a new frame is the method for which we build the frame, the parameters, and the additions (for which we cannot assume any default values; we simply do not know what's inside this data structure at this point). We set the program counter pc to the program counter of the first statement of the body, if the method has a body, otherwise, to a default value NoBodyPC. Initially, there are no local variables defined in the method, and we choose to set the return value to Normal None which stands for no return value and normal termination. At this point, it really doesn't matter what we choose as return value, as the method execution hasn't even been initiated when creating the frame for it.

```
Module Type FRAME.
  (* Parametric module, to be defined upon declaration *)
  Declare Module Adds : ADDS.

  (* Implementation of the module *)
  Record t : Type := make {
    params : ParamDict.t;
    vars  : VarDict.t;
    pc : PC;
    ret  : ReturnVal;
    adds : Adds.t
  }.

  Definition this (fr : t) : option Object :=
    match ParamDict.get (params fr) paramThis with
    | Some (Ref loc) ⇒ Some loc
    | _ ⇒ None
    end.

  ... (* other setters and getters omitted *)

  Definition build ( callee : Method) (params : ParamDict.t) (adds : Adds.t) : t :=
    let pc' := match METHOD.body callee with
      | Some body ⇒STATEMENT.pc (METHODBODY.compound body)
      | None ⇒ NoBodyPC
    end in
    make params VarDict.empty pc' (Normal None) adds.
End FRAME.
```

Listing 2.29: The module type for a method frame

Additions

Both the state and the frame feature a module of type **ADDS** to store auxiliary information. From what we have seen, this module features a type t as the type of the abstract data type. Consequently, we define the module type **ADDS** as in listing 2.30. We simply define a parameter t and do not specify any other construct of the module. An implementing module can add additional elements as needed.

```
Module Type ADDS.
```

```
2   Parameter t : Type.
3   End ADDS.
```

Listing 2.30: The module type for additions

Notations

We introduce notations to dramatically simplify the access and update of fields of the program state. We define the notations on the program state according to the following conventions.

Accessor Notations Accessing a field[1] of the state or the method frame can be done by "*constr@field*". Where *constr* refers to a variable of type State.t or Frame.t and *field* refers to a field defined in a construct or its auxiliary data structures. Such expressions can be chained: For example, if we want to access a field this defined in the method frame of state st, we write "st@fr@this".

Update Notations To update a field in the state or method frame, we use the notation "*constr* [*field* := *value*]", where *constr* is either of type State.t or Frame.t, *field* is the field of the construct to be updated and *value* is the new value for the field. Again, we can chain updates and also mix it with access notations:

st [fr := st@fr [ret := result]][h := h']

This term updates the frame and the heap of state st. We access the frame of st by "st@fr" and update the field ret with the value result. The updated frame is then stored as new frame of st. In this updated state, we set h' as heap.

Notations for Operations We introduce special notations for more specific operations on fields of the state or frame. The general form is as follows: "*constr* [*field* : *op value*]", where *value* is the value which is used by operation op to update field.

For instance, if the type of a field is a set, we provide the following set-operations as notations.

- "*constr* [*field* :+ *value*]" adds value to the set represented by *field*.

- "*constr* [*field* :∪ *value*]" unions the sets *value* and *field* and stores the result into *field*

- "*constr* [*field* :∩ *value*]" intersects the sets *value* and *field* and stores the result into *field*

---

[1]By "field" we refer to a field of the record in the state, *not* a Java field!

2.5.2 Domain constructs

In this section, we introduce two abstract data types: a general purpose dictionary and a heap model. We use the dictionary to represent local variables and parameters. It will also become handy for several other constructs that we will introduce later on. The Coq standard library does feature a dictionary, but requires the type of the keys to feature decidable equality, which is necessary to constructively define the dictionary. However, for our purpose, this only adds unnecessary complexity to the formalization.

A General Purpose Dictionary

The module type DICT in listing 2.31 features two parameters ₄ Key and ₅ Val that have to be set to the types for the keys and the values when declaring a concrete dictionary. The dictionary stores key-value pairs of the specified types and provides the usual operations to update and query the dictionary. ₈ The functions get $d\ k$ retrieves the value assigned to the supplied key k if it exists in the dictionary d. Otherwise, it yields None. ₉ The function update $d\ k\ v$ updates or adds the pair $k \to v$ to dictionary d and yields the updated dictionary, depending on if the key k was already in the dictionary. ₁₀ The function remove $d\ k$ yields a dictionary in which the key-value pair for key k has been removed from dictionary d, if the key existed in the dictionary in the first place. We describe the behavior of these functions with the following axioms: ₂₀ get_update_same states that looking up a value for a key that has been updated yields the updated value. ₂₄ get_remove_none states that looking up a removed key in a dictionary always yields None. ₂₂ get_update_old states that updating a key with a value preserves all other key-value pairs in the dictionary. Analogously, ₂₆ get_remove_old states that removing a key from a dictionary leaves all other key-value pairs unchanged.

Beside these basic operations, we provide some more sophisticated querying functions for the dictionary. ₁₂ The function In $v\ d$ is a predicate that is true if value v is stored in dictionary d; that is, there exists at least one key-value pair that has v as value. ₁₃ The function singleton is a shorthand for creating dictionaries with one key-value pair.

₁₄,₁₅ The functions content and keys yield a list of all values and a list of all keys in a dictionary, respectively. The order of the elements in the list is not specified, but is of course deterministic, since content and keys are functions. ₂₈,₃₀ The axioms content_1 and keys_1 specify the behavior of the the two functions. content_1 states that a value is in the list yielded by content if and only if the value is stored in the dictionary. keys_1 states that a key is in the list yielded by keys if and only if there exists a key-value pair for the given key in the dictionary.

₁₆ The function filter $d\ f$ yields a list of values that are associated to keys for which the predicate f holds. ₃₂ The axiom filter_1 describes this behavior.

₁ **Module Type DICT.**

```
2   Parameter t : Type.
3
4   Parameter Key : Type.
5   Parameter Val : Type.
6
7   Parameter empty   : t.
8   Parameter get     : t → Key → option Val.
9   Parameter update  : t → Key → Val → t.
10  Parameter remove  : t → Key → t.
11
12  Definition In (d : t) (v : Val) : Prop := ∃ k, get d k = Some v.
13  Definition singleton (k : Key) (v : Val) : t := update empty k v.
14  Parameter content : t → list Val.
15  Parameter keys    : t → list Key.
16  Parameter filter  : t → (Key → Prop) → list Val.
17
18  Axiom get_empty :
19     ∀ v, get empty v = None.
20  Axiom get_update_same :
21     ∀ d k v , get (update d k v) k = Some v.
22  Axiom get_update_old :
23     ∀ d k k' v , k ≠ k' → get (update d k v) k' = get d k'.
24  Axiom get_remove_none:
25     ∀ d k, get (remove d k) k = None.
26  Axiom get_remove_old:
27     ∀ d k k', k ≠ k' → get (remove d k) k' = get d k'.
28  Axiom content_1: ∀d v,
29     List.In v (content d) ↔ In v d.
30  Axiom keys_1 : ∀ d k,
31     List.In k (keys d) ↔ get d k ≠ None.
32  Axiom filter_1 : ∀ d f v,
33     List.In v ( filter  d f) ↔ (∃ k, get d k = Some v  ∧ f k).
34  End DICT.
```

Listing 2.31: The abstract data type for a dictionary

We can now declare data structures to represent a local variable store and the parameters of a method, using the dictionary, as shown in listing 2.32 below.

```
1   Parameter Var : Set.
2   Parameter Param : Set.
```

```
3
4   Declare Module VarDict : DICT
5     with Definition Key := Var
6     with Definition Val := Value.
7
8   Declare Module ParamDict : DICT
9     with Definition Key := Param
10    with Definition Val := Value.
```

Listing 2.32: Definition of a local variable and method parameter store

The Heap Model

We reuse Bicolano's heap model with some adjustments. The heap model is based on an axiomatized object store model presented in [73]. The model introduces an inductive data type Location, see listing 2.33, to access three different constructs in the heap: static fields, instance fields, and array elements. Static fields can be directly addressed by their field signature; instance fields need the target object together with the field signature. Naturally, array cells can be addressed by the array object and the offset of the cell.

```
1   Inductive Location : Set :=
2     | StaticField    ( fsig : FieldSignature )
3     | InstanceField  ( obj : Object ) ( fsig : FieldSignature )
4     | ArrayElement   ( obj : Object ) ( pos : Int.t ).
5
6   Declare Module LocDec : DecidableType
7                    with Definition t := Location
8                    with Definition eq := eq (A := Location).
9
10  Declare Module LocSet : WS with Module E := LocDec.
```

Listing 2.33: The inductive data type Location to access different constructs in a heap.

We often want to store sets of locations in a data type. To this end, we define two modules for locations. Firstly, a module LocDec that defines a decidable type over locations. We define parameter t and eq of module type DecidableType from the standard library. Naturally, we set t to be Location. We set eq to the built in Leibnitz equality. Secondly, we define a module LocSet that defines a mathematical set of locations. We specify the module E in module type WS from the standard library to be the decidable type for locations that we just defined before. We also introduce notations for all common set operations for better readability of terms with set operations.

The abstract data type sketched in listing 2.34 defines a heap model with the following four functions. The function **get** *h loc* yields the value at the heap location specified by *loc*. This only succeeds if *loc* is compatible to what is actually stored at that location in *h*. The function **update** *h loc v* updates the location denoted by *loc* in *h* by with *v* and yields the updated heap. The function **typeof** *h obj* yields the runtime type of object with the identifier *obj* or None if there is no allocated object or array with this identifier in the heap. Thus, we can use the function **typeof** to check if an object identifier refers to an allocated object or not. The function **new** *h p t* yields a tuple of the newly allocated location in the heap and the updated heap, or None if there are no more locations that can be allocated. Those four functions are described by a total of thirteen axioms that define the behavior of the heap model. In the proof in chapter 4, we will make use of some of these axioms, and will explain them as needed.

```
Module Type HEAP.
  Parameter t : Type.
  Parameter get     : t → Location → option Value.
  Parameter update : t → Location → Value → t.
  Parameter typeof : t → Object   → option ObjectType.
  Parameter new    : t → Program → ObjectType → option(Object ∗ t).
  ...
End HEAP.
```

Listing 2.34: Excerpt of the axiomatized heap model

Basic Data Types

Values A value can either be a boolean or a number, or a reference, or **null**; listing 2.35 shows the inductive definition to represent values.

Instead of adding the value **null** as a separate constructor we could instead introduce it as a special object identifier. But as most subsequent definitions need to distinguish between references that point to an address in the heap and null anyway, it's easier to keep Null as a constructor so that we get a separate case when performing pattern matching over a value.

```
Inductive Value : Type :=
  | Bool  (b : Prop)
  | Num   (n : num)
  | Ref   (o : Object)
  | Null.
```

Listing 2.35: Definition of values

Boolean Type There are two alternatives for representing the Java type `boolean` in Coq. We can either use the existing inductive type bool of sort **Set** from the Coq standard library or we can directly use the sort **Prop**; that is, conflate the representation of `booleans` with the notion of true and false at the prover level.

The type bool has the advantage that we can use pattern matching on a variable of this type when defining a function. It is the natural choice if we aim to produce a computable implementation of the functions that operate on the data type. The library already defines functions on the data type to represent propositional logic. However, we cannot express first order logic terms with this data type because of the lack of quantifiers.

The sort **Prop** is the type of propositions in Coq. The advantage of using sort **Prop** to represent the Java `boolean` type is that we can directly map any JML first order logic term to a proposition.

In particular, the possibility to use Coq's quantifiers in boolean terms simplifies many semantic definitions drastically. For this reason, we decided to use **Prop** to represent `boolean` values.

However, to specify the semantics of some constructs, we actually want to use the type bool instead of a proposition. For example, if we apply a filter to a list in Coq, the filter needs to be of type bool. To facilitate the use of such constructs, we introduce an axiomatized function from **Prop** to bool, see listing 2.36. The function is partially defined: if we can prove P, the function P2b P yields true of type bool. If ¬ P is provable, the function P2b P yields false. Otherwise we do not know the value of P2b P.

```
Parameter P2b : Prop →bool.
    Axiom P2b_true: ∀ (P : Prop) , P → P2b P = true.
    Axiom P2b_false: ∀ (P : Prop) , ¬P →P2b P = false.
```

Listing 2.36: An axiomatized function from Prop to bool

Number Types We use the Bicolano formalization of Java numbers in Coq[2]. Listing 2.37 shows the definition of an abstract data type for Java numbers in the module type NUMERIC. The definition is based on the type Z from the Coq standard library which can represent arbitrarily large integer numbers. The module type defines the range of numbers that can be represented, as a function of the parameter power. Furthermore, the function smod defines the behavior in the case of overflow and underflow. The operations on numbers are then specified as axiomatized functions. We only show the example of the operation add. In Java, we always calculate exactly and then fit the number into the valid range. This is what axiom add_prop states.

---

[2]Not including floating point numbers, as discussed in section 2.3

```
Module Type NUMERIC.
  Parameter t : Set.
  Parameter toZ : t → Z.
  Parameter power : Z.
  Definition half_base := 2^power.
  Definition base := 2 * half_base .
  Definition range (z : Z) : Prop := −half_base ≤z < half_base .
  Parameter range_prop : ∀ x:t , range (toZ x).
  ...
  Definition smod (x:Z) : Z :=
    ...

  Parameter add : t →t → t.
  Axiom add_prop : ∀i1 i2 ,
    toZ (add i1 i2) = smod (toZ i1 + toZ i2).

  ...
```

Listing 2.37: Representation of Java numbers in Coq

We can now define modules of type NUMERIC for each Java number type with the corresponding value for power. Finally, we combine all (covered) numeric types in Java into one inductive data type num, for easier handling. See listing 2.38 below.

```
Declare Module Byte   : NUMERIC with Definition power := 7.
Declare Module Short  : NUMERIC with Definition power := 15.
Declare Module Int    : NUMERIC with Definition power := 31.

Inductive num : Set :=
  | I  : Int.t → num
  | B  : Byte.t → num
  | Sh : Short.t → num.
```

Listing 2.38: Declaration of the different modules for Java numbers.

We define a set of widening and narrowing operators on numeric values. The function i2s is an example for a narrowing operation from **int** to **short**. In listing 2.39, we show the function signature and its axiomatization. The first axiom defines the behavior of i2s if the resulting **short** is positive, that is, if the last 16 bits of the integer represent a value in the interval $[0 .. 2^{15})$. The second axiom defines the behavior for the interval $[2^{15} .. 2^{16})$.

```
1   Parameter i2s : Int.t → Short.t.
2
3   Axiom i2s_prop1 : ∀ i ,
4     ( Int.toZ i ) mod 2^16 < 2^15 →
5     ( Int.toZ i ) mod 2^16 = Short.toZ (i2s i ).
6
7   Axiom i2s_prop2 : ∀ i ,
8     2^15 ≤( Int.toZ i ) mod 2^16 →
9     ( Int.toZ i ) mod 2^16 − 2^16 = Short.toZ (i2s i).
```

Listing 2.39: An axiomatized narrowing operation from integers to shorts.

References A reference points to an object in the heap. As we do not deal with pointers in Java, it is sufficient to define a data type for object identifiers. Thus, we introduce the type Object of sort **Set**.

2.6 A Formal Semantics of JML in Coq

In this section, we introduce the interface to JML specifications and its implementation. As discussed at the beginning of this chapter, the interface provides direct access to JML specifications at the cost of being less in control of how the interface is used by an application. Thus, we strive to document the JML interface thoroughly and clearly, and keep the implementation as simple and readable as possible.

2.6.1 An Interface to JML Specifications

Listing 2.40 shows the module type JML that defines the JML interface. A module that implements the interface needs to provide the following elements.

- *An implementation of the program State.* The underlying domain defines the program state for Java, which needs to be extended with additional data structures in order to express the semantics of JML constructs such as the pre-heap. The module needs to provide an implementation of the two modules FrameAdds and Adds, which define the local and global auxiliary data structures, respectively. With an implementation of these additions, the module defines a fully implemented program state.

- *A definition of the initial State.* The module needs to provide an implementation of the function InitState , which yields the initial state of programs. The function yields the state in the **main** method is called. Depending on the implementation of the semantics, auxiliary data structures may need to be built up at this point to get a proper state to start with.

- *A definition of how to build new frames.* Similarly to the initial state, a new frame for an invoked method needs to be built up by the implementation of the JML semantics. The module provides an implementation of the function **NewFrame**. The function takes the invoked method, its parameters, and the current state as input and yields the frame in which the first statement in the method body can be executed.

- *An implementation of the JML semantics.* Last but not least, the module needs to provide an implementation of the modules **AnnotationTable** and **Assignables**. The two modules define the meaning of the supported JML constructs, using the syntax definition, the underlying domain, and the auxiliary data structures for the program state as defined above. In the two subsequent paragraphs, we inspect the module types of these two modules and explain the individual function signatures.

```
1  Module Type JML.
2  (* To be implemented *)
3  Declare Module FrameAdds : ADDS.
4  Declare Module Adds : ADDS.
5
6  (* Define Frame and State *)
7  Declare Module Frame : FRAME with Module Adds := FrameAdds.
8  Declare Module State : STATE with Module Frame := Frame
9                                 with Module Adds := Adds.
10
11 (* To be implemented *)
12 Parameter InitState : ParamDict.t → State.t.
13 Parameter NewFrame : Method →ParamDict.t →State.t →Frame.t.
14
15 Declare Module AnnotationTable : ANNOTATION_TABLE State.
16 Declare Module Assignables : ASSIGNABLES State.
17 End JML.
```

Listing 2.40: The module type JML defines the program state and gives access to JML specifications. An implementation of this module can be used as parameter to an operational semantics for Java.

The Annotation Table Interface

The annotation table shown in listing 2.41 provides access to the predicates generated from the JML specifications, that either need to be asserted or can be assumed at given program points by the application of the semantics. The functions of the annotation table are pretty much self-explanatory. Nevertheless, we provide a short description of the functions and discuss in which situations to apply them.

- The functions Precondition and Postcondition yield the predicate defined by JML specifications that is supposed to hold in the pre- and post-state of the corresponding method, respectively. The predicate not only includes the directly related method specification clauses such as requires, ensures, or signals, but also object invariants and initially clauses. An application of the JML semantics can assume that the predicate yielded by Precondition actually holds in the pre-state of a method, and must assert the predicate yielded by Postcondition in the post-states(s) of the method. Furthermore, the two functions can be used to verify method calls: the predicate yielded by Precondition of a callee needs to be asserted before calling it, and the predicate yielded by Postcondition of a callee can be assumed upon method return.

- If the supplied program counter points to either an assert or assume statement, the function LocalAssertion yields the predicate argument of the construct, which the application of the semantics can use as follows. A verification environment needs to prove assert statements, and uses assume statements to help the verification of the current goal. A runtime assertion checker should check assert statements and may ignore assume statements.

- For any kind of loop, the function LoopInvariant yields the conjunction of all loop invariants defined for the loop. The predicate needs to hold at the beginning and end of each loop iteration. Thus, in case of a loop that does not contain a **break** statement, the predicate yielded by LoopInvariant needs to hold after the loop terminated. In the presence of a **break** statement, the JML reference manual suggests to precede the **break** by an assert statement that defines what property holds upon exiting the loop via the **break** statement, since the loop invariant doesn't need to hold at that point.

It may be surprising that the signatures of Postcondition, LocalAssertion, and LoopInvariant only feature one state although we need access to the pre-state of the method, for instance to evaluate \old expressions. The reason is that we can store the necessary information to reconstruct a pre-state in the auxiliary data structures of the current method frame. There is a good reason behind this decision: If we wanted to support \old expressions with a label as second argument, which indicates to execute expression in the program state at the labeled position instead in the pre-state of the method, we would need access not only to the pre-state of the method, but also to the states at given labeled positions in the method. In our approach, we can achieve this by adding the information to reconstruct those states into the auxiliary data structures of the program state and we do not need to change the signature of the JML semantics interface just in order to accommodate the additional feature.

```
1  Module Type ANNOTATION_TABLE (State : STATE).
2    Parameter Precondition:
3        Program →Class → Method →State.t → Prop.
4    Parameter Postcondition:
5        Program →Class → Method →State.t → Prop.
6    Parameter LocalAssertion:
7        Program →Class → Method →PC →State.t → option Prop.
8    Parameter LoopInvariant:
9        Program →Class → Method →PC →State.t → option Prop.
10 End ANNOTATION_TABLE.
```

Listing 2.41: The interface of the annotation table

The Interface for Frame Conditions

We briefly recapitulate some important properties of `assignable` clauses: `assignable` clauses cannot be checked at a given point of the method, but needs to be preserved throughout method execution. Not only do we need to ensure throughout method execution that we only assign to assignable locations, these locations also depend on dynamic data groups that change during method execution. Fresh locations from new objects are assignable even if not mentioned in the `assignable` clause. Invoked methods not only have to obey the own `assignable` clause, but also must not change locations that are not assignable in any transitive caller.

To deal with all aspects of `assignable` clauses, we define the module type ASSIGNABLE that provides functions that need to be used by the application of the semantics at appropriate places. For each function, we define the point at which it needs to be applied in order to serve its purpose.

- The function FieldUpdateCheck needs to be called before assigning to a field. The function yields a predicate that holds if the field is assignable in the current situation. The parameter of type Location refers to the field that is about to be updated.

- The function MethodCallAction needs to be called upon method invocation and allows the semantics to update its auxiliary data structures in the method frame to reflect the changes of assignable locations from the `assignable` clause of the callee. The parameters of types Class and Method specify the callee. The yielded state is an updated copy of the state provided as parameter.

- The function NewObjectAction needs to be called upon object creation. The semantics can update its auxiliary data structures to ensure that all locations of the new object are assignable for the current method. The parameter of type Object refers to the object identifier of the newly created object.

- The function MethodReturnAction needs to be called upon method return and gives the semantics the possibility to perform clean up operations on its auxiliary data structures. The first parameter of type State.t refers to the post-state of the callee, whereas the second parameter of type State.t refers to the state of the caller as of the point of invocation of the callee.

- The function FieldUpdateAction needs to be called upon a field update. Any change in the heap structure also changes the content of dynamic data groups. If the semantics uses auxiliary data structures that reflect dynamic data groups, it needs to update them at this point. The parameter of type Location refers to the field to be updated and the parameter of type Value refers to the new value that will be assigned to the field.

```
1  Module Type ASSIGNABLES (State : STATE).
2    Parameter FieldUpdateCheck:
3            Program →Location → State.t → Prop.
4    Parameter MethodCallAction:
5            Program →Class → Method →State.t → State.t.
6    Parameter NewObjectAction:
7            Program →Object → State.t → State.t.
8    Parameter MethodReturnAction:
9            Program →State.t → State.t → State.t.
10   Parameter FieldUpdateAction:
11           Program →Location → Value → State.t → State.t.
12 End ASSIGNABLES.
```

Listing 2.42: The interface to handle frame properties

2.6.2 The Definition of the JML Semantics

In this section we describe the implementation (definition) of the modules AnnotationTable and Assignables. This implementation defines the semantic meaning of the supported

JML constructs. We place emphasis on faithfulness to the JML reference manual and readability of the definitions – we do not intend to produce a semantics that can be computed efficiently or exported as program. Thanks to the modular structure of our formalization, these aspects can be added as applications of the formalization at any time later on.

As usual, we present the definition of the semantics starting with the top-most definitions from the annotation table and the **Assignables** module, and dive into details as we go along. We highlight interesting aspects while avoiding repetitive or uninteresting parts of the semantics' definition.

Additions to the Program State

In order to express the semantics of JML constructs, we enrich the Java method frame with additional data structures. Listing 2.43 shows the module **FrameAdds**, an implementation of the module type **ADDS**, which we use to build up a JML method frame. The module accommodates the following data structures: a set of heap locations, a set of object identifiers, a tuple of a heap data type and a parameter dictionary, and a dictionary containing quantified variables.

The function **assignables** yields the set of heap locations that can be assigned to throughout the method execution. The set of object identifiers that we get from function **fresh** refers to the objects that have been freshly allocated during the method execution; this includes objects created in (transitive) callees of the method. The function **pre** provides the means to reconstruct the pre-state of the current method. It yields the heap and the parameter dictionary. As a last accessor function, we introduce **quants** that yields a dictionary of variables. The JML semantics uses Variables from this dictionary to evaluate quantifiers in JML expressions. We instantiate the type **t** : **Type**, declared in ADDS, to be the type of the record, that is **t_rec**.

The remainder of the module defines functions that facilitate accesses to and updates of individual elements of the record. We highlight three functions that work on the set of assignable heap locations and omit the other accessor and update functions, which behave similarly, for the other data structures.

The function **set_assignables** is a typical setter, which takes the current frame fr and a set of locations x and yields a new frame in which the assignable locations have been set to x. Using this function, we define more useful functions that directly provide set-operations on assignable locations in the frame. Function **inter_assignables** takes a frame fr and a set of locations and yields a frame that contains as assignable locations the intersection of the pre-existing assignable locations and the provided set x. [15,17] We can see the use of notations to use the set intersection symbol "∩" to represent the function **AMSet.inter** and the union of a singleton set "∪ {x}" to represent the function **AMSet.add**.

2.6. A FORMAL SEMANTICS OF JML IN COQ

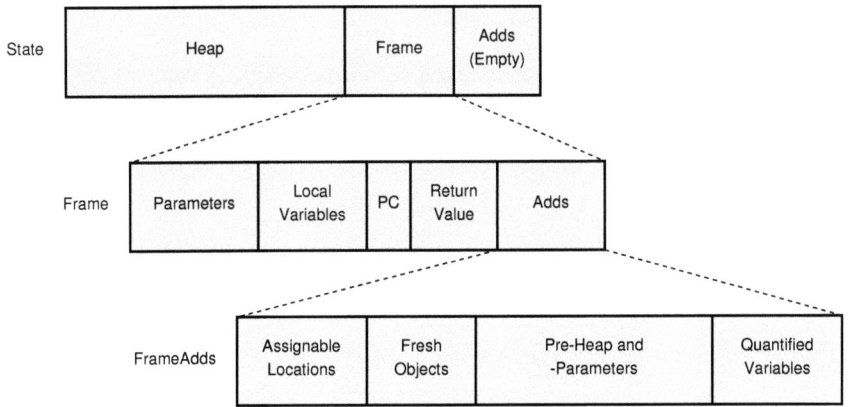

Figure 2.3: A state with no global auxiliary data structures and several auxiliary data structures on the level of method frames. All data types are now defined, thus, all boxes are gray. The size of the boxes does not correspond with the size of the data structure.

```
Module FrameAdds <: ADDS.

  Record t_rec : Type := make {
    assignables : AMSet.t;
    fresh : LocSet.t;
    pre : Heap.t * ParamDict.t;
    quants : VarDict.t
  }.

  Definition t := t_rec.

  Definition set_assignables (fr : t) (x : AMSet.t) : t :=
    make x (fresh fr) (pre fr) (quants fr).
  Definition inter_assignables (fr : t) (x : AMSet.t) : t :=
    set_assignables fr ((assignables fr) ∩ x).
  Definition add_assignable (fr : t ) (x : Address) : t :=
    set_assignables fr ((assignables fr) ∪ {x}).

  ...

End FrameAdds.
```
Listing 2.43: The auxiliary data structures for the frame

This implementation of the JML semantics doesn't need to store any data into global auxiliary data structures. Therefore, we instantiate the data type t of module Adds in listing 2.44 to be an inductive type Singleton that only contains one simple constructor. Thus, any variable of type Adds.t is equal to any other. Therefore, if the heaps and the frames in a two states are equal, the whole states are equal.

```
Module Adds <: ADDS.
  Inductive Singleton : Type :=
  | singleton : Singleton .
  Definition t := Singleton .
End Adds.
```

Listing 2.44: A minimalistic implementation of module Adds

Definition of the Initial State

We set up the initial state of a program as shown in listing 2.45. 11 We use the predefined but unspecified heap InitHeap and 8 the predefined method InitMethod whose body invokes main with the corresponding arguments. For each concrete program run, the InitMethod needs to be specified according to the command line arguments. Apart from InitHeap and InitMethod, everything is naturally set to empty initial values.

```
Definition InitState : State.t :=
  let adds := FrameAdds.make
                LocSet.empty
                ObjSet.empty
                (InitHeap, ParamDict.empty)
                VarDict.empty in
  let frame := Frame.build
                InitMethod
                ParamDict.empty
                adds in
  State. build InitHeap frame Adds. singleton .
```

Listing 2.45: The initial state of the program.

Definition of New Frames

To perform a method invocation, an operational semantics or any other application of the JML semantics needs to build a new frame for the callee. 7 We initialize the frame using the function build from data type FRAME that we've presented in listing 2.29 on page 57. The auxiliary data structures are initialized as follows: ₃ the assignable locations are initially the set of effectively assignable locations $\mathcal{A}^{\text{effective}}$ of the caller; that is, the union of its assignable and fresh locations. Upon evaluation of the assignable clause(s) of the callee, this set will be intersected with the evaluated locations, but it will never be extended to more assignable locations. ₄ Naturally, the set of newly allocated objects is initialized to the empty set. ₅ We store the current heap, which is the pre-heap of the method and the parameters to the field pre. ₆ Furthermore, we initialize the quantified variables to an empty dictionary. Even if we use the method in a quantified expression, we cannot access the quantified variables within the method, but would need to pass them as parameters to the method.

```
Definition NewFrame (m:Method) (p:ParamDict.t) (st:State.t) : Frame.t :=
  let adds := FrameAdds.make
                st@fr@assignables ∪ ObjSet2LocSet st@fr@fresh
                ObjSet.empty
                (st @h , p)
                VarDict.empty in
  Frame.build m p adds.
```

Listing 2.46: The definition of how to build a new frame

Implementation of the Annotation Table Interface

Precondition Listing 2.47 shows the implementation of the function Precondition of the AnnotationTable module. The precondition of a method is a conjunction of three predicates.

₂₋₇ The first part defines which object invariants have to hold at this point. As we implement the visible state semantics for invariants, all object invariants are assumed upon method entry, except for the invariants of the current object if we are in a constructor of the object. To that end, we perform a case split on the kind of method. If the method is a constructor, we quantify over all invariants of all object but **this**. If the method is not a constructor, we quantify over all invariants of all objects.

Furthermore, we quantify over all static invariants in our program. In our formalization, we ignore the issues of static initialization and assume that all types are fully initialized upon program start.

Finally, we state as the last part of the precondition, that there needs to be at least one specification case for this method that defines a requires clause that holds in the current state. We have already discussed the definition of DefinedCase on page 45. The predicate holds if the supplied specification case sc is defined for method m in class c, that is, sc is either declared in m of class c or any super-class of c.

```
1  Definition Precondition (p : Program) (c : Class) (m : Method) (st : State.t):Prop:=
2    match METHOD.kind m , st @fr @this with
3    | Constructor, Some loc ⇒
4        ∀ o : Location, o ≠ loc → EvalObjectInvariant p m o st
5    | _ , _ ⇒
6        ∀ o : Location,  EvalObjectInvariant p m o st
7    end
8    ∧
9    ∀ c', EvalStaticInvariant  p c' m st
10   ∧
11   ∃ sc , DefinedCase c m sc ∧ EvalRequires p m sc st.
```

Listing 2.47: The definition of the precondition of a method

───────── A MADE-TO-MEASURE COQ TUTORIAL ─────────

Part 9   Pattern Matching on Several Variables

The pattern matching that we perform in the definition **Precondition** mentions two comma-separated variables on which we perform a matching simultaneously. This is a very convenient short cut instead of nesting two matchings. A case matches, if and only if all constructors match. For each pattern, we can use the default match "_" independently. Internally, the 2-7 pattern matching is rewritten as nested matchings, e.g.:

```
match METHOD.kind m with
| Constructor ⇒
    match st @fr @this with
    | Some loc ⇒ ∀ o , o ≠ loc → EvalObjectInvariant p m o st
    | _ ⇒ ∀ o : Location, EvalObjectInvariant p m o st
    end
| _ ⇒ ∀ o : Location, EvalObjectInvariant p m o st
end
```

Listing 2.48 shows the definition of the function EvalObjectInvariant. At first glance, we can see that the signature of the function doesn't match its use in listing 2.47. The reason is that all evaluation functions for the JML semantics are defined within a section that declares the following three variables to specify the whereabouts of the current evaluation: variable p of type **Program**, variable c of type **Class**, and a variable m of type **Method**. We explain Coq sections in more details in the next tutorial.

If the method is declared as helper, we directly yield True, that is, we do not evaluate the invariants in this case. If we want to evaluate the invariants of object o for a non-helper method m, we generate a predicate that states the following. ₆ If the type of object o in the heap is an object with a class or interface name cn, and ₇ if this name cn belongs to a class or interface t specified in the program, then ₈ for all invariants ₉ defined in object o, ₁₀ check the invariants hold in a state in which we set `this` to the object o.

As explained in section 2.3, the coverage of the syntax is nearly complete, whereas we only define the semantics for JML level 0. Thus, the universe type modifier um show up in the type, but we ignore it in the evaluation function.

If any of the premises (₆₋₉) of this predicate doesn't hold, the predicate obviously holds, which is the desired behavior. That is, we do not evaluate the invariants for a non-allocated object o, or in an inconsistent state where the type of o mentioned a non-existent class or interface.

₁₀ We have an interesting application of the notations introduced in subsection 2.5.1. With the term "st [fr := st@fr [this := o]]", we update the state st with a new frame, which we produce by updating the parameter this in the old state st@fr with o. Without our notations, this term would have the following form:

(State. set_fr st (Frame.set_param (State. fr st) paramThis (Ref o)))

```
1  Definition EvalObjectInvariant (o : Object) (st : State.t) : Prop :=
2    if METHOD.isHelper m then
3      True
4    else
5      ∀ cn um t,
6      Heap.typeof st@h o = Some (Heap.ObjectObject cn um) →
7      LookupTypedef p cn = Some t →
8      ∀ inv ,
9      DefinedInvariant t inv →
10     EvalPredicate (INVARIANT.pred inv) st[fr := st@fr [ this := o ]].
```

Listing 2.48: The evaluation function for object invariants

The evaluation function for `requires` clauses in listing 2.49 is straight-forward. We access the predicate of the requires clause of the specification case sc, which yields the type optional Expression, see listing 2.12 on page 42. We perform a pattern matching on the type optional, presented in listing 2.13 on page 43. We use notations for the two constructors. (: expr :) denotes that the requires clause is specified and contains the expression expr as predicate. If the requires clause is specified, we evaluate the predicate, otherwise, we yield the predicate NotSpecifiedRequires which is set to True. However, an application of the semantics might want to set the defaults differently, in which case the definition for NotSpecifiedRequires can be changed accordingly.

```
Definition EvalRequires (sc : SpecificationCase ) (st : State.t) : Prop :=
  match REQUIRES.pred (CASE.requires sc) with
  | (: expr :)        ⇒ EvalPredicate expr st
  | \ not_specified   ⇒ NotSpecifiedRequires
  end.
```

Listing 2.49: The evaluation function for `requires` clauses

A MADE-TO-MEASURE COQ TUTORIAL
Part 10   Sections

Sections in Coq provide a nice way of simplifying the signatures of definitions considerably. In the case above, most evaluation functions need access to the abstract data types for the current program, class, and method. We could have added them as parameters to each evaluation function, but this makes the signatures of the definitions cumbersome. It is better to introduce a section with the mentioned variables, see listing 2.50. Within the section, all definitions can access these variables. With the 8 **Check** command, we ask Coq to print out the signature of EvalObjectInvariant ; 9 the comment shows the output. Unsurprisingly, EvalObjectInvariant is a function from Location to State.t to Prop. If we print the signature of the same function after the section EvalHelpers has been closed, we get a more complex signature from Program to Method to Location to State.t to Prop. As we can verify in listing 2.48, the body of EvalObjectInvariant uses the variables p and m, so the two additional arguments are added at the beginning.

```
Section EvalHelpers.
  Variable p : Program.
  Variable c : Class.
  Variable m : Method.
  Definition EvalObjectInvariant (o : Location) (st : State.t) : Prop :=
    ...

  Check EvalObjectInvariant.
  (* Output: Location → State.t → Prop *)
End EvalHelpers.

Check EvalObjectInvariant.
(* Output: Program → Method → Location → State.t → Prop *)
```

Listing 2.50: The usefulness of Coq sections

Postcondition The definition for postconditions, shown in listing 2.51, consists of a conjunction of three predicates, preceded by the definition of variable st' to represent the pre-state of the current method.

₃₋₁₀ The first part of the postcondition describes which object invariants need to be considered, depending on the kind of method for which we compute the postcondition. In the case of a constructor, we quantify over the evaluation of all object invariants. Additionally, we evaluate all `initially` clauses of the current object in this case. The postcondition of a finalizer excludes the object invariants of the object that is being finalized. For a normal method execution, the postcondition includes all object invariants.

As in the precondition, we evaluate the static invariants of all types in the second conjunct, without considering static initialization issues.

Finally, ₁₅₋₂₂ we define in which cases the method specification clauses for normal and exceptional termination apply. We only need to consider the specification cases that are defined for method m and whose `requires` clause holds in the pre-state of the method. For these cases, we evaluate the `ensures` clause if the method terminated normally, or the `signals` clause as well as the `signals_only` clause if the method terminated exceptionally. The field ret of the method frame yields a ReturnVal which is an inductive type with the two constructors Normal val and Exception e. Thus, we can perform a pattern matching on the return value to determine if the method terminated normally or exceptionally.

```
1   Definition Postcondition (p : Program)(c : Class)(m : Method)(st : State.t): Prop :=
2     let st' := pre_state m st in
3       match METHOD.kind m , st @fr @this with
4       | Constructor, Some loc ⇒
5           (∀ o : Location,  EvalObjectInvariant p m o st) ∧
6           EvalInitially  p c m st
7       | Finalizer , Some loc ⇒
8           ∀ o : Location, o ≠ loc → EvalObjectInvariant p m o st
9       | _ , _  ⇒ ∀ o : Location,  EvalObjectInvariant p m o st
10      end
11    ∧
12    ∀ c', EvalStaticInvariant  p c' m st
13    ∧
14    ∀ sc, DefinedCase c m sc →
15      match Frame.ret st@fr with
16      | Normal _   ⇒
17          EvalRequires p m sc st' →
18          EvalEnsures p m sc st
19      | Exception _ ⇒
20          EvalRequires p m sc st' →
```

```
21      ( EvalSignals  p  m  sc  st  ∧  EvalSignalsOnly  p  sc  st )
22      end.
```

Listing 2.51: The definition of the postcondition of a method

The evaluation function for ensures clauses is comparable to the function EvalRequires, shown in listing 2.49. However, the evaluation functions for signals and signals_only clauses differ quite a bit and we present them in the following paragraphs. The function EvalInitially is straight-forward. It quantifies over all initially clauses defined in the current object.

Listing 2.52 shows the evaluation function for signals clauses. ₂ We extract the signals clause from the specification case and assign it to the variable s. ₃ The premise sets the value of e to the exception object stored in the frame. As we call EvalSignals within the Exception case of a pattern matching on the return value, we know for sure that the premise holds. ₄ We store the returned exception as parameter to the method frame which can be accessed by the predicate of the signals clause. The last part of the evaluation function is again similar to the evaluation function for requires clause. Either the clause is specified and the predicate evaluated, or the clause is not specified and the function yields the default value NotSpecifiedSignals.

```
1   Definition EvalSignals (sc : SpecificationCase ) (st : State.t ) : Prop :=
2     let  s := CASE.signals sc  in
3     ∀ e,  Exception e = Frame.ret st@fr →
4     let  fr' := (Frame.set_param st@fr (SIGNALS.exception s) (Ref e)) in
5     match SIGNALS.pred s with
6     | (:expr:)         ⇒ EvalPredicate  expr  st [ fr:=fr ']
7     | \ not_specified  ⇒ NotSpecifiedSignals
8     end.
```

Listing 2.52: The evaluation function for signals clauses

The function for the signals_only clause is evaluates to True, if and only if the the exception from the return value is a subtype of one of the types declared in the signals_only clause. We see this behavior expressed in ₄,₅ listing 2.53. The function assign_compatible, defined as part of the heap model, tests if the object at location loc could be assigned to the type t, that is, the runtime type of loc is a subtype of t.

```
1   Definition EvalSignalsOnly (sc: SpecificationCase ) (st :State.t ) : Prop:=
2     let  s := CASE.signalsOnly sc  in
3     ∀ loc,  Exception loc = Frame.ret st@fr →
4     ∃ t,   t ∈ (SIGNALS_ONLY.types s) ∧
```

```
       assign_compatible p st@h (Ref loc) t.
```

Listing 2.53: The evaluation function for `signals_only` clause

Local Assertions and Assumptions As described in the paragraph on the annotation table interface on page 67, The JML semantics offers access to the predicate of an `assume` or `assert` statement, and the interface description describes how to use the predicates to reflect the JML semantics. The function LocalAssertion yields the predicate of the `assume` or `assert` statement, if there is such a JML statement at the given program counter, otherwise it yields None.

Loop Invariants The function LoopInvariant yields a predicate consisting of the conjunction of all loop invariants, if the statement at program counter pc is a loop. If the loop does not contain a `maintaining` clause, the function yields the default value NotSpecifiedLoopInvariant. As for local assertions and assumptions, it's up to the application of the semantics to use the predicate as described in the annotation table.

Evaluation of JML Expressions

In the annotation table functions, we use function EvalPredicate to evaluate JML predicates into Coq propositions. In JML, predicates are boolean expressions. Thus, the function EvalPredicate is a synonym for the function EvalBoolExpression shown in listing 2.54. In the following, we present how JML expressions are evaluated. JML expressions are a subset of Java expressions with additional JML operators and primary expressions. JML expressions need to be side effect free, that is, a JML expression is not supposed to change any existing element in the state. However, JML expressions can allocate new objects as long as side effects cannot be observed, for instance by comparing object identities. This behavior is called weak-purity. Therefore, JML expressions can only allocate new objects in the state and change their fields. To faithfully map this behavior of weak-purity, Darvas et al. discuss this matter in detail [24, 25]. In their approach, JML expressions not only yield a value when evaluating, but also track the store changes during the evaluation of the expression. This is necessary to create new objects in specifications and access their fields later on in specifications. In our current formalization of JML expressions, we do not track the state changes during the evaluation of JML expressions. Thus, we cannot access locations from objects created within specifications.

We provide three functions to evaluate expressions. One function to evaluate boolean expressions, one to evaluate expressions of a reference type, and one to evaluate numeric expressions. As expressions can be nested, and because the three kinds of expressions are mutually dependent, we need to define the evaluation functions as three Fixpoints that are defined together using the keyword with, as described in tutorial 6 on page 47. As usual, we want to explain the essential and interesting aspects of the evaluation of JML expressions. In the listing 2.54 we show the JML expressions that we want to discuss in the following paragraphs, but we omit large parts of the **Fixpoint** definitions, indicated by ellipsis points "...".

The three functions have a common structure: each function performs a pattern matching on the expression e. For some expressions, the function directly defines the evaluation of the expression. Among others, the expressions ₈ e1 <: e2 [3] and ₂₄ this are examples for this approach. This is reasonable for simple definitions. If the evaluation of an expression is more complex, we call an evaluation function to evaluate that kind of expression. Examples for this approach are ₅ BinaryCondBoolExpr and ₁₄ the evaluation of the JML primary expression \fresh, which call the evaluation functions EvalBinaryCondBoolOp and EvalFresh, respectively.

Before we discuss the evaluation of some interesting kinds of expression, let's have a closer look at the arguments of the function ₄ EvalExpression. The first arguments are the functions EvalBoolExpression, EvalRefExpression, and EvalNumExpression. This way, the function EvalExpression, which is defined earlier in the program text has access to the three evaluation functions to evaluate nested boolean, reference, and numeric expressions. Thus, we combine the two techniques presented in the subsection "Statements and Blocks" in 2.4.1 on page 45 and tutorial 6 on page 47 to deal with the mutually recursive nature of expressions.

In tutorial 10 on page 76 how to use sections to introduce variables that can be accessed by all definitions within the section and need to be provided as additional arguments from outside the section.

```
1   Fixpoint EvalBoolExpression (e : Expression) (st : State.t) : Prop :=
2     match e with
3     | var _ | param _ | field _ _ | method _ _ _ | \result ... ⇒
4       v2b (EvalExpression EvalBoolExpression EvalRefExpression  EvalNumExpression e st)
5     | BinaryCondBoolExpr op e1 e2 ⇒
6       EvalBinaryCondBoolOp EvalBoolExpression op e1 e1 st
7
8     | e1 <: e2 ⇒
9       types_compatible p (EvalType EvalRefExpression e1 st)
10                                  (EvalType EvalRefExpression e2 st)
11    | \old e ⇒
12      EvalBoolExpression e ( pre_state m st)
13
14    | \fresh flist ⇒
15      EvalFresh EvalRefExpression  flist  st
16
```

---

[3]e1 <: e2 states that the evaluation of e1 yields a subtype of the evaluation of e2

```
17      | \forall    qvar ; r ; e  ⇒
18          ∀ v, EvalQuantifier EvalBoolExpression qvar r e v st
19          ...
20      end
21
22      with EvalRefExpression (e: Expression) (st: State.t) : option Location :=
23      match e with
24      | this ⇒
25          v2l (ParamDict.get(Frame.params st@fr) paramThis)
26
27      | null ⇒
28          None
29      ...
30      end
31
32      with EvalNumExpression (e : Expression) (st : State.t) : num :=
33      match e with
34      | BinaryIntExpr op e1 e2 ⇒
35          EvalBinaryNumOp op (EvalNumExpression e1 st) (EvalNumExpression e2 st)
36      | Quantification q v r e ⇒
37          | ( EvalGeneralizedQuantifier EvalBoolExpression EvalNumExpression q v r e st)
38      ...
39      end.
```

Listing 2.54: The evaluation functions for boolean, reference, and numeric expressions

Evaluation of Expressions Common to all Types There are quite some JML Expressions that can be evaluated the same way, regardless of the type of the expression. Examples are the evaluation of local variables, parameter, field access, method calls, or access to the special \result variable, to name some interesting candidates. In listing 2.54, we show 4-6 these cases in the function EvalBoolExpression. A nearly identical handling for these cases is also present in EvalRefExpression and EvalNumExpression, but we omit them in the listing. We propagate the evaluation of these expressions to the function EvalExpression, shown in listing 2.55. At that point, we are not interested in the arguments of the different constructors, since we just forward the whole expression e to EvalExpression. Thus, we use underscores to match the right number of arguments, without storing them in variables. The function EvalExpression yields an option Value. Depending on which function we call it from, we know whether the value should be a boolean, reference, or number. In the case of EvalBoolExpression (for which we expect to get a boolean value), the function v2b extracts the boolean value from its input of type option Value. If input is not a boolean value, the function yields the default value for booleans, UndefinedProp.

The definition of EvalExpression in listing 2.55 is very similar to the definition of the typed evaluation function above with the difference, that the function yields a Value instead of a boolean, reference or number. Local variable and parameter access is straight-forward and can be evaluated in one line, we simply retrieve the value stored in the corresponding dictionary in the program state. We discuss the evaluation of fields and methods in the following two paragraphs. The evaluation of the JML variable \result extracts the value from the ret field of the method frame. If the method terminated normally, EvalResult yields the returned value if there is any; in case of exceptional termination, the function builds a Value from the yielded exception object reference.

```
1  Definition EvalExpression (e: Expression) (st: State.t) : option Value :=
2    match e with
3    | var l                  ⇒ VarDict.get st@fr@vars l
4    | param par              ⇒ ParamDict.get st@fr@params par
5    | field  fsig o          ⇒ EvalFieldAccess fsig o st
6    ...
7    | method msig o params   ⇒ EvalMethodInvocation msig o params st
8    | \ result               ⇒ EvalResult st
9    | _                      ⇒ None
10   end.
```

Listing 2.55: The evaluation functions for expressions common to booleans, references and integers

Field Access The function EvalFieldAccess shown in listing 2.56 yields the value of the static or instance field identified by fsig. In case of an instance field, the second argument contains an expression for the target of the field access, which evaluates to a heap location. Note that the data type FieldSignature not only contains a field identifier, but also the class name in which the field is defined, see listing 2.9 on page 40. Therefore, we only need fsig to access a static field in the heap.

If we try to access a field in a non-wellformed expression, the function yields None instead of a value. This is the case if we try to access an instance field without a target expression, if the field specified by fsig doesn't exist in the target object, if the target expression doesn't evaluate to a object reference, and if there doesn't exist a static field with the given signature.

```
1  Definition EvalFieldAccess ( fsig  :  FieldSignature ) ( target  :  option Expression )
2                             ( st : State.t ) : option Value :=
3    match target with
4    | Some target' ⇒
```

2.6. A FORMAL SEMANTICS OF JML IN COQ

```
5   match EvalRefExpression target' st with
6     | None        ⇒ None
7     | Some loc ⇒ Heap.get st@h (Heap.InstanceField loc fsig )
8   end
9   | None ⇒Heap.get st@h (Heap.StaticField fsig )
10  end.
```

Listing 2.56: The evaluation function for field access

Method Invocation Listing 2.57 shows the part of EvalMethodInvocation that deals with dynamic method invocation. We omit static method invocation as it is very similar but simpler than the dynamic invocation. We also omit all the helper functions used to build up the parameters, but shortly describe them in the text.

Firstly, ₃ we evaluate the parameters of the method. The variable actuals contains a list of Expressions that the function EvalParams evaluates into a list of Values. We store that list into the variable pv. ₄ We then perform a pattern-matching on target to decide if we perform a dynamic or static method invocation. ₅ If target contains an expression, we assume dynamic method invocation. ₈ We evaluate the target to an object reference and ₈ retrieve the type of the target object. If the target evaluates to a proper heap location, ₁₀ the function Lookup tries to find a method with signature msig in the class denoted by cn or one of its super-classes. On success, ₁₁ the function yields the class name cn' in which the method could be found and the abstract data type of the method in question, m'. ₁₂ If we retrieve the abstract data type c' for the class with the name cn', we build a new method frame to invoke m'. ₁₄ With the function lv2params, we build a dictionary of all parameters. The function retrieves the list of parameters from m' and assigns a list of values to the parameters. Since we perform a dynamic method invocation, the first parameter is **this**. Thus, we add a reference value of the target object to the list pv. ₁₇ With this parameter dictionary we can now create the frame for method m'. At this point, everything is set up to actually execute the method.

A method in a JML expression is always *pure*, that is, deterministic and side effect free. Such a method behaves like a mathematical function. In our semantics, we declare a function EvalPureMethod which yields the result of the method invocation.

```
1   Definition EvalMethodInvocation (msig : MethodSignature) (target:option Expression)
2                       ( actuals : list  Expression ) (st : State. t) : option Value :=
3   let pv := EvalParams (METHODSIGNATURE.parameters (msig)₂) actuals st in
4   match target with
5     | Some target' ⇒
6     match EvalRefExpression target' st with
7       | Some target' loc ⇒
```

83

```
 8      match Heap.typeof st@h target'loc with
 9      | Some (Heap.LocationObject cn um) ⇒
10        match Lookup p cn (msig)₂ with
11        | Some (cn', m') ⇒
12          match PROG.class p cn with
13          | Some c' ⇒
14            let params := lv2params m' ((l2v (Some target'loc )):: pv) in
15            let fr' := NewFrame m' params st in
16            EvalPureMethod p c' m' st[ fr:=fr ']
17            ...
18    end.
```

Listing 2.57: The evaluation function for method invocation

We can use the method's specifications to axiomatize the behavior of the function EvalPureMethod. The axiom EvalPureMethod_def in listing 2.58 describes the evaluation function in terms of its pre- and postcondition. This axiom is delicate, as it can introduce inconsistency in the case of a spurious postcondition that doesn't hold for any return value. Rudich et al. discuss the issue of well-formedness of pure method specifications in [75].

```
1  Axiom EvalPureMethod_def:
2    ∀ p c m st ,
3      Precondition p c m st →
4      Postcondition p c m
5        st[ fr := st@fr[ ret := Normal (EvalPureMethod p c m st)]].
```

Listing 2.58: The axiom EvalPureMethod_def

———————— A MADE-TO-MEASURE COQ TUTORIAL ————————

Part 11   Axiomatized Functions

In listing 2.57, we use a function ₁₂ Lookup to retrieve the method for a given method signature and class name. The signature of Lookup below indicates that we use option as return type. That is, the function may or may not find a method.

Program →ClassName →ShortMethodSignature →option(ClassName ∗ Method).

Bicolano, from which we use the formalization of classes and methods to a great extent, does not feature such a function Lookup. However, it features a predicate lookup as shown in listing 2.59 [4]. The predicate holds if the tuple ClassName ∗ Method corresponds to the dynamically-bound method for signature msig in class cn in program p.

---
[4]This version of lookup is already a refactored, nicer version of the original Bicolano lookup, but with the same signature.

2.6. A FORMAL SEMANTICS OF JML IN COQ

```
1  Inductive lookup(p:Program) (cn:ClassName) (msig:ShortMethodSignature):
2                                              (ClassName * Method) →Prop :=
3   | lookup_no_up :
4     ∀ meth ,
5     findMethod p (cn, msig) = Some meth →
6     lookup p cn msig (cn, meth)
7   | lookup_up :
8     findMethod p (cn, msig) = None →
9     ∀ super res , direct_subclass_name p cn super →
10    lookup p super msig res →
11    lookup p cn msig res .
```

Listing 2.59: The inductive definition of the predicate lookup

Such a predicate is useful in proofs and in inductive definitions, but we cannot use it in a function definition, as it doesn't yield the method we're looking for, but just states weather or not a method is the right one.

The constructor ₃ lookup_no_up covers the base case if a method with signature msig is declared in the class with name cn. In this case, lookup trivially holds. The constructor ₇ lookup_up describes the step case if the class with name cn doesn't define a method msig. In this case, lookup holds for some tuple res if the predicate holds in the direct super-class super.

We axiomatize the function Lookup as shown in listing 2.60 The axiom Lookup_def states that Lookup yields some method if and only if the predicate lookup holds for that method. The axiom Lookup_undef states that the function Lookup yields no method if and only if the predicate lookup does not hold for any cn' and m.

```
1  Axiom Lookup_def:
2    ∀ p cn msig cn' m ,
3    Lookup p cn msig = Some (cn',m) ↔ lookup p cn msig (cn', m).
4
5  Axiom Lookup_undef:
6    ∀ p cn msig ,
7    Lookup p cn msig = None ↔ (∀ cn' m, ¬ lookup p cn msig (cn', m)).
```

Listing 2.60: The axiomatization of Lookup

To axiomatize a function based on a predicate, two important properties need to be ensured:

- The predicate needs to behave like a function. That is, for the parameter of the predicate that acts as return value of the function, there is only one possible value

85

CHAPTER 2. A JML FORMALIZATION IN COQ

for which the predicate holds.

- Coq functions are always total, that is, we need to ensure that there exists a value for the return type for which the predicate holds in any possible environment. We can use option T as return type of the function to manage it.

To show the first property, we need to show that there is only one possible cn' and m for which the predicate lookup holds in a given environment specified by p, cn and, msig.

To show the importance of this property, we try to show that our axioms are inconsistent with the following lemma:

Lemma Lookup_evil:
∀ p cn msig cn1 cn2 m1 m2,
lookup p cn msig (cn1, m1) →
lookup p cn msig (cn2, m2) →
(cn1, m1) ≠ (cn2, m2) →
False.

As this is the first time we show how to do a proof in Coq, we perform every step in detail to give the interested reader a feeling for how proofs are done in Coq. However, for the sake of readability, the proof obligations are already quite simplified, e.g., we remove hypotheses from the goals if we do not use them any more. In proofs later on, we would not go into such details.

Proof. After introducing the premises as hypotheses, our goal is simply "**False**". To prove the proof obligation, we need to find a contradiction in its hypotheses.

H1:   lookup p cn msig (cn1,m1)
H2:   lookup p cn msig (cn2,m2)
H3:   (cn1,m1) ≠ (cn2,m2)
―――――――――――――――――――――
False

Apply axiom Lookup_def on both hypotheses.

H1   Lookup p cn msig = Some (cn1,m1)
H2   Lookup p cn msig = Some (cn2,m2)
H3   (cn1,m1) ≠ (cn2,m2)
―――――――――――――――――――――
False

Rewrite H1 in H2.

H2   Some (cn1,m1) = Some (cn2,m2)
H3   (cn1,m1) ≠ (cn2,m2)
―――――――――――――――――――――
False

Use the inversion tactics in H2, see [19, section 10.5]

$$\frac{\begin{array}{ll}\text{H3} & (\text{cn1},\text{m1}) \neq (\text{cn2},\text{m2}) \\ \text{H4} & \text{cn1} = \text{cn2} \\ \text{H5} & \text{m1} = \text{m2}\end{array}}{\text{False}}$$

Use the elim tactics in H3, which puts the negation of H3 as goal.

$$\frac{\begin{array}{ll}\text{H4} & \text{cn1} = \text{cn2} \\ \text{H5} & \text{m1} = \text{m2}\end{array}}{(\text{cn1},\text{m1}) = (\text{cn2},\text{m2})}$$

Rewrite H4 and H5 in the goal.

$$\frac{}{(\text{cn2},\text{m2}) = (\text{cn2},\text{m2})}$$

Finally, Coq is able to prove the goal with the tactic trivial . □

In order to "defuse" this lemma, we need to show that its premise never holds without using the axioms we're about to justify.[5] We need to prove that H1, H2, and H3 from the lemma always lead to a contradiction, for instance by showing that (cn1, m1) and (cn2, m2) are always equal if H1 and H2 hold, which is exactly the first property we discussed above.

So if we want to axiomatize a function as in listing Lookup_def, we state the following lemma, listing 2.61, which is relatively easy to prove.

```
Lemma lookup_func:
  ∀ p cn msig m m',
  lookup p cn msig m →
  lookup p cn msig m' →
  m = m'.
Proof.
intros .
induction H.
  inversion H0.
  subst; rewrite H in H1; inversion H1; trivial .

  rewrite H in H1; inversion H1.

  inversion H0.
  rewrite H3 in H; inversion H.
```

---

[5] It is a good idea to put the lemma before the axioms in the Coq source, so that there is no way the lemma could use them.

```
17    apply IHlookup; clear IHlookup.
18    inversion H1; inversion H4.
19    rewrite H10 in H7.
20    inversion H9; inversion H12.
21    unfold PROG.defined_Class in H13, H16.
22    rewrite H7 in H16; rewrite H16 in H13; inversion H13.
23    rewrite H20 in H18; rewrite H18 in H15; inversion H15.
24    rewrite H21 in H11; rewrite ← H11 in H8; rewrite H8.
25    trivial .
26  Qed.
```

Listing 2.61: Lemma lookup_func that ensures that lookup is only valid for one method.

Again, as it's the first time, we show the proof script of this lemma and explain it in detail, to give the reader an impression of the Coq development.

Proof. We prove the lemma by induction on the structure of ₃ "lookup p cn msig m". ₉₋₁₂ The base case, that is, constructor lookup_no_up, is fairly simple to prove by ₉ splitting up the term ₄ "lookup p cn msig m'" into its two constructors. If we compare both base cases, we ₁₀ easily figure out that the resulting method needs to be the same. If we have constructor lookup_no_up for ₃ and lookup_up for ₄, we can ₁₂ show a contradiction in the hypotheses.

The induction step case, that is, constructor lookup_up, is a bit more interesting. Again, ₁₄ we split the term ₄ "lookup p cn msig m'" into its two inductive cases. ₁₅ If the cases do not match, we again get contradicting hypotheses. If we compare both constructors lookup_up, we get the following goal.

...	
H1	direct_subclass_name p cn super
H2	lookup p super msig res
H0	lookup p cn msig r'
IHlookup	lookup p super msig r' → res = r'
H4	direct_subclass_name p cn super0
H5	lookup p super0 msig r'

res = r'

₁₇ We apply the induction hypothesis IHlookup which has the premise "lookup p super msig r'" that is nearly identical to hypothesis H5. We now need to prove that this premise holds. ₁₈₋₂₄ The remainder of the proof uses the slightly awkward inductive definition direct_subclass_name from Bicolano to show that super and super0 are equal, which is clear when looking at H1 and H4 for a language with single inheritance. Proving this fact involves a lot of unfolding of definitions and rewriting of hypotheses, but we do not want to discuss this in details. We can then use the fact super = super0, to rewrite the goal to "lookup p super0 msig r'" which is identical to H5 and the goal can therefore be proven by ₂₅ trivial . □

Java Operators The only operator evaluation function that we look at is used in ₄₃₋₄₄ listing 2.54. The function EvalBinaryNumOp evaluates a binary operation on numbers to a numeric value. We pass the operator and the result of the evaluations of the operands to the function.

Listing 2.62 shows the definition of this function. It takes care of the conversion of the different numeric types of the operands and the result, as described in chapter 5 of the Java language specification [36]. We perform a simultaneous matching on both operands and apply widening and narrowing operations where necessary.

The type of the result is the larger type of the two operands. To compute the value, both operands are converted to integers and handed to the function EvalBinaryIntOp which yields the result of the integer operation. The definition of this function is not very interesting, as it simply calls the corresponding functions of the abstract data type for numbers, described in paragraph about Java numbers on page 63.

```
 1  Definition EvalBinaryNumOp (op : BinaryIntOp) (n1 n2 : num) : num :=
 2    match n1 , n2 with
 3    | I i1 , I i2   ⇒ I (    EvalBinaryIntOp op      i1         i2 )
 4    | I i1 , B b2   ⇒ I (    EvalBinaryIntOp op      i1    (b2i b2))
 5    | I i1 , Sh s2  ⇒ I (    EvalBinaryIntOp op      i1    (s2i s2))
 6    | B b1 , I i2   ⇒ I (    EvalBinaryIntOp op (b2i b1)        i2 )
 7    | B b1 , B b2   ⇒ B (i2b (EvalBinaryIntOp op (b2i b1) (b2i b2)))
 8    | B b1 , Sh s2  ⇒ B (i2b (EvalBinaryIntOp op (b2i b1) (s2i s2)))
 9    | Sh s1, I i2   ⇒ I (    EvalBinaryIntOp op (s2i s1)        i2 )
10    | Sh s1, B b2   ⇒ B (i2b (EvalBinaryIntOp op (s2i s1) (b2i b2)))
11    | Sh s1, Sh s2  ⇒ Sh(i2s (EvalBinaryIntOp op (s2i s1) (s2i s2)))
12    end.
```

Listing 2.62: The evaluation functions for binary integer operators

The \fresh Expression We focus on the definition of the construct \fresh, representative for many other JML operators. The JML primary expression \fresh takes a list of expressions as parameters and expresses that the evaluations of the parameters are references to objects that have been freshly allocated during method execution. That is, in the pre-state of the method, these objects were not yet allocated.

We discuss the definition of \fresh shown in listing 2.63, starting with the innermost constructs. We evaluate each expression in the list flist to a heap location by mapping the evaluation function for reference expressions to each element of flist. The innermost pattern matching replaces the option Location yielded by EvalRefExpression with a Location. 6 If EvalRefExpression yields None, which is the only other option to Some loc, we yield the location UndefinedLocation. For all locations in the computed list, the heap function typeof should then yield None in the pre-heap. Thus, the object is not allocated in that heap. For this definition to be correct, we need to specify that UndefinedLocation is not allocated, which is a natural choice.

```
Definition EvalFresh ( flist : list Expression) (st : State.t) : Prop :=
  ∀ loc ,
    loc ∈ (map (fun e ⇒
              match EvalRefExpression e st with
              | Some loc ⇒ loc
              | _        ⇒ UndefinedLocation
              end) flist ) →
  Heap.typeof (st@fr@preheap) loc = None.
```

Listing 2.63: The evaluation function for \fresh expressions

Quantified Expressions We define the function EvalQuantifier to evaluate the body of quantified expressions. A quantified expression has the form "*quant* qvar ; r ; e", where *quant* is one of \forall and \exists. The variable qvar is the variable we quantify over, r is a range predicate that specifies the valid range for values of qvar and e is the quantified expression.

In listing 2.54 we show 17 the case for the simplified version of \forall that only quantifies over one variable qvar. In JML, a quantifier can mention a list of quantified variables. We desugar these expressions into nested quantified expressions with only one variable each. We use the Coq quantifiers ∀ and ∃ to quantify over the value v, which is passed as argument to the function EvalQuantifier.

The definition of the function in listing 2.64 reveals what happens to the value v that we quantified over. We store the value v assigned to the key qvar into the dictionary quants of the frame additions. Then we evaluate the range predicate r and the expression e in a state with the updated frame into two Coq propositions. The function EvalQuantifier holds, if the evaluation of r implies the evaluation of e.

```
Definition EvalQuantifier (qvar : Var) (r : Expression) (e : Expression) (v : Value)
                                                      (st : State.t) : Prop :=
  let fr' := st@fr[quants:= VarDict.update st@fr@quants qvar v] in
```

```
4   let e'  := EvalBoolExpression e st[fr:=fr'] in
5   let r'  := EvalBoolExpression r st[fr:=fr'] in
6   r' → e'.
```

Listing 2.64: The evaluation function for universal and existential quantification

Implementation of the Frame Conditions Interface

The implementation of the frame condition interface reflects the semantic understanding of `assignable` clauses in the presence of static and dynamic data groups.

Listing 2.65 shows the definition of function FieldUpdateCheck. The function describes a proposition that is equivalent to True if the assignment is permitted by the `assignable` clause. Concretely, the definition states that ₂ the field is in the set of assignable locations or ₄ the field's target is a freshly allocated object. The function LocInObjSet extracts the object identifier from the location loc and checks if the set st@fr@fresh contains that object identifier.

```
1   Definition FieldUpdateCheck (p : Program) (loc : Location) (st : State.t) : Prop :=
2     loc ∈ st@fr@assignables
3   ∨
4   LocInObjSet loc st@fr@fresh .
```

Listing 2.65: The implementation of the function FieldUpdateCheck

Listing 2.66 shows the definition of function MethodCallAction. The method updates the set of assignable locations in the method frame according to its specification.

Upon method frame creation for the callee, the set of assignable locations in the new frame has been initialized to the assignable locations from the caller. Now, ₂ we evaluate the `assignable` clause of the callee to a set of locations, locs, and ₃ intersect the two sets. Thus, the new content of assignables is the locations that can be assigned to in the current method as well as all transitive callers. In the presence of data groups, the evaluation of the `assignable` clause is tricky. We devote the next subsection to this matter.

```
1   Definition MethodCallAction (p:Program)(c:Class)(m:Method)(st:State.t): State.t :=
2     let locs := UnfoldDatagroups p st@h (EvalAssignableClause p c m st) in
3     st[fr := st@fr[ assignables :∩ locs ]].
```

Listing 2.66: The implementation of the function MethodCallAction

Listing 2.67 shows the definition of function NewObjectAction. The method frame contains an auxiliary data structure fresh to store newly allocated objects. We keep this data structure up to date by adding the object identifier obj to the set of new objects upon object creation.

```
1  Definition NewObjectAction (p : Program) (obj : Object) (st : State.t) : State.t :=
2    st [ fr := st@fr [ fresh :+ obj ]].
```

Listing 2.67: The implementation of function NewObjectAction

Listing 2.68 shows the definition of function MethodReturnAction. The function builds the program state of the caller after the execution of the callee has terminated. We take the global data structures from the post state of the callee and update the fresh objects in the method frame of the caller. Thanks to our notations, all of these operations can be written in one relatively simple term. st_c refers to the post-state of the callee and st refers to the state of the caller as of method invocation. We replace the method frame of st_c by the frame from the caller, but not before we union the sets of fresh objects from the caller and the callee. Thus, we get a program state that represents the post state of the call, from the callers point of view.

```
1  Definition MethodReturnAction (p : Program)(st_c : State.t)(st : State.t):State.t :=
2    st_c [ fr := st@fr [ fresh :∪ st_c@fr@fresh ]].
```

Listing 2.68: The implementation of function MethodReturnAction

Listing 2.69 shows the definition of function FieldUpdateAction. As this implementation of the semantics of `assignable` clauses doesn't use any auxiliary data structures that depend on the value of fields, there is nothing to do in this function.

Although not used in this implementation, we keep the function in the interface for frame conditions, as we might want to express the semantics of `assignable` clauses differently, using auxiliary data structures that depend on the current structure of the dynamic data groups, see chapter 4.

```
1  Definition FieldUpdateAction (p:Program)(loc:Location)(v:Value)(st:State.t):State.t :=
2    st .
```

Listing 2.69: The implementation of function FieldUpdateAction

Evaluation of Assignable Locations

The definition MethodCallAction uses the two functions EvalAssignableClause and UnfoldDatagroups to retrieve the heap locations that are declared assignable in the callee's specification.

The function EvalAssignableClause shown in listing 2.70 yields the locations directly represented by the `assignable` clauses of all specifications whose `requires` clause holds, we call them *valid* cases. The yielded set does not include the locations that are implicitly assignable via a data group. The function ₃ ValidStoreRefs yields the list of assignable store refs of all valid specification cases. It yields the store ref \nothing if either all valid specification cases declare assignable \nothing or some of the cases are assignable \not_specified and the application of the JML semantics decides to treat undefined assignable clauses as assignable \nothing. This can be achieved by defining the parameter NotSpecifiedAssignableClause to be \nothing. ValidStoreRefs yields the store ref \everything if there is at least one valid specification case that contains assignable \everything or one with assignable \not_specified and the application of the JML semantics decides to treat undefined assignable clauses as assignable \everything. This is the default setting in our semantics.

We then perform a pattern matching on the result of ValidStoreRefs. The two cases \nothing and \everything are trivial. The third case puts all locations denoted by the list of store refs into the resulting set of locations. The function s StoreRef2Location yields a singleton set if the store ref denotes a single location in the heap, that is, a field or an array location, and a set of several locations if the store ref denotes all fields of an object or a range of array elements. Beside the fact that a store ref can denote several locations, its evaluation is essentially the same as evaluating a field or array access. StoreRef2Location evaluates the target to an object identifier if the store ref is not a static field, and then builds a location for each field identifier or array index.

```
1  Definition EvalAssignableClause (p:Program)(c:Class)(m:Method)(st:State.t): LocSet.t:=
2  match ValidStoreRefs p c m st with
3  | \nothing      ⇒ LocSet.empty
4  | \everything   ⇒ AllLoc st@fr@preheap
5  | StoreRefs srl ⇒
6      fold_right
7        (fun sr locs ⇒
8           LocSet.union (StoreRef2Location p st@fr sr) locs)
9        LocSet.empty
10       srl
11 end.
```

Listing 2.70: The function EvalAssignableClause

Unfolding of Data Groups The function UnfoldDatagroups shown in listing 2.71 takes the set of heap locations yielded by EvalAssignableClause and *unfolds* the data groups of these locations, that is, adds all locations that are contained in the data groups to the set of assignable locations.

We provide an axiomatic definition of UnfoldDatagroups, based on FieldInDg p h f dg, that holds if field f is directly or transitively contained in the data group dg in the environment specified by program p and heap h.

The axiom UnfoldDatagroups_def states that ₃ a field f is in the set yielded by the function UnfoldDatagroups p h dgs if and only if ₅ there exists a data group dg in the set dgs that contains the field f, where dgs is the set of locations that should be unfolded.

```
1  Parameter UnfoldDatagroups: Program →Heap.t →LocSet.t → LocSet.t.
2  Axiom UnfoldDatagroups_def: ∀ p h f dgs,
3     f ∈ (UnfoldDatagroups p h dgs)
4     ↔
5     ∃ dg, dg ∈ dgs ∧ FieldInDg p h f dg.
```

Listing 2.71: An axiomatization of function UnfoldDatagroups

Data Group Membership Listing 2.72 shows the inductive definition of predicate FieldInDg. The definition features a step case and three base cases. FieldInDg_step defines transitivity: if field f is in a data group dg', and dg' is in dg, then f is also in dg. FieldInDg_same defines reflexivity: a field is always in its own data group. The two remaining rules define the cases that field f is directly contained in dg, either statically or dynamically.

```
1   Inductive FieldInDg (p:Program)(h:Heap.t):Location→ Location→ Prop :=
2   | FieldInDg_step : ∀ f dg dg',
3       FieldInDg p h dg' dg →
4       FieldInDg p h f dg' →
5       FieldInDg p h f dg
6   | FieldInDg_same : ∀ f dg,
7       f = dg →
8       FieldInDg p h f dg.
9   | FieldInDg_static : ∀ f dg,
10      direct_FieldInDg_static p f dg →
11      FieldInDg p h f dg
12  | FieldInDg_dynamic : ∀ f dg pivot,
13      direct_FieldInDg_dynamic p h f dg pivot →
14      FieldInDg p h f dg
```

Listing 2.72: The inductive definition of predicate FieldInDg

We can determine static data group membership on a purely syntactical level. Field f is statically contained in dg exactly when the following three propositions are true.

1. The locations f and dg are instance fields.

2. The two fields f and dg are defined in the same object.

2.6. A FORMAL SEMANTICS OF JML IN COQ

3. The field f features a static data group declaration, that is, an "in" clause, that mentions the field dg.

Listing 2.73 shows the definition of the predicate direct_FieldInDg_static as an inductive data type. ₄,₅ We express the first proposition by defining that f and dg are equal to instance fields with fresh variables for object identifiers and field signatures. ₆ The second property is expressed by stating that the just-mentioned object identifiers are equal. The third property is slightly more difficult to express, as we need to extract the information from the DATA_GROUP data type accessed by the function dataGroups in the FIELD data type, see 2.4.1 on page 40. ₇ We define the variable field to be the field data type with signature field_fsig in program p. ₈ The field's list of data group declarations contains a data group dg_decl that is ₉ static and ₁₀ contains the field signature of dg.

```
Inductive direct_FieldInDg_static  (p : Program) : Location → Location → Prop :=
| direct_FieldInDg_static_def :
    ∀ dg f dg_obj dg_fsig f_obj f_fsig  field dg_decl ,
    (* 1 *) f = Heap.InstanceField f_obj f_fsig →
            dg = Heap.InstanceField dg_obj dg_fsig →
    (* 2 *) dg_obj = f_obj →
    (* 3 *) findField p f_fsig = Some field →
            dg_decl ∈ (FIELD.dataGroups field) →
            DATA_GROUP.isDynamic dg_decl = false →
            dg_fsig ∈ (DATA_GROUP.dataGroups dg_decl) →
    direct_FieldInDg_static  p f dg.
```

Listing 2.73: The inductive definition of predicate direct_FieldInDg_static

Dynamic data groups depend on the value of pivot fields that defines the relationship between the data group and the field. Field f is dynamically contained in data group dg via the pivot field pivot exactly when the following four propositions are true.

1. The locations f, dg, and pivot are instance fields.

2. The fields pivot and dg are defined in the same object.

3. The field pivot points to the object in which f is defined. For this, we need to have the heap in the environment.

4. The field pivot features a dynamic data group declaration (a "maps ... \into" clause) that mentions the field signature of dg as data group and the field signature of f as target.

In listing 2.74 we present the inductive definition of direct_FieldInDg_dynamic. It is very similar to the predicate for static data groups. Again, the numbers in comments relate the premises of the inductive definition to the items above.

```
1  Inductive direct_FieldInDg_dynamic (p : Program) (h : Heap.t) :
2                              Location → Location → Location → Prop :=
3  | direct_FieldInDg_dynamic_def :
4      ∀ dg f dg_obj dg_fsig f_obj f_fsig  pivot_obj  pivot_fsig   pivot_field
5        pivot_loc  dg_decl ,
6      (* 1 *) f = Heap.InstanceField f_obj f_fsig →
7              dg = Heap.InstanceField dg_obj dg_fsig →
8              pivot = Heap.InstanceField pivot_obj pivot_fsig →
9      (* 2 *) dg_obj = pivot_obj →
10     (* 3 *) Heap.get h pivot = Some (Ref f_obj)→
11     (* 4 *) findField p pivot_fsig = Some pivot_field →
12             dg_decl ∈ (FIELD.dataGroups pivot_field) →
13             DATA_GROUP.isDynamic dg_decl = true →
14             DATA_GROUP.pivotTarget dg_decl = Some (FieldDg f_fsig) →
15             dg_fsig ∈ (DATA_GROUP.dataGroups dg_decl) →
16     direct_FieldInDg_dynamic p h f dg pivot.
```

Listing 2.74: The inductive definition of predicate direct_FieldInDg_dynamic

2.7 Summary

In this chapter we presented a formalization of JML in Coq, which is suitable for both meta-reasoning and program verification. Its extendible and modular definition allows easy integration of new aspects and constructs. Furthermore, the separation of the JML semantics from the operational semantics of Java enables to use the formalization as part of an already existing verification environment. As opposed to other formal JML definitions, our formalization faithfully describes the behavior of `assignable` clauses.

Chapter 3

An Efficient RAC for Assignable Clauses

In this chapter we present the first algorithm to check `assignable` clauses at runtime, in the presence of dynamic data groups. Dynamic data groups turn the checking of `assignable` clauses into a difficult and inherently non-modular task. A data group contains different members over time and can get very large, only bounded by the number of allocated objects in the heap.

Following the description of the semantics of `assignable` clauses in section 1.8.2 on page 21, we could come up with a naïve way of implementing a runtime assertion checker: upon method invocation, we create a set of assignable locations and unfold all data groups in that set. We intersect the resulting set with the set of effectively assignable locations of the caller (because the frame conditions from both the caller and the callee need to be respected). Furthermore, we keep track of a set of fresh locations which we update upon object creation and pass to the caller upon method return (because the caller can update locations that are freshly allocated in the callee). Checking if a location is assignable would be a simple lookup in the set of assignable locations and the fresh set. The time and memory overhead of this approach is linear to the number of locations in the assignable and fresh sets for each method invocation.

This approach has two major shortcomings. Firstly, unfolding all data groups mentioned in an `assignable` clause in the pre-state of a method is very expensive if the data groups are large (which is a realistic assumption). Secondly, it is often the case that many of these locations would not be updated during the execution of the method. That is, we might spend a significant effort in unfolding a huge data group without ever actually using most of the gained information. We discuss both issues in more detail in section 3.4 on page 107.

Overview. Section 3.1 explains the approach we choose to overcome the issues described above. Section 3.2 introduces an example that we will use in the following sections to explain the algorithm. Section 3.3 introduces the algorithm to check `assignable` clauses with static data groups. In this section, we concentrate on the representation of `assignable` clauses as well as the efficient operations based on bitsets and hash-based data structures. Section 3.4 starts with observations on dynamic data groups followed by the algorithm to check `assignable` clauses with dynamic data groups. Section 3.5 introduces two optimizations that are easy to accomplish and necessary to achieve the goal that the algorithm does not perform worse than the naïve implementation in any case. We conclude the chapter with section 3.6 where we briefly discuss the implementation of the runtime assertion checker in Java, present an experimental evaluation of the algorithm for an example that showcases a difficult data structure to handle, and discuss the theoretical results on time and space overhead.

3.1 Approach

Our algorithm concentrates on minimizing the time overhead while keeping the memory footprint acceptable. While it is not possible to define an algorithm for this task that clearly performs better than the naïve version in every case, it is certainly possible to come up with a solution that can check `assignable` clauses with only little time overhead and moderate memory consumption in the average case. In the worst case, we want our algorithm to perform no worse than the naïve implementation of the semantics discussed at the start of this chapter. In order to achieve our goal, we attack the problem from three sides.

- We provide efficient implementations of two operations that are heavily used in our algorithm: checking if an `assignable` clause mentions a certain location or data group, and collecting all static data groups that contain a location. We introduce new data structures for assignable maps and for static data groups, based on bitset operations, to achieve this goal.

- We reduce memory consumption and runtime overhead by introducing the concept of *lazy unfolding* of dynamic data groups to avoid unnecessary overhead. Instead of unfolding the data groups of an `assignable` clause in the pre-state of the method, we track the changes to dynamic data groups during method execution and only store the difference between the pre-state and the current state. We can decide at compile time which operations trigger a change to the dynamic data groups and instrument the code at that point to store the changes.

- We optimize time complexity by caching the result of checking whether a location is assignable, as this information can be reused within the same method.

3.2 Running Example

We introduce a running example which we refer to in the subsequent sections in order to illustrate how our algorithm works. The example introduces a balanced binary tree implementation of an in-memory data store. We assume the typical situation for a data store: it contains a large number of items and the content of the store changes frequently.

The store can be accessed through the public interface of class `Store`, which we present in listing 3.1. The store features two public fields `struct` and `footprint` of type `JMLDataGroup`. The type `JMLDataGroup` indicates that the only purpose of the fields is the data groups that they implicitly define. The data group `struct` contains all heap locations that are used to structure the storage, but not the items. The data group `footprint` contains all heap locations that refer to data currently being stored. Using these two data groups, we can define frame conditions for the interface methods of the store, without revealing implementation details.

Let's look at the specification of the method $_{14}$ `put`. The $_{11}$ `assignable` clause allows the method to change the internal structure of the store arbitrarily, but no other heap location can be assigned to. Most notably, no data from the stored items can be updated.

The implementation of `put` $_{18}$ delegates the task to the root node of the internal tree, if the store already contains at least one item, or $_{16}$ creates a new root node containing the first item.

The tree consists of nodes of type `Node`. The field `root` is $_5$ statically contained in the data group `struct` of the store. Furthermore, `root` features a data group `struct`, which we $_6$ declare to be dynamically contained in data group `struct` of the store. Finally, `root` also features a data group `footprint`, which we $_7$ declare to be dynamically contained in data group `footprint` of the store.

We declare the method $_{22}$ `contains` to be pure, which allows us to use it in specifications. It yields `true` if the store contains a node with an item equal to `i`.

```
1  public class Store {
2    public JMLDataGroup struct;                    // 0
3    public JMLDataGroup footprint;                 // 1
4
5    private Node root; //@ in struct;              // 2
6    /*@ maps root.struct \into struct; */
7    /*@ maps root.footprint \into footprint; */
8
9    /*@ public normal_behavior
10   @    requires true;
11   @    assignable this.struct;
12   @    ensures this.contains(i);
```

99

```
13       @*/
14       public void put(Item i){
15         if (root == null){
16           root = new Node(i);
17         } else {
18           root.insert(i);
19         }
20       }
21
22       public /*@ pure */ boolean contains(Item i){ ... }
23
24       ... // Other fields and methods omitted.
25     }
```

Listing 3.1: Excerpt of the class Store. We highlight the field declarations and the methods put to add new items into the store, and contains to query the presence of an item in the store. We provide an enumeration of the fields in the comments behind the field declarations, which will help to explain the algorithm in the next sections.

Listing 3.2 shows an excerpt of class Node. As we have seen in the definition of the root node in Store, the Node class features the two data groups struct and footprint. Moreover, a node has two children, left and right that contain subtrees of nodes, as well as the payload of type Item.

The fields left and right are part of the structure of the store, thus we [5,9] declare them to be statically contained in struct. Furthermore, the struct data group of the left subtree is declared to be [6] dynamically contained in the struct data group of the current node. Similarly, left.footprint is dynamically contained in the data group footprint of the current node. The same applies to the data groups struct and footprint of the right subtree. Furthermore, we declare that the data group footprint of the item is dynamically contained in the data group footprint of the current node.

The class Node provides a [17] constructor, which allows us to directly initialize a node with a given item. The method [20] insert is used by the put method of Store to insert a new item into the tree at the appropriate position. For both the constructor and the method insert, we provide a lightweight method specification that only mentions the assignable clause. Furthermore, the Node class features a private method [22] balance in order to rebalance the tree after insertion and deletion of nodes. We choose not to provide any specifications for this internal method.

```
1    class Node {
2      JMLDataGroup struct;                              // 0
3      JMLDataGroup footprint;                           // 1
```

```
    private Node left; //@ in struct;                    // 2
    /*@ maps left.struct \into struct; */
    /*@ maps left.footprint \into footprint; */

    private Node right; //@ in struct;                   // 3
    /*@ maps right.struct \into struct; */
    /*@ maps right.footprint \into footprint; */

    Item item;                                           // 4
    /*@ maps item.footprint \into footprint; */

    //@ assignable this.item;
    Node(Item i) { item = i; }

    //@ assignable this.struct;
    void insert (Item i) { ... }

    private void balance() { ... }

    ...  // Other methods omitted.
}
```

Listing 3.2: Excerpt of the class Node. We highlight the field declarations, the insert method and a private method balance. Again, we provide an enumeration of the fields in the comments behind the field declarations.

Finally, we introduce the class Item shown in listing 3.3. The class features a data group footprint which contains the fields id and payload. If an item is stored in a node, the data group footprint of Item is contained in the data group footprint of the node, as we can see in 14 listing 3.2.

The class features a method copy which behaves similarly to clone. If the other item is selected, the fields id and payload of this item are set to point to the same objects. Furthermore, the other item is deselected.

The assignable clause of the method allows the update of any location contained in footprint as well as the field selected of other.

```
public class Item implements Comparable {
  public JMLDataGroup footprint;                         // 0

  private String id; //@ in footprint;                   // 1
```

```
     private /*@ spec_public */ boolean selected;         // 2

     private Object payload; //@ in footprint;            // 3

     /*@ public normal_behavior
       @     requires other != null && other.selected = true;
       @     assignable this.footprint, other.selected;
       @     ensures this.equals(other);
       @*/
     public void copy(Item other){
         id = other.id;
         payload = other.payload;
         other.selected = false;
     }
     ... // Other fields and methods omitted.
}
```

Listing 3.3: Excerpt of the class Item. The class stores an arbitrary payload under a given id. We provide an enumeration of the fields in the comments behind the field declarations, which will be used in section 3.3.1.

3.3 Checking Assignable Clauses with Static Data Groups

As a first step, we present an algorithm to check assignable clauses in the presence of *static* data groups only. Thus, we do not have to deal with the non-modularity introduced by dynamic data groups. However, we need to come up with a very efficient way of checking static data group membership, since we use this operation very frequently when checking assignable clauses with dynamic data groups, as presented in the next section.

3.3.1 Data Structures

Our goal is to check assignable clauses in the presence of static data groups in constant time. The following operations are involved in the check for field updates:

1. Looking up all assignable fields of a given object.

2. Looking up all data groups that contain a given location.

3. Deciding whether or not the intersection between two sets of fields of an object is empty.

3.3. CHECKING ASSIGNABLE CLAUSES WITH STATIC DATA GROUPS

We introduce the following data structures to perform all three tasks in constant time.

Field Identifiers

We enumerate the fields of a class such that at runtime, even in the presence of inheritance, every field of an object has a unique number. In listings 3.1, 3.2, and 3.3 from the running example, we show these numbers in comments behind field declarations, to help the reader to understand the algorithm.

We use the assigned numbers as positions in bitsets and arrays. Thus we start numbering with 0 and increment the number by one for each field. If the class inherits fields from a super type other than Object, the first field gets as number the total number of fields from the super-types.

Assignable Locations

As explained in section 1.8.2, the evaluation of assignable clauses leads to a set of locations. We represent this set by a map from objects to bitsets, in which the keys of the map are the objects of the locations, and each bit of the bitset represents a field of that object. The position of the bit corresponds to the number assigned to the field. If a field of an object is declared to be assignable, its corresponding bit is set.

As opposed to the semantic description of data groups in section 1.8.2, we do not unfold the data groups mentioned in the assignable clause. To clarify the difference to the semantics, we introduce the notation $\mathcal{A}_m^{declared}$ to refer to the locations that are explicitly declared to be assignable in m. Thus, as opposed to the set $\mathcal{A}_m$, $\mathcal{A}_m^{declared}$ doesn't contain the locations that stem from unfolding the data groups.

This design allows us to perform the first operation mentioned in section 3.3.1 in constant time, as we use a hash map as the underlying data structure for $\mathcal{A}_m^{declared}$, and there are only a handful of elements in the hash map.

Example. For method copy of class Item in listing 3.3, we represent the assignable clause this.struct, other.selected by the following assignable map:

$$\mathcal{A}_{copy}^{declared} = \{\text{this} \mapsto [\checkmark \ \cdot \ \cdot \ \cdot\,], \text{other} \mapsto [\,\cdot \ \checkmark \ \cdot \ \cdot\,]\}$$

The first bit in the bitset of object this represents field footprint and the second bit in the bitset of object other represents field selected.

To retrieve the bitset of a given object o in an assignable map $\mathcal{A}$, we write $\mathcal{A}[o]$. We overload the notation to query whether or not a *location* is mentioned in a set $\mathcal{A}$. That is, $\mathcal{A}[o.f]$ yields *true* if $o.f$ is in $\mathcal{A}$ and *false* otherwise. If the map does not contain an object o, $\mathcal{A}[o]$ yields an empty bitset. To store object o with bitset bs in $\mathcal{A}$, we write $\mathcal{A}[o] \leftarrow bs$.

Example. $\mathcal{A}_{\text{copy}}^{\text{declared}}[\text{other}]$ yields $[\cdot\checkmark\cdot\cdot]$, that is, `other.selected` is declared to be assignable, whereas $\mathcal{A}_{\text{copy}}^{\text{declared}}[\text{other.struct}]$ simply yields *false*.

Fresh Locations

If an object is newly created, all locations of that object are *fresh*. To represent the set of fresh locations $\mathcal{F}^{\triangleleft}$, we need to save only the set of newly allocated objects, which implicitly gives us the set of fresh locations.

The query $\mathcal{F}^{\triangleleft}[o]$ yields *true* if the object o is newly allocated since the beginning of the current method execution, and *false* otherwise.

Static Data Groups

For each field, we use a bitset to represent the data group(s) the field belongs to. That is, we equip every class with an array of bitsets.

Example. For class `Item`, we represent the static data groups by the following array.

$$\begin{array}{l} \texttt{footprint} \\ \texttt{id} \\ \texttt{selected} \\ \texttt{payload} \end{array} \left[\begin{array}{l} [\checkmark\cdot\cdot\cdot] \\ [\checkmark\checkmark\cdot\cdot] \\ [\cdot\cdot\checkmark\cdot] \\ [\checkmark\cdot\cdot\checkmark] \end{array}\right]$$

To access the data groups that *statically* contain field f of class c, we write $\mathcal{D}^{\text{static}}[c@f]$. For simplicity, we may also write $\mathcal{D}^{\text{static}}[o.f]$ to get the static data groups of field f of class c, where o is of type c.

Example. $\mathcal{D}^{\text{static}}[\texttt{Item@id}]$ yields $[\checkmark\checkmark\cdot\cdot]$, which means that `id` is in the data group of `footprint` (the first bit) and of course in its own data group (the second bit).

We set up the data structures for static data groups such that we can perform the second and third operation described in section 3.3 in constant time. The second operation involves one array access, and the third operation involves computing the intersection of two bitsets, which is possible in constant time.

We can safely assume constant time operations on bitsets, because we have an upper bound on the number of fields that we can define in a class. Thus, we only need a fixed sized bitset, which results in constant time operations. Usually, a class doesn't declare more than 64 fields. In this case we can even fit the bitset into one double-word and get a very good performance.

3.3.2 Code Instrumentation

An `assignable` clause restricts assignments throughout a method execution. This implies that checks of the `assignable` clause need to be performed throughout a method execution and not only in pre- and post-states. In the following, we present the code instrumentation to build up the necessary data structures and to check the validity of a field update. The relevant statements are: field updates (as these might violate the assignable clause), object creation (to track fresh locations), method invocation (to evaluate assignable clauses in the pre-state of a method and merge assignable sets), and method return (to update the assignable sets from the caller).

Method Invocation

Upon invocation of method m from within method m', we evaluate the assignable clause of m to the set $\mathcal{A}_m^{\text{declared}}$. For all locations $o.f$ in the assignable clause, we enable the bit that represents f in the bitset $\mathcal{A}_m^{\text{declared}}[o]$. To do this, we perform the following update: $\mathcal{A}_m^{\text{declared}}[o] \leftarrow \mathcal{A}_m^{\text{declared}}[o] \cup \mathcal{B}(f)$ where $\mathcal{B}(f)$ is the bitset in which only the bit for field f is enabled.

Furthermore, we compute the intersection of the $\mathcal{A}_m^{\text{declared}}$ and the *merged* assignable locations of m', which we denote by $\mathcal{A}_{m'}^{\text{merged}}$. The merged assignable locations correspond to the effective assignable locations $\mathcal{A}_{m'}^{\text{effective}}$ defined in the semantics, but without unfolding of data groups. Thus, in an environment where m' is called by m'', we define:

$$\mathcal{A}_{m'}^{\text{merged}} = \mathcal{F}_{m'}^{\triangleleft} \cup \left(\mathcal{A}_{m'}^{\text{declared}} \cap \mathcal{A}_{m''}^{\text{merged}} \right)$$

This merging can be performed efficiently. However, we do not discuss its details, as we will have to replace this aspect of the algorithm when dealing with dynamic data groups below.

Example. For method copy of class Item, we have shown in section 3.3.1 that $\mathcal{A}_{\text{copy}}^{\text{declared}}$ is {this $\mapsto$ [✓ · · ·], other $\mapsto$ [· ✓ · ·]}. Let us assume that $\mathcal{A}_{m'}^{\text{merged}}$ is set to the map {this $\mapsto$ [✓ · · ·], store $\mapsto$ [· ✓ ·]}, where m' is the caller of copy, and store refers to an object of type Store. The intersection of the assignable maps $\mathcal{A}_{\text{copy}}^{\text{declared}} \cap \mathcal{A}_{m'}^{\text{merged}}$ would then yield the map: {this $\mapsto$ [✓ · · ·]}

Field Update

Updating a field is the only way to violate an assignable clause. According to the semantics defined in section 1.8.2, we need to check before an update of a location $o.f$ in a method m called by m' if $o.f$ is in the set $\mathcal{A}_m^{\text{effective}}$. This is the case if either the object o has been freshly allocated during the execution of m and therefore is a member of the set $\mathcal{F}_m^{\triangleleft}$, or $o.f$ is in the set $\mathcal{A}_m$ and it was already assignable in m' upon invocation of m.

Checking if $o.f$ is in the set of fresh locations $\mathcal{F}_m^{\triangleleft}$ is performed by $\mathcal{F}_m^{\triangleleft}[o]$. Checking if $o.f$ is assignable in the set of assignable locations $\mathcal{A}_m$ is performed by $\mathcal{A}_m^{\text{declared}}[o] \cap \mathcal{D}^{\text{static}}[o.f] \neq \emptyset$. That is, we get the bitset representing the assignable fields of object o

CHAPTER 3. AN EFFICIENT RAC FOR ASSIGNABLE CLAUSES

in $\mathcal{A}_m^{\text{declared}}$ and intersect it with the bitset representing the data groups that contain f. If the intersection of the two bitsets is not empty, either $\mathcal{A}_m^{\text{declared}}$ contains $o.f$, or it contains at least one data group that contains $o.f$. Checking if $o.f$ was already assignable in m' can be done similarly by $\mathcal{A}_{m'}^{\text{merged}}[o] \cap \mathcal{D}^{\text{static}}[o.f] \neq \emptyset$. We can combine the last two checks by accessing the bitset representing the assignable fields of object o of $\mathcal{A}_m^{\text{declared}} \cap \mathcal{A}_{m'}^{\text{merged}}$ and then computing the intersection with the static data group:

$$\mathcal{F}_m^\triangleleft[o] \;\vee\; (\mathcal{A}_m^{\text{declared}} \cap \mathcal{A}_{m'}^{\text{effective}})[o] \cap \mathcal{D}^{\text{static}}[o.f] \neq \emptyset$$

In the paragraph on method invocation above, we have shown that we can compute $\mathcal{A}_m^{\text{declared}} \cap \mathcal{A}_{m'}^{\text{effective}}$ once and for all upon method invocation. Therefore, all of the remaining operations for a field update can be performed in constant time, which means that we can check the `assignable` clauses for field updates in constant time in the presence of static data groups only.

Example. We continue the example from the section on method invocation on the preceding page where $\mathcal{A}_{\text{copy}}^{\text{declared}} \cap \mathcal{A}_{m'}^{\text{merged}}$ results in the map {`this` $\mapsto [\checkmark \cdot \cdot \cdot]$}. The body of method `copy` performs three field updates. For the first assignment, 16 `id = other.id` we evaluate the check as follows:

$$\underbrace{\mathcal{F}_m^\triangleleft[\text{this}]}_{\textit{false}} \;\vee\; \underbrace{\underbrace{(\mathcal{A}_m^{\text{declared}} \cap \mathcal{A}_{m'}^{\text{merged}})[\text{this}]}_{[\checkmark \,\cdot\,\cdot\,\cdot\,]} \cap \underbrace{\mathcal{D}^{\text{static}}[\text{Item@id}]}_{[\checkmark\checkmark\,\cdot\,\cdot\,]}}_{[\checkmark\,\cdot\,\cdot\,\cdot\,]} \neq \emptyset$$

So, the field update can be performed. Similarly, the assignment to `payload` can be performed. However, we are not allowed to perform the third assignment 18 `other.selected = false` even though it would be allowed by the `assignable` clause of `copy`. The reason is, that the location `other.selected` was not assignable in m' upon invocation of `copy`.

Object Creation

On creation of a new object o in method m, all locations of o are fresh in m and in every transitive caller m_i of m. According to the semantics of fresh sets, we would have to add all fields of o to $\mathcal{F}_m^\triangleleft$ as well as to each $\mathcal{F}_{m_i}^\triangleleft$. Since any caller of m can observe newly allocated locations only *after* m returns, we add o only to $\mathcal{F}_m^\triangleleft$ and update the callers later. Because of this simplification, the instrumentation of object creation can be performed in constant time and produces a memory overhead linear in the number of newly allocated objects.

Method Return

Before a method m may return to its caller m', the set of fresh locations $\mathcal{F}_m^\triangleleft$ needs to be added to $\mathcal{F}_{m'}^\triangleleft$. This operation can be done with time overhead linear in the number of objects in $\mathcal{F}_m^\triangleleft$ and does not increase the memory overhead as $\mathcal{F}_m^\triangleleft$ will be consumed by the garbage collector eventually.

3.4 Checking Assignable Clauses with Dynamic Data Groups

We extend the algorithm for checking `assignable` clauses to deal with *dynamic* data groups, that is, data groups that contain fields from other objects and therefore depend on the heap. From the running example in section 3.2, we observe two properties of dynamic data groups that we describe in this section. These properties not only hold for this individual example, but apply in the general case. As dynamic data groups are inherently non-modular, we need to base the design of our algorithm on these observations, in order to profit in the average case from a dramatic speed up.

Data Group Size versus Data Groups per Location We typically use dynamic data groups to refer to the locations in all objects of a data structure. The data groups `struct` and `footprint` in the running example showcase this use of dynamic data groups. The more objects we add to the data structure, the bigger such data groups get, independently of the particular kind of the data structure. However, the number of data groups that contain a given location differs a lot depending on the data structure, and is typically related to the lookup time complexity. Table 3.1 compares the number of locations in a data group versus the number of data groups that contain a location. In all cases, we assume that the data structure contains n elements and the data group in question contains a fixed number of locations per element. In this setting, we always get $O(n)$ locations in the data group.

Data Structure	# locations per data group	# data groups per location
List	$O(n)$	$O(n)$
Tree	$O(n)$	$O(\log n)$
Hashtable	$O(n)$	$O(1)$
Graph	$O(n)$	$O(1) \ldots O(n)$

Table 3.1: Comparison of data group size versus the number of data groups that contain a location.

In case of a linked list, the locations at the tail of the list are contained in all data groups of the elements in front. Thus, we also get $O(n)$ for the number of data groups that contain a given location. The situation is more interesting for trees. Still, the number of locations in a data group is linear in the number of nodes in the tree. However, there are only $O(\log n)$ data groups that contain a given location, namely the transitive parents of the node containing the location. In case of data structures based on hash tables, we look at an even greater difference between the two numbers. If the hash table is not degraded, that is, the overflow lists in the buckets are not large, we look at a constant number of data groups that contain a given location. If we look at a graph structure, the topology and the connectedness of the nodes in the graph greatly influence the number of data groups that contain a given field. A completely connected graph results in $O(n)$ data groups that contain a location, whereas in a star topology, we get a constant number of data groups for a given location.

To sum up, it is often much easier to ask the question of which data groups contain a given location, rather than asking the question of which locations are contained in a data group. This holds especially for tree-like and hash-based data structures, whereas linked lists present a case in which the difference is minimal.

Specificness of Assignable Clauses Dynamic data groups allow us to be unspecific in `assignable` clauses. Instead of mentioning the exact locations that a method can or will update, we talk about possibly unspecific groups of locations.

The assignable clause we use in the specification of method `put` in class `Store` on page 99 is quite unspecific. We allow assignment to all fields, that make up the internal structure of the store. On the one hand, this is because we do not want to reveal implementation details of the store and thus need to find a way of abstracting away from these. On the other hand, we simply do not know at compile time exactly which locations might be changed. We need to allow the method to update anything that might get updated in any situation.

From the `assignable` clause of a method, we can conclude which parts of the heap definitively stay unchanged. This information is usually more interesting than to exactly pinpoint the heap locations that actually might get changed. The main purpose of the `assignable` clause of method `put` is to guarantee that *only* the structure of the store might get changed, and not the content of the stored items or anything else.

A central implication of using unspecific assignable clauses is that the implementation of the method often assigns to only a small fraction of the locations that may be assigned to. In the case of the method `put`, it only assigns to one single `left` or `right` field to add an item if no balancing happens, and a couple of `left` and `right` fields if we need to rotate subtrees in order to balance the tree. But in no case will the method update all locations mentioned in `struct` or even a number of the same magnitude.

Conclusions from the Observations From the first observation we learn that in many data structures, the number of data groups that contain a location can be many magnitudes smaller than the number of locations in a data group. The second observation shows that we often assign to a small fraction of the locations that are actually declared to be assignable. Therefore, we avoid unfolding data groups in the pre-state of a method, and rather find out upon field assignment if there exists a data group mentioned in the assignable clause that contains the field. This decision raises the following three issues:

- We have to spend more effort to check if a field is assignable, as the information is not directly available.

- We can no longer merge sets of assignable locations. If we were merging two sets that contain partially overlapping dynamic data groups we would have to unfold the data groups to find out which locations are in the intersection. Since we decided not to unfold data groups, we cannot merge anymore.

- As the content of dynamic data groups may change over time, we need to keep track of all changes in dynamic data groups in order to reconstruct the assignable locations as in the pre-state of the method.

In the following sections, we explain how we can efficiently cope with these issues.

3.4.1 Data Structures

We do not change any of the existing data structures for checking assignable clauses, but add data structures to represent dynamic data groups. We design our data structures such that it is possible to quickly find all data groups that dynamically contain a location.

Dynamic Data Groups

To represent dynamic data groups, we add an array of sets of tuples of two locations to each object. With this data structure, we store for each field of the object a set of data groups that dynamically contain the field along with the pivot field on which the data group is defined. We call this data structure *back-links*; from the location back to the data groups. The first location in the tuple is the pivot field and the second location in the tuple is the data group that contains the field.

Example. For the object g of class Node (see Fig. 1.2 on page 25), we represent the dynamic data groups with the following array:

$$\begin{array}{l} \texttt{struct} \\ \texttt{footprint} \\ \texttt{left} \\ \texttt{right} \\ \texttt{item} \end{array} \begin{bmatrix} \{(\texttt{c.right}, \texttt{c.struct})\} \\ \{(\texttt{c.right}, \texttt{c.footprint})\} \\ \{\} \\ \{\} \\ \{\} \end{bmatrix}$$

The entries for the fields struct and footprint contain a back-link to their respective data groups: struct is directly contained in the data group c.struct via the pivot c.right, similarly, footprint is directly contained in the data group c.footprint via the same pivot.

We do not introduce back-links for fields that are not *directly* contained in a data group. Thus, because the fields `left` and `right` are indirectly contained in the data group `c.struct` via `struct`, we do not introduce a back-link for them. For the same reason, `item` doesn't get a back-link.

With this back-link data structure and the bitset representation of static data groups, we can efficiently compute the set of all data groups that contain a given location. We introduce the notation $\mathcal{D}_h[o.f]$ to refer to the set of dynamic *and* static data groups that contain $o.f$ directly or indirectly in heap h. As opposed to static data groups, the content of a dynamic data group changes along with the heap. Thus, we need to provide the heap as argument to specify in which heap the content of the data group is evaluated.

Example. We assume the heap structure as shown in Fig. 1.2 for heap h (the left part). We want to retrieve all data groups that contain `g.right`: firstly, `g.struct` is a data group that statically contains `g.right`. Secondly, the data group `c.struct` dynamically contains `g.struct` via pivot `c.right`, and thus also contains `g.right`. Finally, `a.struct` dynamically contains `c.struct` via pivot `a.left`. Thus, the yielded set of data groups is the following:

$$\mathcal{D}_h[\texttt{g.right}] = \{\texttt{g.struct}, \texttt{c.struct}, \texttt{a.struct}\}$$

In the algorithm for checking assignable clauses in the presence of dynamic data groups, we will have to ignore back-links that use certain pivot fields. Thus, we add another parameter that specifies the excluded pivots to the notation to access data groups of a field. We write $\mathcal{D}_h^{\mathcal{X}}[o.f]$ to refer to all data groups that contain location $o.f$ in heap h without using any of the e$\mathcal{X}$cluded pivot fields. To facilitate this restriction, we store the pivot fields along with the data groups in the back-link data structure.

Example. If we exclude the pivot `a.left` when computing the data groups in the situation of the previous example we get the following set of data groups:

$$\mathcal{D}_h^{\{\texttt{a.left}\}}[\texttt{g.right}] = \{\texttt{g.struct}, \texttt{c.struct}\}$$

The data group `a.struct` is no longer in the resulting set of data groups for field `g.right`, because `a.left` is on the path from `a.struct` to `g.right`.

We are going to explain in more details how we compute the set of data groups $\mathcal{D}[o.f]$ for location $o.f$ in section 3.5.

Stack of Assignable Maps and Fresh Locations

Since we can no longer merge `assignable` clauses from the caller and the callee efficiently upon method invocation, we now have to check for each field update whether the updated location is assignable in all methods on the call stack. To facilitate this check, we provide access to the assignable maps of all methods on the call stack by passing a stack of assignable maps to the callee (rather than one merged assignable map). Furthermore, we provide access to the fresh locations of all methods on the call stack.

The notations to refer to the assignable map or the fresh locations of a method stay unchanged. With $\mathcal{A}_{m_i}^{declared}$, we denote the assignable map for some method m_i on the call stack and with $\mathcal{F}_{m_i}^{\triangleleft}$, we denote the set of fresh locations of that method.

Stack of Updated Pivots

In our algorithm we need to keep track of changes to the dynamic data groups during method execution. Therefore, we introduce a stack of sets of updated pivots. For all methods on the call stack we can access the set of pivots that have been updated since their respective pre-states.

We are going to use these sets to identify the back-links that we want to exclude when checking the assignability of a heap location. Thus, we introduce the notation $\mathcal{X}_{m_i}$ to refer to the set of updated (and therefore excluded) pivots for some method m_i on the call stack.

3.4.2 Code Instrumentation

In order to support dynamic data groups, we need to change the code instrumentation for field updates and method invocations, whereas object creation and method return stay unchanged.

Method Invocation

Upon an invocation of method m we evaluate the assignable clause of m to the map $\mathcal{A}_m^{declared}$ as described in section 3.3.2, but we do not intersect the assignable sets of the caller and the callee. Instead, we push the map of assignable locations $\mathcal{A}_m^{declared}$ to the assignable stack that already contains the assignable maps of all (transitive) callers. Furthermore, we push empty sets to the stack of fresh locations and updated pivots. Upon method invocation, no object has been newly allocated and no pivot field has been updated yet in method m.

Field Update

The runtime checks introduced before a field update are considerably more complex when dealing with dynamic data groups than for static data groups only. Without the concept of merged assignable maps, we need to check explicitly for each method on the call stack, if a location is assignable in that method. Furthermore, we need to compute if a field is contained in an assignable data group possibly via many indirections.

CHAPTER 3. AN EFFICIENT RAC FOR ASSIGNABLE CLAUSES

Before updating a location $o.f$ in method m, we need to check that for every method m_i on the call stack of m, $o.f$ is either fresh or contained in the set of assignable locations. More formally:

$$\forall m_i \cdot m_i \hookrightarrow^* m \rightarrow o.f \in \mathcal{F}_{m_i}^\triangleleft \vee o.f \in \mathcal{A}_{m_i}.$$

Checking $o.f \in \mathcal{F}_{m_i}^\triangleleft$: Since we do not update the set of fresh locations for all transitive callers of m (see the section on object creation on page 106), it is not sufficient to check if $\mathcal{F}_{m_i}^\triangleleft[o]$ yields *true* to determine if o as been newly allocated during the execution of m_i. We need to check if there exists a (transitive) callee m_k in which o has been newly allocated. We write $\exists m_k \cdot m_i \hookrightarrow^* m_k \wedge \mathcal{F}_{m_k}^\triangleleft[o]$.

Although this looks more complicated than directly putting fresh locations into the set of fresh location of all callers, it allows us to simplify the runtime assertion checker implementation considerably: when checking the assignability of $o.f$, we evaluate the assignability for the top most method on the call stack (that is, the most current method) and work our way down the stack. As soon as we find a method m_k in which o has been newly created and $o.f$ was assignable in all methods between the current one and m_k, we know that $o.f$ is assignable and we can stop. For any transitive caller of m_k down to the `main` method of the program, m_k is the witness for which the condition from the last paragraph holds.

Checking $o.f \in \mathcal{A}_{m_i}$: Since we do not unfold dynamic data groups upon method invocation, we need to perform additional computation to check if $o.f$ is assignable upon field assignment. The location $o.f$ is in the assignable map $\mathcal{A}_{m_i}$ of method m_i, if we find a data group dg that both dynamically contains the location $o.f$, and is mentioned in the assignable clause of method m_i. We can write $\exists dg \cdot dg \in \mathcal{D}_{h_0(m_i)}[o.f] \wedge dg \in \mathcal{A}_{m_i}^{\text{declared}}$, where $h_0(m_i)$ refers to the pre-heap of method m_i. As `assignable` clauses are to be evaluated to a set of locations in the pre-state of a method, and this involves the unfolding of data groups, we need to use the pre-heap when determining the data groups that contain $o.f$.

To sum it up, we check the following assertion at runtime prior to an update of location $o.f$ in method m:

$$\forall m_i \cdot m_i \hookrightarrow^* m \rightarrow$$
$$\exists m_k \cdot m_i \hookrightarrow^* m_k \wedge \mathcal{F}_{m_k}^\triangleleft[o] \quad \vee$$
$$\exists dg \cdot dg \in \mathcal{D}_{h_0(m_i)}[o.f] \wedge \mathcal{A}_{m_i}^{\text{declared}}[dg]$$

The time complexity for finding a data group that dynamically contains $o.f$ is linear in the size of $\mathcal{D}[o.f]$ multiplied by the number of methods on the call stack. However, we can dramatically speed up this lookup by introducing caches for finding dynamic data groups, see Sec. 3.5.

Example. Again, we consider the heap structure on the left side of Fig. 1.2. We now discuss the situation in which the `insert` method of class `Node` adds a new node to `d.left`, that is, no balancing needs to take place. Let's assume that insert has been called via a.insert by the method put of the Store object store that contains node a as root. Naturally, at the bottom of the method stack, we have the main method, which we choose to annotate with assignable \nothing.

Table 3.2 shows the stack of assignable maps, the fresh sets, and the list of data groups that contain c.left. According to the formula above, we check for each method m_i on the call stack the following condition before updating d.left: either $\mathcal{A}_{m_i}^{declared}$ mentions a data group of d.left, or the object d has been newly allocated during the execution of m_i. The set $\mathcal{D}_{h_0(m_i)}[\text{d.left}]$ evaluates to the same set in case of the top three methods on the stack. For the pre-heap of method main the object d is not allocated, thus $\mathcal{D}_{h_0(\text{main})}[\text{d.left}]$ yields only the data groups that statically contain the location, that is, {d.struct}.

m_i	$\mathcal{A}_{m_i}^{declared}$	$\mathcal{F}_{m_i}^{\triangleleft}$	$\mathcal{D}_{h_0(m_i)}[\text{d.left}]$
d.insert	d.struct	-	d.struct, a.struct, store.struct
a.insert	a.struct	-	d.struct, a.struct, store.struct
store.put	store.struct	-	d.struct, a.struct, store.struct
⋮			
main	-	store, a, ..., h	d.struct

Table 3.2: The Call Stack for the update of d.left

We can easily verify that c.left is assignable: d.insert mentions d.struct in its assignable clause, with is a data group that contains d.left according to the value of $\mathcal{D}_{h_0(\text{d.insert})}[\text{d.left}]$. Similarly, the check succeeds for the methods a.insert and store.put. Both methods mention a data group that contains c.left. For method main the check succeeds as object d has been newly allocated during the execution of main and is therefore in the set of fresh locations.

In the example above, we concentrate on the back-link data structure, which enables the efficient evaluation of $\mathcal{D}_{h_0(\text{d.insert})}[\text{d.left}]$ and thus an efficient way of checking assignable clauses with dynamic data groups. In the following example, we want to perform a similar experiment, but focus on object creation issues.

Example. We want to verify that the following method doesn't break any involved assignable clause:

```
//@ assignable \nothing
void createStore(Item i){
  Store store = new Store();
  store.put(i);
  ...
```

```
6 }
```

The interesting check happens when the constructor of class `Node` assigns the item `i` to field `item`. Let's again look at the method call stack, table 3.3.

m_i	$\mathcal{A}_{m_i}^{\text{declared}}$	$\mathcal{F}_{m_i}^{\triangleleft}$	$\mathcal{D}_{h_0(m_i)}[\text{d.left}]$
`root.Node`	`root.item`	-	`root.footprint, store.footprint`
`store.put`	`store.struct`	`root`	`root.footprint`
`createStore`	-	`store`	`root.footprint`
⋮			

Table 3.3: The Call Stack for the update `root.item = i`

For the constructor of class `Node`, the assignment is fine because the `assignable` clause directly mentions the field `item`. For the method `put` the assignment is fine because the object `root` has been newly created in this method. Interestingly, the assignment is also permitted in method `createStore` although the method neither mentions the field or its data groups in the `assignable` clause nor does it contain the object `root` in its fresh set. The reason is that the object has been newly allocated in a callee of `createStore`, namely the method `put`. Therefore, the following condition holds with witness `store.put` for m_k, and thus the check for `createStore` succeeds: $\exists m_k \cdot \texttt{createStore} \hookrightarrow^* m_k \wedge \mathcal{F}_{m_k}^{\triangleleft}[\text{root}]$

Updating a Pivot Field Whenever we update a pivot field of a data group, we change the content of the data group. This is a problem because upon a method call, we do not unfold the data groups mentioned in the `assignable` clause of the callee, even though the semantics of `assignable` clauses prescribes that the set of assignable locations is to be determined in the pre-state of the method. In the above assertion for the field update check, we circumvent the problem by assuming that we can compute the set of data groups for a location using the pre-heap of the method. However, the runtime assertion checker can not rely on the availability of the complete pre-heap for each method in the call stack. Consequently, the solution is to track any change to the content of the data groups mentioned in the `assignable` clauses of all method on the call stack.

We apply a technique that we call *lazy unfolding*. The first time we update a pivot field of a data group that is directly or indirectly contained in an assignable map $\mathcal{A}_{m_i}^{\text{declared}}$ during the execution of a method m_i, we perform the following two operations in order to preserve the content of assignable data groups in m_i:

1. We add the pivot field to the set of excluded pivots $\mathcal{X}_{m_i}$. As we described in the section on dynamic data groups on page 109 we can provide this set of excluded pivots to the computation $\mathcal{D}_h^{\mathcal{X}_{m_i}}[o.f]$, which yields all data groups that contain location $o.f$ without using any of the pivots mentioned in $\mathcal{X}_{m_i}$.

3.4. CHECKING ASSIGNABLE CLAUSES WITH DYNAMIC DATA GROUPS

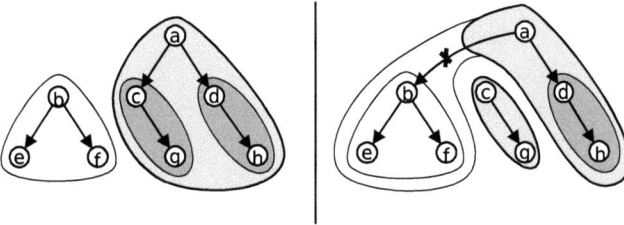

Figure 3.1: The same situation as in Fig. 1.2. The cross depicts the excluded pivot field.

2. We add the location to which the pivot pointed before the update directly to the map of assignable locations $\mathcal{A}_{m_i}^{\text{declared}}$. Therefore, the location stays assignable although the pivot field points to a different location after the update.

The following formula describes the main property of the lazy unfolding:

$$\forall o.f \cdot \exists dg \cdot dg \in \mathcal{D}_h^{\mathcal{X}_{m_i}}[o.f] \wedge \mathcal{A}_{m_i}^{\text{declared}}[dg] \leftrightarrow$$
$$\exists dg \cdot dg \in \overbrace{\mathcal{D}_{h'}^{\mathcal{X}_{m_i} \cup \{p\}}}^{1.}[o.f] \wedge \underbrace{\left(\mathcal{A}_{m_i}^{\text{declared}} \cup \{g\}\right)}_{2.}[dg]$$

The property states that the lazy unfolding does not influence the assignability of any field. The variable p refers to the pivot field which points to location g in heap h before it gets updated. The heap h' is the resulting heap from the field update. We identify the two involved operations of the lazy unfolding.

With the lazy unfolding, we manage to eliminate the occurrence of $h_o(m_i)$ in the check. According to the property above, we preserve the content of assignable data groups upon pivot field update. Any other change to the heap does not influence dynamic data groups. Thus, we can replace the pre-heap by the current heap in $\mathcal{D}_h^{\mathcal{X}_{m_i}}[o.f]$.

$$\forall m_i \cdot m_i \hookrightarrow^* m \rightarrow$$
$$\exists m_k \cdot m_i \hookrightarrow^* m_k \wedge \mathcal{F}_{m_k}^{\triangleleft}[o] \quad \vee$$
$$\exists dg \cdot dg \in \mathcal{D}_h^{\mathcal{X}_{m_i}}[o.f] \wedge \mathcal{A}_{m_i}^{\text{declared}}[dg]$$

Example. Fig. 3.1 shows how the lazy unfolding works. The left side depicts the heap structure before we perform the assignment `a.left = b` whereas the right side depicts the situation after the update. The shapes around the objects visualize the `struct` data groups of the different objects. The grayed out data groups depict the assignable data groups if we assume the `assignable` clause of the method we're looking at mentions `a.struct`. To preserve the assignable locations of the pre-state, we add `c.struct` explicitly to the assignable map, which preserves the assignability of the locations of objects `c` and `d`.

115

Furthermore, we add a.left to the set of excluded pivots which makes the back-link from b.struct to a.struct invalid, which essentially renders the locations of objects b, e, and f not assignable. Looking at the locations in the gray shapes, one can see that we effectively preserved the assignability of locations in the state on the left-hand side although the data group changed in the meantime.

3.5 Optimizations

As we have shown in the last section, the time overhead to check if a location o.f is assignable depends on the height of the call stack and on the size of the set of data groups $\mathcal{D}[o.f]$. For every update of location o.f, we check if o.f is assignable in all assignable maps on the stack. For each method on the stack, this involves to compute the set $\mathcal{D}[o.f]$ and to check if it contains a data group that is mentioned in the assignable map. There are two simple but effective optimizations:

- Stop computing the set $\mathcal{D}[o.f]$ as soon as an assignable data group has been found.

- Determine the assignable data groups during the computation and store the result.

The first optimization is very straight-forward. To evaluate $\mathcal{D}[o.f]$, we collect all data groups that are reachable via back-links from o.f. For each data group that we find, we can directly check if it is assignable. If yes, we can stop the evaluation.

The second optimization requires us to represent the set $\mathcal{D}[o.f]$ such that we can determine which data groups in the set are assignable if we eventually find a data group that is mentioned in an assignable map. In the example below, we show how the implementation of the runtime assertion checker represents $\mathcal{D}[o.f]$ and what data groups can be marked as assignable.

To store this information, we equip each assignable map with a cache that stores all the additional information from the queries since the method invocation. The information in the cache stays valid during method execution. Therefore, caches become especially useful if we assign to the same set of locations several times in a method, for instance when doing a computation in a loop.

Example. In order to highlight the usefulness of caches and to explain the details on how to collect the data groups of a field, we need to introduce a heap data structure in which a pivot field is not always directly contained in exactly one data group. Nothing prevents us from creating a heap structure as shown on the left side in Fig. 3.2 using six objects of class Node: a ... f. The heap data structure is not a tree, but an directed graph that even includes cycles.

In this situation, we want to check if the location f.left is assignable if $\mathcal{A}_{m_i}^{\text{declared}}$ contains a.struct. According to the formula of the check, we need to find a witness for dg for which the following condition holds: $\exists dg \cdot dg \in \mathcal{D}_h^{\{\text{a.left}\}}[\text{f.left}] \land \mathcal{A}_{m_i}^{\text{declared}}[dg]$.

3.5. OPTIMIZATIONS

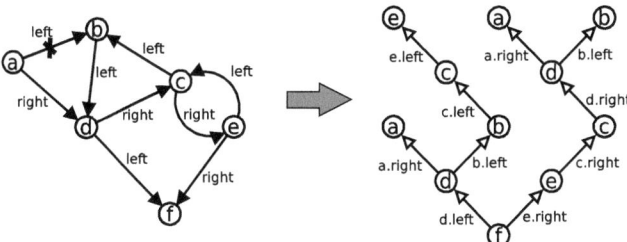

Figure 3.2: Generation of the tree of data groups for field f.left. The labeled circles denotes objects, black arrows denote pivot fields, white arrows denote back-links.

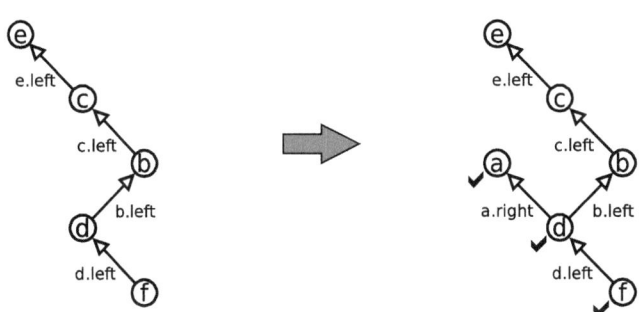

Figure 3.3: Intermediate and final step of the tree generation with early stop and caching.

Intuitively, we can see that the set $\mathcal{D}_h^{\{\text{a.left}\}}[\text{f.left}]$ contains the data group struct from all objects in the graph. That is, f.left is assignable as it is contained in a.struct.

As explained earlier, the implementation of the runtime assertion checker computes this set using the back-link data structure. The implementation represents the set as a tree of data groups, which we show on the right side of Fig. 3.2. The advantage is that the tree preserves the information via which pivot fields f.left is contained in a data group. To build the tree, we need to detect cycles in the data group structure and break them up. We do this by not inserting a data group to the tree if it has already been added earlier as a transitive parent. Therefore, the tree can contain duplicates, but cycles are broken up. Furthermore, back-links over excluded pivot fields are ignored.

Building the tree of data groups is the most expensive operation in the check for assignable locations, thus we seek to stop early when building the tree. As soon as we find a data group that is mentioned in the assignable clause, we can stop building up the tree.

Fig. 3.3 shows the process of building the tree. We collect data groups of f.left using a depth first strategy. Whenever a data group is contained in several other data groups via different back-links, we pick one and continue to search for a data group that is contained in the assignable map. On the left side of the figure, we already collected the struct data groups of the objects f and d, and chose to continue with b, c and e. Here we need to break a cycle and do not add c again. Thus, we cannot continue the search for an assignable data group on that branch and need to find another path.

We need to go all the way back to the node d where we had more than one back-link to choose from. This time, we choose a and find that its data group struct is in fact assignable. In this process, we not only learned that f.left is assignable, but we can also deduce that any data group on the path from a.struct to f.left is for sure assignable. The right side of Fig. 3.3 shows the end result. We store into the cache of the assignable map that the data groups a.struct, d.struct, and f.struct are in fact assignable as well as the field f.left. The next time the evaluation of $\mathcal{D}[o.f]$ hits any of these data groups, a lookup in the cache will immediately yield that the data groups are assignable.

One might be tempted to mark the data groups on the unsuccessful branch as non-assignable. However, this is not always correct due to the fact that we removed some edges to avoid cycles. In fact, the data groups e.struct, c.struct, and b.struct are indeed assignable.

3.6 Implementation and Evaluation

As a proof of concept, we implemented the algorithm described in this paper to check assignable clauses in Java programs. To test the efficiency of our algorithm, we chose a doubly-linked list, where the nesting of data groups is as deep as the number of nodes in the list: every node is equipped with a struct data group that contains the next and previous fields and dynamically contains the struct field of the successor node. The list itself also features the fields head and tail as well as the data group struct that contains the struct data group of the head in the list. This data structure represents the worst case for our algorithm, as the fields in the list contain $O(n)$ data groups if there are n nodes in the list, see table 3.1 on page 107.

We performed experiments with different list operations to measure the performance of our algorithm[1]. The most interesting experiment has been to reverse large doubly-linked list, which involves operations on every node of the list and changes the structure of the dynamic data groups completely. In fact, every pivot field gets assigned to, which leads to a complete unfolding of the data group. This is the worst case scenario for our algorithm, which tries to avoid unfolding as much as possible.

Surprisingly, we need only a bit more than one seconds to add 10'000 nodes to a list and reverse it with the runtime assertion checker enabled. We spend around 80% of the time to add the nodes, and 20% of the time to reverse the list. The memory footprint is around 20MB before reversing the list and grows to 25MB during reversing because of the caches that get filled in the process. If we switch off runtime assertion checking for the same example, the program terminates within half a second and uses around 2.5MB. When repeating the experiment with 20'000 nodes, time and memory consumption doubles for both versions.

For the doubly-linked list, the runtime overhead of our checker is a factor of 2 and the memory overhead is a factor of 10. For the main applications of runtime assertion checking (to prepare static verification and to reproduce possibly spurious verification errors), we consider this overhead acceptable, especially for recursive data structures such as our doubly-linked list. We expect the overhead to be significantly smaller for non-recursive aggregate structures, where dynamic data groups are not nested as deeply.

Encouraged by the good performance of the prototype, we integrated our algorithm into OpenJML [68] which allowed us to extend our experiments. Beside others, we implemented the tree data structure and ran the runtime assertion checker on them. There are two practical issues that deserve attention.

Firstly, the compiled library code doesn't contain the code instrumentations necessary to check assignable clauses. Therefore, library code called by our own methods might not respect the assignable clauses defined in these methods. This can be fixed by annotating the library code and recompile it with our runtime assertion checker.

Secondly, the performance of the checks can be significantly influenced by both the specification and the implementation. We want to illustrate this with an example that uses the doubly linked list that we introduced at the beginning of this section. With this data structure, we can achieve the greatest differences due to the fact that the data structure poses a worst case scenario.

Example. As described above, each node in the list has a data group struct that contains

---
[1] On a desktop computer with a single core 3.4 GHz CPU

all previous and next fields of the trailing nodes. The following example is somewhat artificial, but nicely shows what influences the overhead introduced by the runtime assertion checker. We do not discuss the efficiency or usefulness of the code itself, but concentrate on the runtime assertion checking aspects.

We want to create a linked list that contains the numbers 0 to 10000 in ascending order. We show four implementations that all produce the same list, but with different impacts for the runtime assertion checker overhead.

Our first implementation adds the numbers using a method addTail which adds the given number at the tail of the list. Its assignable clause is unnecessarily unspecific and permits to change any location in the data group list.struct.

```
for (int i = 0 ; i ≤ 10000 ; i++) {
    list.addTail(i);
}

//assignable list.struct;
void addTail(int i) { ... }
```

The fact that we add nodes to the tail in combination with the unspecific assignable clause of addTail leads to a quadratic overhead for the runtime assertion checker. Each time the loop invokes addTail, $\mathcal{A}_{\text{addTail}}^{\text{declared}}$ is set to list.struct with empty caches, and no lazy unfolding yet. Thus, each time, the runtime assertion checker needs to check if the next field of the last node is assignable, which it can only do by traversing through the back-links from the last node all the way back to the first node and finally the list object itself. Only then, the checker can confirm that the field is assignable. As soon as the method addTail terminates, this information gets lost. Upon the next invocation, the same query is going to be performed again, for one more node in the list. We would require some kind of global cache to avoid computing the same results over and over again, but this cache would be very hard to keep up to date and would only accelerate the checker in a small number of situations, like this artificial example.

We can significantly speed up the checker if we provide a more specific assignable clause to addTail. The overhead of the runtime assertion checker becomes linear, as the list does not have to be traversed each time a node is added:

```
//assignable list.tail, list.tail.next;
void addTail(int i) { ... }
```

The checker also creates only a linear overhead if we append elements at the head of the list rather than the tail, even with an unspecific assignable clause for addHead. In this case, the function addHead writes to this.head and this.head.previous (as well as the fresh locations of the newly created node). In both cases, the checker can reach list.struct in linear time, independently of the size of the list.

```
for (int i = 10000 ; i ≥ 0 ; i--) {
  list.addHead(i);
}

//assignable list.struct;
void addHead(int i) { ... }
```

The last version that we present to create such a list does not involve to call a method to add new nodes to the list, but inlines the code in the loop. In this case, we assume that `list.struct` is assignable in the current environment.

```
for (int i = 10000 ; i ≥ 0 ; i--) {
  Node n = new Node(i);
  if (list.tail = null){
    list.head = list.tail = n;
  } else {
    n.previous = list.tail;
    list.tail = list.tail.next = n;
  }
}
```

In this case, we also generate only a linear overhead to check assignability although it is again unspecific. The reason is that during execution of the method, all nodes in the list are freshly created and put into the set of fresh locations. Thus, checking if `n.previous` is assignable is trivial. Furthermore, the assignments to `list.tail` and `list.tail.next` can be checked in linear time.

3.7 Theoretical Results

Our algorithm depends mainly on the following factors: the size of the set of dynamic data groups that contain a location ($|\mathcal{D}|$), the size of the assignable sets ($|\mathcal{A}|$), and the size of the call stack ($|cs|$).

Time Complexity Field update is the only operation that may generate a significant time overhead. The check if a location is assignable has a time complexity of $\mathcal{O}(|\mathcal{D}| \times |cs|)$ if the result is not cached in any assignable map, and $\mathcal{O}(|cs|)$ if the result is cached in all assignable maps. That is, the caches have a big impact on the performance if we have a deep nesting of `assignable` clauses. We also see that we do not have a good solution for recursive method calls, where $|cs|$ gets big.

In our running example, $|\mathcal{D}|$ is logarithmic to the number of nodes in the tree, which leads to a very good performance.

Memory Overhead The data structures that produce a significant memory overhead are the ones for storing the sets of assignable locations, including caches, as well as the fresh sets. That is, the memory overhead depends on the number of assignable locations mentioned in the `assignable` clauses, the amount of lazy unfolding, and of course the number of methods on the call stack. We get an overhead of $\mathcal{O}(|\mathcal{A}| \times |cs|)$, where the size of $\mathcal{A}$ depends on how much unfolding happened already.

In our running example, if we have a method with an `assignable` clause stating 'a.struct' $|\mathcal{A}|$ initially contains only the location `a.struct` and our memory overhead is very small. For each `left` or `right` pointer that we assign to in a method, we add one more location to that set, and, if we completely reorder the whole tree, end up in a complete unfolding of the data group.

3.8 Summary

In this chapters we presented an algorithm to efficiently check JML's assignable clause in the presence of dynamic data groups at runtime. Due to the non-modularity of dynamic data groups, this is a difficult task that requires to avoid to compute unnecessary information. We implemented this algorithm in OpenJML and performed experiments that show that our approach works for reasonably large data structures. With this algorithm, we made it possible to deal with non-modular data abstraction at runtime.

Chapter 4

Correctness Proof of the RAC for Assignable Clauses

In this chapter, we formally prove the correctness of the runtime assertion checker for `assignable` clauses, which we introduced in the last chapter. We show that the runtime assertion checker is equivalent to the JML semantics for the chosen Java and JML subset. A formal proof of a runtime assertion checker involves formalizing an operational semantics for JML ($\mathcal{S}_{sem}$) as well as an operational semantics for Java with the runtime assertion checks and instrumentations ($\mathcal{S}_{rac}$) and to prove that both semantics are bisimular. That is, the two semantics behave equivalently.

Fig. 4.1 depicts the property described above. The predicate $\mathcal{R}_{rac}^{sem}$ describes the bisimulation relation. For any st_{sem} and st_{rac}, if $\mathcal{R}_{rac}^{sem}(st_{sem}, st_{rac})$ holds, the two states are in a bisimulation relation. We say: st_{sem} and st_{rac} *correspond*. The diagram reads as follows: If st_{sem} and st_{rac} correspond, and we perform a step in both semantics, then the resulting states st'_{sem} and st'_{rac} still correspond.

This proof is a good evaluation of the JML formalization, presented in chapter 2. The next section introduces the proof strategy and shows how the proof can be formalized as application of the JML semantics.

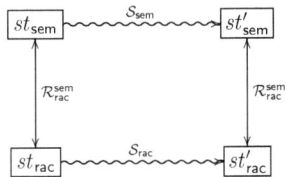

Figure 4.1: The property that we want to prove.

4.1 Approach

We prove the correctness of the runtime assertion checker with a refinement strategy. Each refinement is one more step away from the JML semantics, as defined in section 2.6.2, into the direction of the algorithm presented in chapter 3. For each refinement, we prove that the semantics defined in the refinement is bisimilar to the semantics defined in the last refinement (or the JML semantics, in case of the first refinement). Therefore, we can chain together the refinements and argue that the last refinement, which is the most concrete model of the algorithm, is in fact bisimilar to the JML semantics. The following enumeration lists the refinements and shortly explains what aspect of the algorithm is covered in the refinement.

1. Do not unfold data groups in the pre-state of the method: we replace the flat set of assignable locations (see section 2.6.2 on page 70) by a stack of assignable locations (see section 3.4.1 on page 110).

2. Introduce the concept of lazy unfolding. The first time a pivot field gets updated, we unfold all assignable data groups that use that pivot field (see the paragraph on updating pivot fields in section 3.4.2 on page 114). In other words, we save the pre-state of the involved assignable data groups.

3. Introduce the back-link data structures to quickly find all data groups that dynamically contain a location (see section 3.4.1 on page 109).

Fig. 4.2 gives an overview of the involved parts of the correctness proof in Coq. It is an extension of Fig. 2.1. The parts that we have already seen are Syntax & Domain, which we do not show in details in this figure, the JML Semantics Interface, as well as the JML Semantics Definition, which implements the interface and operates on the JML Program State.

We provide three refinements of a runtime assertion checker for assignable clauses. Each refinement is an implementation of the JML Semantics Interface and operates on its own implementation of the program state: RAC1 State, RAC2 State, and RAC3 State. The first refinement, introduced in section 4.5, accesses the pre-heap of each method in the call stack in order to unfold the data groups in the right state for each set of assignable locations in the stack. The second refinement, introduced in section 4.6, eliminates the need for saving the whole pre-heap of each method by introducing the lazy-unfolding. However, without the back-link data structure, it's not possible to define the lazy unfolding constructively, we need to axiomatize it. This is fine, since we constructively define the lazy unfolding in the third refinement, introduced in section 4.7.

On top of the four different implementations, that is, definitions of the JML Semantics Interface, we define a very stripped down Java operational semantics, introduced in section 4.3. It supports just the interesting aspects of the language to prove the correct checking of assignable clauses, as discussed in 3. In section 4.4, we prove that the operational semantics is deterministic. The operational semantics takes an implementation of the JML Semantics Interface as argument, and applies the functions from the interface at the appropriate places. As we only prove the correctness of the runtime assertion checker for assignable clauses, we do not apply the functions of the annotation table, but only the functions of the frame conditions interface. In fact, we can now very easily create the different operational semantics described above. Thus, S_{sem} is the operational semantics parametrized with the JML Semantics Definition, whereas S_{rac} is the operational semantics parametrized with the 3rd Refinement of RAC, which is why we also call it S_{rac3}. In the same manner, we can create S_{rac1} and S_{rac2}.

Having defined the different operational semantics, we can now perform the bisimulation proofs for all involved semantics. For each refinement, we prove that the two neighboring semantics are bisimilar, which in the end allows us to conclude that S_{sem} and S_{rac} are in fact bisimilar, and therefore, the main theorem on the following page holds.

Correctness Proof of Runtime Assertion Checker for Assignable Clauses			
			Proof of 3rd Refinement
		Proof of 2nd Refinement	
	Proof of 1st Refinement		Proof of Determinism
	Java Operational Semantics		
JML Semantics Definition	1st Refinement of RAC	2nd Refinement of RAC	3rd Refinement of RAC
JML Program State	RAC1 State	RAC2 State	RAC3 State
JML Semantics Interface			
Syntax & Domain			

Figure 4.2: Overview of the correctness proof of the runtime assertion checker. Again gray boxes depict parts that are defined in a constructive way, whereas white boxes may contain axiomatic definitions.

4.2 The Main Theorem

We discussed the intuitive proof goal at the beginning of this chapter and depicted it with Fig. 4.1. We want to define a bisimulation between the JML semantics and runtime assertion checker. That is, the semantics and the runtime assertion checker behave equivalently. The following now formally states the property that we are going to prove in this chapter.

Theorem 4.1. Correctness of Runtime Assertion Checker

If one starts in a state st_{sem} and executes a step in the JML operational semantics to get state st'_{sem}, and given a state st_{rac} that corresponds to state st_{sem}, then there exists a state st'_{rac} that one gets by executing the same step in the runtime assertion checker and that corresponds to st'_{sem}.

Moreover, if one can execute a step in the runtime assertion checker from st_{rac} to st'_{rac}, and st_{sem} corresponds to st_{rac}, then there exists a corresponding st'_{sem} that one gets by executing the same step in the JML operational semantics:

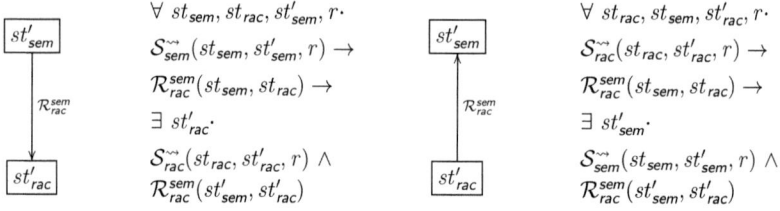

$\mathcal{S}^{\leadsto}(st, st', r)$ is an inductively defined predicate that holds if the state st' is a state that we can reach by performing one step on state st. The variable r is a *step value*. In both cases r is the result of the execution. It contains a Java value if the performed step evaluates an expression. Furthermore, it contains the information if the execution terminated normally or exceptionally. We discuss the type of r below in section 4.3. In the theorem, we use the same step value r in both involved semantics. Thus, we also show that performing steps in both semantics yield the same result value.

The fact that our theorem relies on predicates to model state transitions rather than functions raises an issue: if $\mathcal{S}^{\leadsto}$ is nondeterministic, that is, performing a step on a state can lead to several possible outcomes, our nice commutative diagram from in Fig. 4.1 doesn't reflect the actual situation any more.

Fig. 4.3 visualizes the issue. Let's assume there are several possibilities to perform a step in both semantics. Dotted lines in the diagram depict possible alternatives. In $\mathcal{S}_{sem}$, we happen to take the top most transition, whereas in $\mathcal{S}_{rac}$, we nondeterministically pick the transition on the bottom in a step. Starting from corresponding states, the outcome of performing a step on both semantics may lead to states that do not correspond any more. In the diagram, we can see that the states st'_{sem} and st'_{rac} do not stand in a correspondence relation. However, we could still prove our theorem in this situation, as there *exists* a state that can be reached by performing a step in $\mathcal{S}_{rac}$ and that corresponds to st'_{sem}, we depict this connection in the diagram with dashed lines.

There are two solutions to this problem. We can either restate our theorem and additionally enforce that for any possible state in one semantics, there is a correlation to

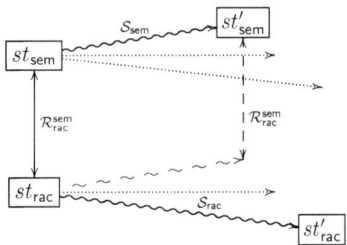

Figure 4.3: The commutative diagram falls apart if the semantics ($\mathcal{S}_{\mathsf{sem}}$ or $\mathcal{S}_{\mathsf{rac}}$) are non-deterministic.

any possible state in the other semantics, or we prove that our semantics is deterministic. Because our semantics $\mathcal{S}_*$ are indeed deterministic, we prefer to separate the two concerns and prove determinism of the operational semantics independently of the correctness proof of the runtime assertion checker.

4.3 An Operational Semantics for Java

We define an operational semantics for Java that we can configure with different implementations (refinements in our case) of the JML semantics:

Module OperationalSemantics (jml : JML).

The module jml provides access to the definition of the program state as well as to the implementation of the annotation table and the frame condition interface, see listing 2.40. The operational semantics uses these definitions at the appropriate places.

We define a deviation system for a big step semantics with four mutually dependent inductive definitions in Coq whose signatures we show in listing 4.1. The definition ExpressionStep defines the evaluation of one step in a Java expression. The definition ListSteps evaluates a list of expressions, for instance the list of method parameters, into a list of values, one expression per step. The definitions StatementStep and BlockStep evaluate statements and block of statements, respectively. With these four definitions, we can describe the evaluation of Java source code.

```
Inductive ExpressionStep (p : Program):
                Expression → State.t → State.t → StepValue → Prop :=
  ...
with ListSteps (p : Program):
           list Expression → State.t → State.t → list StepValue → Prop :=
  ...
with StatementStep (p : Program) :
```

CHAPTER 4. CORRECTNESS PROOF OF THE RAC FOR ASSIGNABLE CLAUSES

```
 8                    Method →BLOCK.t →State.t → State.t → StepValue → Prop :=
 9    ...
10  with BlockStep (p : Program) :
11                    Method →BLOCK.t →State.t → State.t → StepValue→ Prop :=
12    ...
```

Listing 4.1: The inductive data types for an operational semantics in Java

Each of the four definitions use the type StepValue to specify the outcome of the step. The listing 4.2 shows the definition of the inductive data type. The operation semantics uses constructor normal_step to specify that a statement- or block-steps could be executed successfully. The constructor normal_step_v indicates that a step in an expression succeeded and that the evaluation yields the contained value. The last two constructors describe a step that leads to an exceptional state in the evaluation. We choose to provide two separate constructors for Java Errors and Exceptions, as it's likely that a semantics may want to ignore JVM errors and only deal with subtypes of Exception. With the two constructors, a different handling can be defined on a syntactical level by pattern matching.

```
1  Inductive StepValue :=
2    | normal_step : StepValue
3    | normal_step_v : Value → StepValue
4    | exception_step : Object → StepValue
5    | error_step : Object → StepValue.
```

Listing 4.2: The definition StepValue

———————————— A MADE-TO-MEASURE COQ TUTORIAL ————————————

Part 12 Dealing with Mutual Induction in Proofs

To perform a proof by induction on an inductive definition, Coq provides a command induction X, where X is a variable of an inductive type. However, in the presence of mutual induction, the command induction can be applied, but doesn't generate useful induction hypotheses, as it overlooks the mutual dependency.

We need to build our own induction scheme that generates the correct induction hypotheses, see 4.3. Coq provides two commands **Scheme** and **Combined Scheme** to build the predicate mutual_ind that can be used to perform a proof by mutual induction on the deviation system. There is very little documentation on this commands, found at [18].

```
1  Scheme expr_step_ind   := Minimality for ExpressionStep Sort Prop
2    with expr_steps_ind  := Minimality for ListSteps Sort Prop
```

```
3   with stmt_step_ind    := Minimality for StatementStep Sort Prop
4   with block_step_ind   := Minimality for BlockStep Sort Prop.
5
6   Combined Scheme mutual_ind from expr_step_ind, expr_steps_ind, stmt_step_ind,
7                                   block_step_ind .
```

Listing 4.3: Generation of the predicate mutual_ind, to perform proofs by induction on the operational semantics.

The predicate mutual_ind *forces us into a certain form when reasoning about the operational semantics. Listing 4.4 shows the conclusion of* mutual_ind. *To prove a property of the semantics, we need to build a goal with the same shape, so that we can apply* mutual_ind *to it. The properties that we want to prove are* P, P0, P1, *and* P2. *What we get by applying* mutual_ind *are a set of goals, one for each inductive case, with the correct induction hypotheses.*

```
1   mutual_ind: ∀ (p : Program) ,
2   ... (* a premise for each inductive case *) →
3   (∀ e : Expression , ∀ t t0 : State.t , ∀ s : StepValue,
4    ExpressionStep p e t t0 s → P e t t0 s)
5   ∧
6   (∀ l : list Expression, ∀ t t0 : State.t, ∀ l0 : list StepValue,
7    ListSteps p l t t0 l0 → P0 l t t0 l0 )
8   ∧
9   (∀ m : Method, ∀t : BLOCK.t, ∀t0 t1 : State.t, ∀ s : StepValue,
10   StatementStep p m t t0 t1 s → P1 m t t0 t1 s)
11  ∧
12  (∀ m : Method, ∀t : BLOCK.t, ∀t0 t1 : State.t, ∀ s : StepValue,
13   BlockStep p m t t0 t1 s → P2 m t t0 t1 s)
```

Listing 4.4: the conclusion of predicate mutual_ind

In the following, we concentrate only on the first of the four mutual definitions, ExpressionStep, as it contains all interesting constructs that are involved in checking assignable clauses: the method invocation and return, field assignment, and object creation.

Instance Field Assignment Listing 4.5 shows the rule for successful assignment to an instance field. The following properties hold:

3. The current expression is an assignment expression to an instance field.

CHAPTER 4. CORRECTNESS PROOF OF THE RAC FOR ASSIGNABLE CLAUSES

4-7 The evaluation of the target of the assignment expression in state st returns normally and yields a new state st1 and object obj. We set location loc to refer to the field's location. The type of the evaluated target object is a reference type in which a field with signature fsig is defined.

8 The predicate FieldUpdateCheck, defined in the supplied implementation of the frame condition interface, holds. That is, the field is *assignable*. Note that the operational semantics doesn't need to understand how or why a field is assignable, it simply calls the corresponding function from the jml module to answer the question. The implementation of the module, which also provides the definition of State.t, can access its auxiliary data structures to answer the question, while the operation semantics is not even aware of any auxiliary data structures.

9,10 The evaluation of the right-hand side of the assignment in state st1 returns normally and yields a new state st2 and the value v. This value has a Java type that can be assigned to the field.

11 The function FieldUpdateAction is called to update the auxiliary data structures in st2 to reflect the field update. The function is not supposed to change anything else in the state st2.

12 The resulting state st' contains the heap in which the field loc is updated with value v.

```
1  | assignment_instance_field_ok :
2    ∀ e v obj fsig expr target st st1 st2 st' st3 loc cn um,
3    e = Assignment (field  fsig (Some target)) expr →
4    ExpressionStep p target st st1 (normal_step_v (Ref obj)) →
5    loc = (Heap.InstanceField obj fsig ) →
6    Heap.typeof st2@h obj = Some (Heap.ObjectObject cn um) →
7    defined_field  p cn fsig →
8    FieldUpdateCheck p loc st1 →
9    ExpressionStep p expr st1 st2 (normal_step_v v) →
10   assign_compatible p st2@h v (FIELDSIGNATURE.type (snd fsig)) →
11   FieldUpdateAction p loc v st2 = st3 →
12   st' = st3[h:= Heap.update st2@h loc v] →
13   ExpressionStep p e st st' (normal_step_v v)
```

Listing 4.5: The constructor assignment_instance_field_ok of the definition ExpressionStep. The underlined functions are defined in the frame conditions interface of the provided jml module.

130

4.3. AN OPERATIONAL SEMANTICS FOR JAVA

Method Invocation Listing 4.6 shows the rule for the successful call and return of a method that returns a value. Successful meaning that neither the call itself nor the callee raises an error or an exception. Thus the following properties hold:

- 3 The expression at hand is a method call.

- 4-7 The expression o evaluates to the target object for the call, which will be the **this** object in the callee, and a new state st1. The lookup of method signature msig in the type of the target object cn yields a method m'. Furthermore, there exists a class c' with name cn in the program.

- 8-10 The list of parameter expressions evaluate into a list of values and the resulting state st2, none of these evaluations terminate exceptionally or throw an error. The function nv2v transforms the list of StepValues yielded by ListSteps to a list of values, throwing away everything that is not a normal_step_v. Therefore, if the length of the two lists are the same, the original list only contained normal step values.

- 11,12 The variable fr_c1 refers to a new frame initialized with a parameter dictionary that contains the object **this** as well as the computed values of the parameters. State st3 is st2 in which we replace the frame by fr_c1.

- 13 The call to MethodCallAction allows the provided JML semantics to update the auxiliary data structures for the method invocation.

- 14-17 The body of method m' executes normally in a state st_c' and yields a value v.

- 18 The function MethodReturnAction builds the resulting state st' of the method call, using the relevant parts from the callers state st2 and the callees state st_c' and updating the auxiliary data structures.

```
1  | method_vcall_ok:
2    ∀ e st st1 st2 st3 st_c st_c' st' fr_c1 msig o cn um this ps psnv psv v cn' m' ...,
3    e = method msig (Some o) ps →
4    ExpressionStep p o st st1 (normal_step_v (Ref this)) →
5    Heap.typeof st1@h this = Some (Heap.ObjectObject cn um) →
6    lookup p cn (snd msig) (cn' , m') →
7    PROG.class p cn = Some c' →
8    ListSteps p ps st1 st2 psnv →
9    psv = nv2v psnv →
10   length psv = length psnv →
11   fr_c1 = NewFrame m' (lv2params m' ((Ref this)::psv)) st2 →
12   st3 = st2[fr:=fr_c1] →
```

```
13   MethodCallAction p c' m' st3 = st_c →
14   METHOD.body m' = Some body →
15   STATEMENT.type (METHODBODY.compound body) = Compound b →
16   BlockStep p m' b st_c st_c' normal_step →
17   Normal (Some v) = Frame.ret st_c'@fr →
18   MethodReturnAction p st_c' st2 = st' →
19   ExpressionStep p e st st' (normal_step_v v)
```

Listing 4.6: The constructor method_vcall_ok of the definition ExpressionStep. The underlined functions are defined in the frame conditions interface of the provided jml module.

Object Creation Listing 4.7 shows the rule for successful creation of an object of a given type. The following properties hold:

3. The expression at hand is an object creation expression.

4. We successfully retrieve a new object o of the specified type from the heap model, together with a new heap h'.

5. The function NewObjectAction updates the auxiliary data structures in st to reflect the object creation.

6. The resulting state st' contains the new heap h'.

```
1   | new_object_ok:
2   ∀ e o st st' st1 h' cn um,
3   e = new (ReferenceType (TypeDefType cn um)) →
4   Heap.new st@h p (Heap.ObjectObject cn um) = Some (o , h') →
5   NewObjectAction p o st = st1 →
6   st' = st1[h:= h'] →
7   ExpressionStep p e st st' (normal_step_v (Ref o))
```

Listing 4.7: The constructor new_object_ok of the definition ExpressionStep. The underlined functions are defined in the frame conditions interface of the provided jml module.

4.4 Proof of Determinism

We can prove determinism of the operational semantics without knowing the implementation of the parameter jml. That is, no matter what JML semantics we use, the operational semantics is deterministic. We want to prove the following theorem:

Theorem 4.2. Deterministic Operational Semantics

If we perform a step from state st to st' with step value r' in the operational semantics with an arbitrary implementation of the module jml, *and if we also find a state st'' and a step value r'' by executing the same step, then the resulting states and the step values must be equal:*

$$\forall\ st, st', r' \cdot \mathcal{S}^{\leadsto}_*(st, st', r') \to$$
$$\forall\ st'', r'' \cdot \mathcal{S}^{\leadsto}_*(st, st'', r'') \to$$
$$st' = st'' \land r' = r''$$

We express theorem 4.2 in Coq as shown in listing 4.8. We follow the structure given by the mutual induction principle mutual_ind shown in listing 4.3 on page 128. For each of the four mutual inductive definitions, we state the desired property and build the conjunction of the four properties.

```
Theorem OpSem_deterministic:
∀ p,
  (∀ e st st' r',
  ExpressionStep p e st st' r' →
  ∀ st'' r'',
  ExpressionStep p e st st'' r'' →
  st' = st'' ∧ r' = r'')
∧
  (∀ l st st' r',
  ListSteps p l st st' r' →
  ∀ st'' r'',
  ListSteps p l st st'' r'' →
  st' = st'' ∧ r' = r'')
∧
  (∀ m b st st' r',
  StatementStep p m b st st' r' →
  ∀ st'' r'',
  StatementStep p m b st st'' r'' →
  st' = st'' ∧ r' = r'')
∧
  (∀ m b st st' r',
  BlockStep p m b st st' r' →
  ∀ st'' r'',
  BlockStep p m b st st'' r'' →
  st' = st'' ∧ r' = r'').
```

Listing 4.8: Theorem 4.2 in Coq

Proof. We prove the theorem by mutual induction on the deviation system $\mathcal{S}_*^{\leadsto}(st, st', r')$. By applying the predicate mutual_ind, we get a goal for each constructor of the four definitions ExpressionStep, ListSteps, StatementStep, and BlockStep.

Firstly, we need ensure that there are never two different rules in the deviation system that can be applied in the same situation. As our operational semantics only features one rule per language construct, this property is certainly true. Secondly, we need to show that each rule is deterministic, that is, cannot produce more than one possible outcome.

Case Method Call: Let's highlight the case of a method call, which is the most interesting case to prove. Looking at the definition of the method call in listing 4.6 we can see that the following lines can introduce non-determinism, all other lines are function applications that naturally do not lead to non-determinism:

5 ExpressionStep p o st st1 (normal_step_v (Ref this))

7 lookup p cn (snd msig) (cn' , m')

9 ListSteps p ps st1 st2 psnv

17 BlockStep p m' b st_c st_c' normal_step

In case of lines 5, 9, and 17, we can apply the induction hypotheses that we get from mutual_ind. For line 7, we need to show that the predicate lookup behaves like a function, that is, there is only one possible cn' and m' in a given environment. We have already discussed this proof in detail in tutorial 11. Therefore, we can show that a method call is always deterministic.

The proofs of the other cases are analogous. A special note deserves object creation. In our heap model, the allocation of new objects is performed by the *function* Heap.new and is therefore deterministic by definition. □

4.5 First Refinement

"Don't unfold those data groups!"

In the first refinement, $\mathcal{S}_{\text{rac1}}$, we want to avoid unfolding the data groups in the pre-state of a method. We replace the unfolded set of assignable locations with a stack of assignable locations, in which the data groups are not unfolded, as explained in section 3.4.

4.5.1 Additions to the Program State

In order to decide if a location is assignable, we need to be able to judge if a location was contained in an assignable data group in the pre-state. As we do not yet introduce the concept of back-links and lazy unfolding, we store the pre-heaps of all methods along

4.5. FIRST REFINEMENT

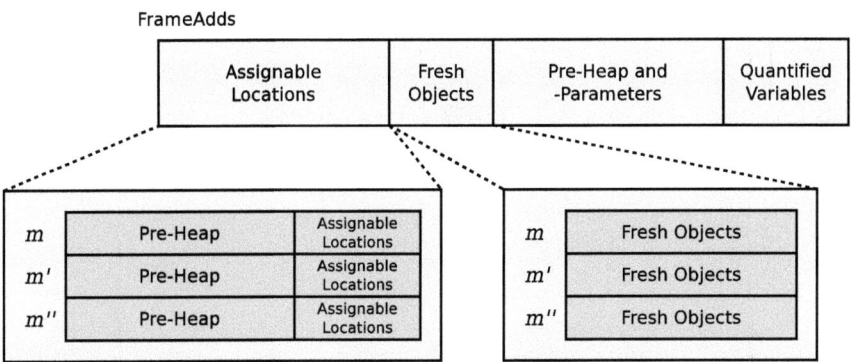

Figure 4.4: The auxiliary data structures FrameAdds of S_{rac1}, in the situation $m'' \hookrightarrow m' \hookrightarrow m$

with the assignable locations. Thus, the type of the assignable field in the auxiliary data structure for frames is stack (Heap.t * LocSet.t). The stack contains the assignable sets of all methods on the call stack. This is necessary as we can not compute the intersection of sets of assignables, see 3.4. The type (Heap.t * LocSet.t) is a tuple in Coq. The function fst applied to a variable of this type yields the first element of the tuple, in our case the heap, and the function snd yields the second element of the tuple, in our case a set of locations. We introduce notations (a)$_1$ for (fst a) and (a)$_2$ for (snd a). The type stack is our implementation of a stack in Coq, which we will highlight below. Analogously, we replace the set of fresh objects by a stack of sets of fresh objects.

Fig. 4.4 depicts the FrameAdds data structure for this refinement. The remaining fields of FrameAdds are left unchanged, as well as the global auxiliary data structure Adds.

Effectively, we make the situation worse in this refinement. Instead of unfolding the data groups in the pre-state and store one set of locations that may contain all allocated locations in the heap, we now store a stack of assignable set, along with a copy of the whole heap for each method in call stack. However, as we discussed in the overview at the beginning of the chapter, it is the first step into the right direction.

4.5.2 The Implementation of a Stack Data Type in Coq

We implement a stack data structure in Coq, based on the data type list from the standard library. All operations and properties of lists are available for stack. Additionally, we add the operations shown in listing 4.9. The meaning of empty, singleton, push, and pop is self-explanatory. ₆ peek yields the top element of the stack without removing it, or None if the stack is empty, whereas ₇ peekd does the same but yields the default-element provided as second parameter if the stack is empty. ₁₀ apply_top applies a function of type A → A to the top most element of the stack, if the stack contains at least one element, otherwise, the unchanged (empty) stack is yielded. Similarly, ₁₁ replace_top replaces the top most element by another.

We add another two operations that are quite specialized, mainly to simplify some definitions in the next refinement. Nevertheless, we introduce them now: The operation ₁₂ truncate removes so many elements from the top of the stack that its size is not bigger than specified by the first parameter. If the stack is not bigger in the first place, truncate doesn't modify the stack. ₁₃ level takes two stacks as parameters and truncates the larger stack to the size of the smaller one, so that the two stacks, yielded as tuple, have the same size.

```
1  Definition stack := list .
2  Variable A : Type .(* The element type of the stack *)
3
4  Parameter empty : stack A →bool.
5  Parameter singleton : A → stack A.
6  Parameter peek : stack A →option A.
7  Parameter peekd : stack A →A → A.
8  Parameter push : A →stack A → stack A.
9  Parameter pop : stack A →stack A.
10 Parameter apply_top : (A → A) → stack A → stack A.
11 Parameter replace_top : A → stack A → stack A.
12 Parameter truncate : nat → stack A → stack A.
13 Parameter level : stack A → stack A → (stack A * stack A).
```

Listing 4.9: The interface of the abstract data type for stacks in Coq, based on list .

――――――――――― A MADE-TO-MEASURE COQ TUTORIAL ―――――――――――

Part 13 Avoiding Undecidability in Implementations

The implementations of the operations above are straight-forward. However, when writing a function in Coq, we often deal with the problem that certain underlying operations yield a value of type **Prop**. In this case, we cannot just perform a syntactic pattern matching on that value, as it might be undecidable.

In the paragraph on the definition of `boolean` in our domain model on page 63, we introduce the axiomatized function P2b: **Prop** →bool to circumvent this problem. However, using this function means that we need to prove that either P or $\neg P$ holds, where P is the proposition passed to the function. With this proof, and the axioms P2b_true and P2b_false we can then continue to evaluate the function.

This sound like additional headache, and we should avoid it as much as possible. To show this, let's have a closer look at a possible (but misguided) implementation of function truncate:

4.5. FIRST REFINEMENT

```
Fixpoint truncate (n : nat) (s : stack A) : stack A :=
  if P2b (n < |s|) then
    match s with
    | _ :: t ⇒ truncate n t
    | -     ⇒ []
    end
  else s.
```

The test $n < |s|$ is of type **Prop**. We use the function P2b to get a bool, which we can use in the if... then... else... construct. While this definition is very readable, using it involves to prove for a given n and s, that $n < |s|$ or its negation $\neg(n < |s|)$ holds. Only then, we can execute the function. As a consequence, we can use this function only in proofs, but not to actually compute a result or even extract it to a program.

To avoid this problems in the first place, we want to define functions in Coq that only depend on decidable types. For our implementation of truncate, we can use the library function

$$\text{nat\_compare: nat} \rightarrow \text{nat} \rightarrow \text{comparison}$$

which yields for two peano numbers a value of the inductive data type comparison with the three constructors Lt, Eq, and Gt. Thus, we can perform a pattern matching on this result. Listing 4.10 shows the actual implementation of truncate in our development.

```
1  Fixpoint truncate (n : nat) (s : stack A) : stack A :=
2    match nat_compare n |s| with
3    | Lt ⇒
4      match s with
5      | _ :: t ⇒ truncate n t
6      | -     ⇒ []
7      end
8    | _ ⇒ s
9    end.
```

Listing 4.10: The implementation of operation truncate.

The use of nat_compare instead of < also raises new issues. In order to prove properties on truncate, we need to reason about the properties of nat_compare a great deal in order to prove simple facts. The standard library provides a good start, but ultimately, we need quite some additional lemmas just to deal with this fact. For instance, the following pretty obvious fact requires a non-trivial proof:

∀ n m, nat_compare n m = Lt ↔ nat_compare m n = Gt.

Or written in mathematical form: $n < m \leftrightarrow m > n$

We prove a selection of useful lemmas about the operations truncate and level. Listing 4.11 shows the lemmas for operation truncate. ₁ Lemma truncate_1 states that the size of the truncated stack is exactly the requested size n, if the stack contained at least n elements before. ₃,₅ The lemmas truncate_nil and truncate_n_nil state that truncate yields [] (nil), if either the requested size n is 0 or the input stack was empty already. ₇ truncate_same states that truncating a stack to its own size doesn't modify the stack after all. ₁ truncate_pop states that truncating a stack to its size minus one is the same as performing the operation pop on the stack. ₁₁ map_truncate states that it does not make a difference if we first apply a function f to all elements of the stack and then truncate, or the other way round. Finally, ₁₄ truncate_truncate states that truncating a stack to some size and then truncate it to an even smaller (or same) size can be replaced by truncating the stack to the smaller size directly.

```
1  Lemma truncate_1:
2  ∀ (n : nat) (s : stack A), n ≤ |s| → n = |truncate n s|.
3  Lemma truncate_nil:
4  ∀ (s : stack A), truncate 0 s = [].
5  Lemma truncate_n_nil:
6  ∀ (n : nat), truncate n [] = [].
7  Lemma truncate_same:
8  ∀ (s : stack A), truncate |s| s = s.
9  Lemma truncate_pop:
10 ∀ (n : nat) (s : stack A), |s| = n+1 → truncate n s = pop s.
11 Lemma map_truncate:
12 ∀ (f : A → B) (n : nat) (s : stack A),
13 map f (truncate n s) = truncate n (map f s).
14 Lemma truncate_truncate:
15 ∀ (n m : nat) (s : stack A),
16 n ≤ m → truncate n s = truncate n (truncate m s).
```

Listing 4.11: A set of lemmas about operation truncate

Listing 4.12 shows the lemmas for operation level. ₁ level_1 states that the size of two leveled stacks is the same. ₃ level_eq states that leveling two stacks of the same size results in the same stacks. ₅,₇ The lemmas level_le and level_ge describe the relation between level and truncate.

```
1  Lemma level_1:
2  ∀ (s s' t t' : stack A), (s', t') = level s t → |s'| = |t'|.
3  Lemma level_eq:
4  ∀ (s t : stack A), (s, t) = level s t ↔ |s| = |t|.
```

4.5. FIRST REFINEMENT

```
5  Lemma level_le:
6  ∀ (s t : stack A), (s, truncate |s| t) = level s t ↔ |s| ≤|t|.
7  Lemma level_ge:
8  ∀ (s t : stack A), (truncate |t| s, t) = level s t ↔ |t| ≤|s|.
```

Listing 4.12: A set of lemmas about operation level

The proofs of all lemmas are performed by induction on the size of the stack.

4.5.3 The Bisimulation Relation

We introduce the bisimulation relation $\mathcal{R}_{rac1}^{sem}$ between $\mathcal{S}_{sem}$ and $\mathcal{S}_{rac1}$ in listing 4.13. The predicate CorrespondingState holds for a st_{sem} and a st_{rac1}, if the heaps of both states are identical, and if the frames correspond. Mind that we do not need to argue that the additions to the state, Adds, are equal, as they are implemented as singleton, that is, the data type contains exactly one value and is therefore two variables of this type are always equal.

```
1  Definition CorrespondingState (p : Program) (st_rac : State.t) (st_sem : Sem.State.t):
2                                                                                Prop :=
3  st_sem@h = st_rac@h  ∧
4  CorrespondingFrame p st_rac@fr st_sem@fr .
```

Listing 4.13: The definition the bisimulation relation $\mathcal{R}_{rac1}^{sem}$ between the semantics $\mathcal{S}_{sem}$ and $\mathcal{S}_{rac1}$.

Listing 4.14 shows the definition of corresponding frames: two frames fr_{sem} and fr_{rac1} correspond, if all fields except for assignables and fresh are equal. 10 The fresh set of $\mathcal{S}_{sem}$ contains the same elements than the top element of the stack fresh in $\mathcal{S}_{rac1}$ Furthermore, 11 the predicate Corresponding− FreshAssignables needs to hold, and 14 we state that the stack of fresh objects is not empty.

```
1   Inductive CorrespondingFrame (p : Program) : Frame.t → Sem.Frame.t → Prop :=
2   | CorrespondingFrame_def:
3      ∀ fr_rac fr_sem,
4      fr_sem@params      = fr_rac@params →
5      fr_sem@vars        = fr_rac@vars →
6      fr_sem@pc          = fr_rac@pc →
7      fr_sem@ret         = fr_rac@ret →
8      fr_sem@pre         = fr_rac@pre →
9      fr_sem@quants      = fr_rac@quants →
10     fr_sem@fresh       [=] peekd fr_rac@fresh ∅ →
```

```
11    CorrespondingFreshAssignables p
12      fr_sem@assignables  fr_sem@fresh
13      fr_rac@assignables  fr_rac@fresh  →
14      fr_rac@fresh ≠ [] →
15      CorrespondingFrame p fr_rac fr_sem .
```

Listing 4.14: The definition of corresponding method frames. For the bisimulation relations of the following refinements, we will omit the 4-10 trivial parts.

In listing 4.15, we show to the most interesting part of the correspondence relation, which describes the relation between the sets of assignable locations and fresh objects in $\mathcal{S}_{\mathsf{sem}}$ and their corresponding stack data structures in $\mathcal{S}_{\mathsf{rac1}}$. The predicate holds if and only if for any heap location loc 4 that is either in the assignable set, or a location of a fresh object in $\mathcal{S}_{\mathsf{sem}}$, the following is true in $\mathcal{S}_{\mathsf{rac1}}$: 6,7 for each method in the call stack, 8-10 either the location's object has been freshly allocated in that method or any of its callees, or 12,13 the location is in the set of assignable locations after unfolding the data groups contained in the set in the method's pre-state.

As the stacks of assignable locations and fresh objects contain an element for each method on the call stack, we can refer to an element that belongs to a given method on the call stack by its position. Thus, we quantify over the number n and restrict its range to valid positions in the stack by the premise 7 n < |a_rac|, in order to quantify over the entries of the stack for all methods on the call stack.

Moreover, we can use the position of an element in these stacks to identify if an element belongs to a callee or a caller of some method in the call stack, as the order of the stack entries corresponds to the order of the methods in the call stack. Thus, by the limitation of m: 9, m ≤ n ∧ m < |f_rac|, we express that m refers to a position in the stacks that corresponds to a callee of the method at position n.

With the function "nth", we get the element at the nth position of a stack, or a default value otherwise. For instance 10 nth m f_rac ∅ yields the mth element in the stack of fresh object sets, or an empty set otherwise.

```
1   Definition CorrespondingFreshAssignables(p:Program)(a_sem:LocSet.t)(f_sem:ObjSet.t)
2               (a_rac : stack (Heap.t * LocSet.t))  ( f_rac : stack ObjSet.t) : Prop :=
3   ∀ ( loc : Location ),
4     loc ∈ a_sem ∨LocInObjSet loc f_sem
5   ↔
6     ∀ (n : nat),
7       n <|a_rac| →
8       (∃ (m : nat),
9          m ≤n ∧ m < |f_rac|
10           ∧ loc ∈ (ObjSet2LocSet (nth m f_rac ∅)))
```

```
11        ∨
12        loc ∈ (UnfoldDatagroups p (nth n a_rac (InitHeap,∅)))₁
13                                  (nth n a_rac (InitHeap,∅))₂).
```

Listing 4.15: The interesting part in this refinement: the relation between the fresh and assignable sets of the two involved semantics.

4.5.4 Implementation of the Frame Conditions Interface

From the five functions in the frame condition interface, we implement tree of them different to the semantics. The first is FieldUpdateCheck, which needs to deal with the fact that the assignable locations have not been unfolded in the pre-state. The second is MethodCallAction, which has less work to do for the same reason. The third is MethodReturnAction, which deals with stacks of fresh object sets rather than just one such set.

The definition of FieldUpdateCheck, shown in listing 4.16, is basically the property defined on the right side in CorrespondingFreshAssignables, see 4.15. It checks if loc or a data group that contains loc is assignable in each element of the assignable stack or if there exists object that has been freshly allocated during the execution of the method that contains the location. The only difference is that we do not check if the location is in the unfolded set of assignable locations, but rather check if there exists a data group that contains the location and that is mentioned in the assignable set. It is natural that the correspondence relation and the field update checks are closely related, as the outcome of this check is the only relevant information that needs to correspond in the two semantics of the bisimulation. To check if a field is contained in a data group, we use the inductive predicate FieldInDg, which we presented in listing 2.72 on page 94.

```
1  Definition FieldUpdateCheck (p : Program) (loc : Location) (st : State.t) : Prop :=
2  ∀ (n : nat),
3      n < |st@fr@assignables| →
4      (∃ (m : nat),
5          m ≤ n ∧ m < |st@fr@fresh|
6          ∧ loc ∈ ObjSet2LocSet (nth m st@fr@fresh ∅))
7      ∨
8      ∃ dg, dg ∈ (nth n st@fr@assignables (InitHeap,∅))₁ ∧
9      FieldInDg p (nth n st@fr@assignables (InitHeap,∅))₂ loc dg.
```

Listing 4.16: The $\mathcal{S}_{rac1}$ implementation of FieldUpdateCheck.

Upon method invocation, the $\mathcal{S}_{rac1}$ definition of MethodCallAction, shown in listing 4.17, evaluates the assignable clause into a set of locations, but does not unfold the data groups. This set, together with the current heap is stored in the stack of assignable locations. The function EvalAssignabeClause is defined to yield the same set of locations than its counterpart in $\mathcal{S}_{sem}$, for corresponding states.

The function MethodCallAction is called in a state that already contains the new frame for the method. This frame features an element on top of the assignable stack that has been initialized with the set LocSetAll, which represents the default assignable clause assignable \everything. Therefore, the implementation behind the notation ":+" does not put a new element on the stack, but *replaces* the top most element of the assignable stack with the new value.

```
1  Definition MethodCallAction (p : Program) (c : Class) (m : Method) (st : State.t) :
2                                                                       State.t :=
3    let locs := EvalAssignableClause p c m st in
4    st [ fr:=st@fr[ assignables :+ (st@h, locs )]].
```

Listing 4.17: The $\mathcal{S}_{rac1}$ implementation of MethodCallAction.

Upon method return, MethodReturnAction of $\mathcal{S}_{rac1}$ adds the set of fresh objects from the caller to his own set of fresh objects, see listing 4.18. The function computes the union of the top most elements of the fresh stacks from caller and callee and *replaces* the top element of the caller with the new set.

With peekd we retrieve the top element of the fresh stack of the callee. In order for this to operate as expected, the stack must not be empty (hence, we added the information at line 14 in listing 4.14). Behind the notation ":∪", we hide the details of the update, which are:

$$\text{apply\_top (ObjSet.union f\_c) fr@fresh}$$

where ObjSet.union f_c is the curried function to compute the union between the given set of fresh objects of the callee and a set provided as argument.

```
1  Definition MethodReturnAction (p:Program) (st_c:State.t) (st:State.t) : State.t :=
2    st_c [ fr:=st@fr[ fresh :∪ (peekd st_c@fr@fresh ∅) ]].
```

Listing 4.18: The $\mathcal{S}_{rac1}$ implementation of MethodReturnAction.

4.5.5 Proof of the First Refinement

The way we build up the different semantics involved in the refinements allows us to apply an elegant way of proving the correctness of each refinement. The semantics only differ in the implementation of the supplied jml module. Therefore, by proving that the different implementations of the functions in the jml module preserve the correspondence between states, we can elegantly show that the two semantics are in fact bisimilar.

In this first refinement, the interesting proofs are the correctness proofs for the functions FieldUpdateCheck and MethodCallAction. Of course, we also provide a correctness proof of all other functions of the frame conditions interface in our formalization. However, these proofs are either not interesting or similar to (but simpler than) the proof for MethodCallAction.

We present the proof of the first refinement as follows: firstly, we show that the function FieldUpdateCheck behaves equivalently for corresponding states and that the S_{rac1} implementation of MethodCallAction preserves the correspondence between states in S_{sem} and S_{rac1}. Secondly, we prove the main theorem for this refinement, which states that the semantics S_{sem} and S_{rac1} are bisimilar.

Correctness Proof of the Frame Condition Implementation

Lemma 4.3. Correct Field Update Check
For corresponding states, the field update checks in S_{sem} and S_{rac1} are equivalent.

```
1  Lemma FieldUpdateCheck_Correct:
2    ∀ loc p st_rac st_sem,
3      CorrespondingState p st_rac st_sem →
4      ( Rac1.Assignables.FieldUpdateCheck p loc st_rac
5        ↔
6        Sem.Assignables.FieldUpdateCheck p loc st_sem ).
```

Listing 4.19: Correctness of S_{rac1} version of FieldUpdateCheck

Proof. By introducing the ₃ premise and by unfolding the involved definitions, we get a hypothesis that states the property defined by Corresponding− FreshAssignables, see 4.15. For reasons that we discussed on page 141, the definitions of FieldUpdateCheck of S_{sam} and S_{race} are equivalent to the left and right side of the full implication of this property, respectively.

The S_{rac1} definition of FieldUpdateCheck differs from the correspondence relation only in the unfolding of data groups:

```
H4 : loc
     ∈ UnfoldDatagroups p (nth n stRac@fr@assignables (InitHeap, ∅))₁
       (nth n stRac@fr@assignables (InitHeap, ∅))₂
```

```
∃ dg,
dg ∈ (nth n stRac@fr@assignables (InitHeap, ∅))₂
∧ FieldInDg p (nth n stRac@fr@assignables (InitHeap, ∅))₁ loc dg
```

Listing 4.20: Proof excerpt

CHAPTER 4. CORRECTNESS PROOF OF THE RAC FOR ASSIGNABLE CLAUSES

Checking the definition of UnfoldDatagroups in listing 2.71 on page 94, we realize that the goal is equivalent to H4. □

Lemma 4.4. Correct Method Call Action

Fig. 4.5 depicts the proof idea for the function MethodCallAction of $\mathcal{S}_{rac1}$. Starting from two corresponding states st_{sem} and st_{rac1}, the application of functions MethodCallAction on these states yields the states st'_{sem} and st'_{rac1}, and these two states correspond.

This only needs to hold if the states st_{sem} and st_{rac1} contain a new method frame. Hence, the the set of fresh objects in st_{sem} is empty, the top element of the fresh stack in st_{rac1} is the empty set as well, and the top element of the assignable stack in st_{rac1} is the set of all locations.

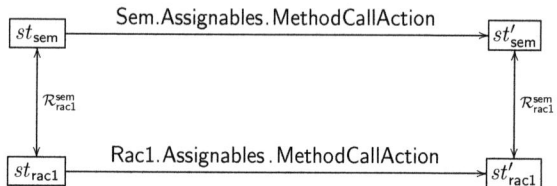

Figure 4.5: MethodCallAction preserves the relation $\mathcal{R}_{rac1}^{sem}$.

```
1  Lemma MethodCallAction_Correct:
2  ∀ p c m st_rac st_rac' st_sem st_sem'  st_rac_assignables  st_rac_fresh ,
3  (    st_sem@fr@fresh = ∅
4   ∧ st_rac@fr@assignables = ((InitHeap, LocSetAll) :: st_rac_assignables )
5   ∧ st_rac@fr@fresh = (∅ :: st_rac_fresh )) →
6
7  CorrespondingState p st_rac st_sem →
8  Sem.Assignables.MethodCallAction p c m st_sem = st_sem' →
9  Rac1.Assignables.MethodCallAction p c m st_rac = st_rac' →
10 CorrespondingState p st_rac' st_sem'.
```

Proof. We start the proof of this lemma by unfolding all involved definitions. The only part of the program state that MethodCallAction touches, is the field assignable in the method frame. Thus, all parts of the correspondence relation that do not mention the assignables field can trivially be discharged.

We are left with the definition of CorrespondingFreshAssignables, for which we need to show equivalence after the update of the assignables field. In $\mathcal{S}_{sem}$, we intersect the existing assignable locations with the unfolded set of assignable locations from the method's specification. In $\mathcal{S}_{rac1}$, we replace the top most element in the assignable stack by a tuple containing the pre-heap of the method and non-unfolded set of assignable locations from method's specification.

Hinit : st_sem@fr@fresh = ∅
    ∧ st_rac@fr@assignables =(InitHeap,LocSetAll):: st_rac_assignables
    ∧ st_rac@fr@fresh = ∅ :: st_rac_fresh
H0 : st_sem@h = st_rac@h
H9 : CorrespondingFreshAssignables p
    st_sem@fr@assignables
    st_sem@fr@fresh
    st_rac@fr@assignables
    st_rac@fr@fresh

CorrespondingFreshAssignables p
  (st_sem@fr@assignables ∩ UnfoldDatagroups p st_sem@h
                                        EvalAssignableClause p c m st_sem))
  st_sem@fr@fresh
  (replace_top (st_rac@h, EvalAssignableClause p c m st_rac)   st_rac@fr@assignables)
  st_rac@fr@fresh

Listing 4.21: Proof excerpt

In order to explain the proof strategy, let's have a look at the unfolded version of the goal:

```
1  ...
2  ─────────────────────────────────────────────
3  ∀ loc : Location,
4    loc ∈ (st_sem@fr@assignables
5         ∩ UnfoldDatagroups p st_sem@h (EvalAssignableClause p c m st_sem)
6         ∨ LocInObjSet loc st_sem@fr@fresh
7  ↔
8    (∀ n : nat,
9       n < |replace_top (st_rac@h, EvalAssignableClause p c m st_rac)
10            st_rac@fr@assignables |) →
11        (∃ m : nat,
12           m ≤n ∧ m < |st_rac@fr@fresh |
13           ∧ loc ∈ ObjSet2LocSet (nth m st_rac@fr@fresh ∅))
14      ∨
15        loc ∈ UnfoldDatagroups p
16            (nth n
17              ( replace_top (st_rac@h, EvalAssignableClause p c m st_rac)
```

```
18              st_rac@fr@assignables ) (InitHeap, ∅) )₁
19         (nth n
20            ( replace_top (st_rac@h, EvalAssignableClause p c m st_rac)
21              st_rac@fr@assignables ) (InitHeap, ∅) )₂)
```

Listing 4.22: Proof excerpt

We discuss both directions of the full implication at line ₇:
"→": We know that ₄,₅ the location loc is both in st_sem@fr@assignables and the unfolded set yielded by EvalAssignableClause because it cannot be in ₆ st_sem@fr@fresh, as this would contradict to the hypothesis Hinit.

We perform a case split on n. If $n = 0$, we choose the right hand side of the ₁₄ disjunction. The 0th element of the stack in which we replaced the top is of course the replacement itself. Therefore, we can rewrite H0 and simplify the access to the first and second part of the tuple to get the goal, where H10 originates in the ₅ premise of the last goal:

```
...
H10 : loc ∈ UnfoldDatagroups p st_sem@h EvalAssignableClause p c m st_sem

loc ∈ UnfoldDatagroups p st_rac@h (EvalAssignableClause p c m st_rac)
```

Listing 4.23: Proof excerpt

We know from H0 that the heaps are equal, furthermore the function EvalAssignableClause yields equal sets of locations for corresponding states, thus we can prove this goal.

If $n > 0$, we look at any but the first stack element. As the first element is the only one that got changed, we can use H9, which states the desired property for the original assignable stacks, to prove the goal.

"←": We need to prove that loc is ₄ in st_sem@fr@assignables *and* ₅ in the unfolded set of assignable locations from the method's specification, because we know from Hinit that loc is definitively not in the ₆ fresh set. In the following, we discuss the proof of both sides of the conjunction.

To prove that loc∈st_sem@fr@assignables, we use the correspondence relation in H9. In order to apply (the unfolded version of) H9 to the goal, we need to show that loc is assignable in st_rac before the update:

```
...

∀ loc : Location,
  (∀ n : nat,
    n < | st_rac@fr@assignables |)
    → (∃ m : nat,
       m ≤ n ∧ m < |st_rac@fr@fresh|
```

```
              ∧ loc ∈ ObjSet2LocSet (nth m st_rac@fr@fresh ∅))
         ∨
              loc ∈ UnfoldDatagroups p
                 (nth n  st_rac@fr@assignables  (InitHeap, ∅) )₁
                 (nth n  st_rac@fr@assignables  (InitHeap, ∅) )₁
```

Listing 4.24: Proof excerpt

Again, we perform a case split on n. If n = 0, we know from the second part of Hinit, that loc is certainly in the unfolded set of the first stack element, as it contains all locations. As the first stack element stays unchanged after the application of MethodCallAction, we can trivially prove the goal for n > 0.

To prove that loc is in the unfolded set of assignable locations in st_sem (this is the second part of the conjunction from before), we set n to 0 and show that the right part of the disjunction (15-21 in listing 4.22) needs to hold because the left part does definitively not hold because of Hinit. Analogously to the forward direction, we can then show that the two unfolded sets are identical. □

Proof of the Bisimulation Property

Theorem 4.5. Correctness of the First Refinement

If one starts in a state st_{sem} and performs a step in the semantics to get state st'_{sem}, and given a state st_{rac1} that corresponds to state st_{sem}, then there exists a state st'_{rac1} that one gets by applying the same step in the runtime assertion checker and that corresponds to st'_{sem}.

Moreover, if one can perform a step in the runtime assertion checker from st_{rac1} to st'_{rac1}, and st_{sem} corresponds to st_{rac1}, then there exists a corresponding st'_{sem} which one gets by performing the same step in the semantics:

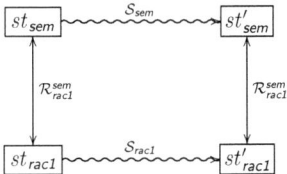

Proof. The proof of both statements is completely symmetrical, we will only discuss the forward direction $\mathcal{S}_{sem} \rightarrow \mathcal{S}_{rac1}$.

Similar to the proof of determinism, we need to state the property for all four inductive definitions of a step and perform a proof by mutual induction. We discuss the three interesting cases method call, field update, and object creation. Of course, we prove both directions of all cases in the formalization.

Case Field Update: Listing 4.25 shows the proof obligation for field update. We rearranged and commented the generated hypotheses for a better understanding.

CHAPTER 4. CORRECTNESS PROOF OF THE RAC FOR ASSIGNABLE CLAUSES

2-11 The hypotheses H – H10 represent define a field update in $\mathcal{S}_{\mathsf{sem}}$, we can directly relate them to the premises of the rule for field assignment in listing 4.5 on page 130.

14 The hypothesis H11 states that the initial states are corresponding.

17-22 H2 is the induction hypothesis for the call to ExpressionStep in H1. Thus, we know that we can evaluate the target of the assignment and preserve the correspondence.

25-29 H5 is the induction hypothesis for the call to ExpressionStep in H4. Thus, the right hand side of an assignment can be evaluated while preserving the correspondence.

```
1   (* Case: perform a field update in OpSem ($\mathcal{S}_{\mathsf{sem}}$) *)
2   H   : e = Assignment (field fsig (Some target)) expr
3   H1  : OpSem.ExpressionStep p target st st1 (normal_step_v (Ref obj))
4   H0  : loc = Heap.InstanceField obj fsig
5   H6  : Heap.typeof st2@h obj = Some (Heap.ObjectObject cn um)
6   H7  : defined_field p cn fsig
7   H3  : Sem.Assignables.FieldUpdateCheck p loc st1
8   H4  : OpSem.ExpressionStep p expr st1 st2 (normal_step_v v)
9   H8  : assign_compatible p st2@h v (FIELDSIGNATURE.type (fsig)$_2$)
10  H9  : Sem.Assignables.FieldUpdateAction p loc v st2 = st3
11  H10 : st' = st3 [h := Heap.update st2@h loc v]
12
13  (* The initial states correspond *)
14  H11 : CorrespondingState p st_rac st
15
16  (* Induction Hypothesis for H1 *)
17  H2 : ∀ st_rac : State.t,
18          CorrespondingState p st_rac st
19          → (∃ st_rac' : State.t,
20              CorrespondingState p st_rac' st1
21              ∧ OpRacl.ExpressionStep p target st_rac st_rac'
22                (normal_step_v (Ref obj)))
23
24  (* Induction Hypothesis for H4 *)
25  H5 : ∀ st_rac : State.t,
26          CorrespondingState p st_rac st1
27          → (∃ st'_rac : State.t,
28              CorrespondingState p st'_rac st2
29              ∧ OpRacl.ExpressionStep p expr st_rac st'_rac (normal_step_v v))
30
```

4.5. FIRST REFINEMENT

```
31  ∃ st'_rac : State.t,
32  CorrespondingState p st'_rac st'
33  ∧ OpRac1.ExpressionStep p e st_rac st'_rac (normal_step_v v)
```

Listing 4.25: Proof excerpt

We want to find an instance for the existential variable in the goal, that is, we need to construct a state st'_rac that corresponds to st' and that can be reached by performing one expression step starting from st_rac.

We construct this state step by step: By H2 and the fact that the premise of H2 holds because of H11, we know that there exists a corresponding state to st1, we call it st1_rac. From this, we can perform the same reasoning with H5 to get a state st2_rac that corresponds to st2. From the definition of FieldUpdateAction, we learn that st2 = st3. We can now create a state st'_rac by updating the heap in st2_rac in the same way as H10 updates st3.

We provide st'_rac as a witness to the existential in the goal. We now have to prove that this witness is the right one, that is, it corresponds to st' and we can indeed perform one step in $\mathcal{S}_{rac}$ that leads to this state.

The first part is trivial, because we just constructed st'_rac from the induction hypotheses H2 and H5 that state that the resulting states are corresponding. We prove the second part by applying the correct rule, that is, inductive constructor from ExpressionStep in $\mathcal{S}_{rac1}$. The correct choice is naturally the same rule that was applied on $\mathcal{S}_{sem}$, thus, we apply the constructor assignment_instance_field_ok with the appropriate instantiation for the universal quantifiers.

Most of the variables are identical in $\mathcal{S}_{sem}$ and $\mathcal{S}_{rac1}$, only the state variables differ. Applying this constructor results in ten new sub-goals to prove, one for each premise of the assignment rule, but most of them can be immediately discharged by the trivial tactic, if the sub-goal exactly matches a hypothesis. Examples are hypotheses H0 or H7 that are not dependent of the semantics used. But also the two induction hypotheses provide the 21-22,29 means to trivially discharge sub-goals that contain the inductive definitions.

We are left with three sub-goals. The first is the $\mathcal{S}_{rac1}$ counterpart of H3:

Rac1.Assignables.FieldUpdateCheck p loc st1_rac

We apply lemma 4.3, to discharge this sub-goal.

The remaining two sub-goals are the counterparts of H6 and H8, that use st2_rac instead of st2 to access the heap. Because we know that st2_rac and st2 correspond, we can rewrite the sub-goals to exactly match H6 and H8.

Case Method Call: Listing 4.26 shows the proof obligation for a method call. We rearranged and commented the generated hypotheses for a better understanding.

Analogous to the case from field update, we split the hypotheses of the generated goal into three categories: 2-17 the premises of the method call rule, 20 the premise of our property that we want to prove, and ₂₃₋₃₈ generated induction hypotheses for the nested calls to perform a step.

```
1  (* Case: perform a method call in OpSem (S_sem) *)
2  H   : e = method msig (Some o) ps
3  H0  : OpSem.ExpressionStep p o st st1 (normal_step_v (Ref this0))
4  H2  : Heap.typeof st1@h this = Some (Heap.ObjectObject cn um)
5  H3  : lookup p cn (msig)₂ (cn', m')
6  H4  : PROG.class p cn = Some c'
7  H5  : OpSem.ListSteps p ps st1 st2 psnv
8  H7  : psv = OpSem.nv2v psnv
9  H8  : length psv = length psnv
10 H9  : fr_c1 = Sem.NewFrame m' (lv2params m' (Ref this0 :: psv)) st2
11 H10 : st3 = st2 [fr := fr_c1]
12 H11 : Sem.Assignables.MethodCallAction p c' m' st3 = st_c
13 H12 : METHOD.body m' = Some body
14 H13 : STATEMENT.type (METHODBODY.compound body) = Compound b
15 H14 : OpSem.BlockStep p m' b st_c st_c' normal_step
16 H16 : Normal (Some v) = st_c'@fr@ret
17 H17 : Sem.Assignables.MethodReturnAction p st_c' st2 = st'
18
19 (* The initial states correspond *)
20 H18 : CorrespondingState p st_rac st
21
22 (* Induction hypotheses for H0, H5, H14 *)
23 H1  : ∀ st_rac : State.t,
24        CorrespondingState p st_rac st
25        → (∃ st'_rac : State.t,
26             CorrespondingState p st'_rac st1
27             ∧ OpRac1.ExpressionStep p o st_rac st'_rac
28                (normal_step_v (Ref this0)))
29 H6  : ∀ st_rac : State.t,
30        CorrespondingState p st_rac st1
31        → (∃ st'_rac : State.t,
32             CorrespondingState p st'_rac st2
33             ∧ OpRac1.ListSteps p ps st_rac st'_rac psnv)
34 H15 : ∀ st_rac : State.t,
35        CorrespondingState p st_rac st_c
36        → (∃ st'_rac : State.t,
37             CorrespondingState p st'_rac st_c'
38             ∧ OpRac1.BlockStep p m' b st_rac st'_rac normal_step)
```

4.5. FIRST REFINEMENT

```
40  ∃ st'_rac : State.t,
41  CorrespondingState p st'_rac st'
42  ∧ OpRac1.ExpressionStep p e st_rac st'_rac (normal_step_v v)
```

Listing 4.26: Proof excerpt

The proof strategy is identical to field update. We construct a state st'_rac that corresponds to st' and that can be reached by performing one step in $\mathcal{S}_{rac1}$ starting from st_rac.

We already have everything we need to construct st'_rac. We use H1 to get st1_rac. From this, we use H6 to get st2_rac. From a lemma that shows that Rac1.NewFrame is correct, that is, preserve the correspondence relation, we can construct a st3_rac that corresponds to st3. Using the lemma 4.4, we set a state st_c_rac to be the corresponding state to st_c. From H15 we get the state st_c'_rac and finally use the correctness lemma for Rac1.Assignables.MethdReturnAction to construct a corresponding state to st'.

We use st'_rac as witness for the existential quantifier in the goal. The ₄₁ left hand side of the conjunction is trivially true, as we have just used the correspondence relation to create st'_rac, and the ₄₂ right hand side can be proven by applying the method call rule of $\mathcal{S}_{rac1}$. This creates sixteen new sub-goals, from which fourteen can be discharged trivially. The remaining two (the counterparts of H2 and H16) can be discharged by unfolding the appropriate correspondence relations to show that the heap (in case of H2) and the return value (in case of H16) are identical in corresponding states.

Case Object Creation: Listing 4.27 shows the proof obligation for object creation. We can prove it by constructing a state st'_rac using Rac1.Assignables.NewObjectAction. The definition is accompanied by a correctness lemma that shows that the function preserves correspondence of states. We use st'_rac as witness and apply the rule for object creation of $\mathcal{S}_{rac1}$. Finally, we unfold the correspondence relation on the initial states to show that st@h and st_rac@h yield the same heap.

```
1   (* Case: object creation in OpSem (𝒮_sem) *)
2   H : e = new (ReferenceType (TypeDefType cn um))
3   H0 : Heap.new st@h p (Heap.ObjectObject cn um) = Some (o, h')
4   H1 : Sem.Assignables.NewObjectAction p o st = st1
5   H2 : st' = st1 [h := h']
6
7   (* The initial states correspond *)
8   H3 : CorrespondingState p st_rac st
9
10  ∃ st'_rac : State.t,
11  CorrespondingState p st'_rac st'
```

12 | ∧ OpRac1.ExpressionStep p e st_rac st'_rac (normal_step_v (Ref o))

Listing 4.27: Proof excerpt

□

4.6 Second Refinement

"LOSE THOSE HEAPS!"

In the second refinement, we define the semantics $\mathcal{S}_{rac2}$ which eliminates the need to store the whole heap for each element of the stack of assignable locations. We realize the *lazy unfolding* of data groups, as introduced in the paragraph on updating pivot fields on page 114.

4.6.1 Additions to the Program State

Once more, we change the signature of the field assignable of the auxiliary data structures for method frames. While it is stack (Heap.t * LocSet.t) in $\mathcal{S}_{rac1}$, we change it to stack (LocSet.t * LocSet.t) in $\mathcal{S}_{rac2}$. The second element of the tuple is the set of assignable locations, which is identical to $\mathcal{S}_{rac1}$. However, the first element of the tuple is now the set of pivot fields that got assigned to during method execution. Thus, data groups using these pivot field should not be considered when checking if a location is contained via dynamic data groups in the set of assignable locations. We name these locations *excluded pivots*.

Fig. 4.6 depicts the FrameAdds data structure for this refinement. The remaining fields of FrameAdds are left unchanged, as well as the global auxiliary data structure Adds.

In this refinement, we set things right again after we introduced additional copies of the whole heap in the last refinement. Now, the auxiliary data structures do not contain any unnecessary information any more.

4.6.2 Dealing with Excluded Pivots

In the presence of excluded pivot fields, we need to adapt the definitions of data group unfolding and membership. If a field is contained in a data group via a dynamic data group defined on an excluded pivot field, we ignore this data group for the field.

Data Group Unfolding and Membership

The definition of UnfoldDatagroups_rac, shown in listing 4.28 is nearly identical to the definition UnfoldDatagroups in listing 2.71 on page 94. The only difference is, that instead of providing the heap in which the data groups should be unfolded, the function expects the current heap and a set of excluded pivots as arguments. From the axiomatization, we

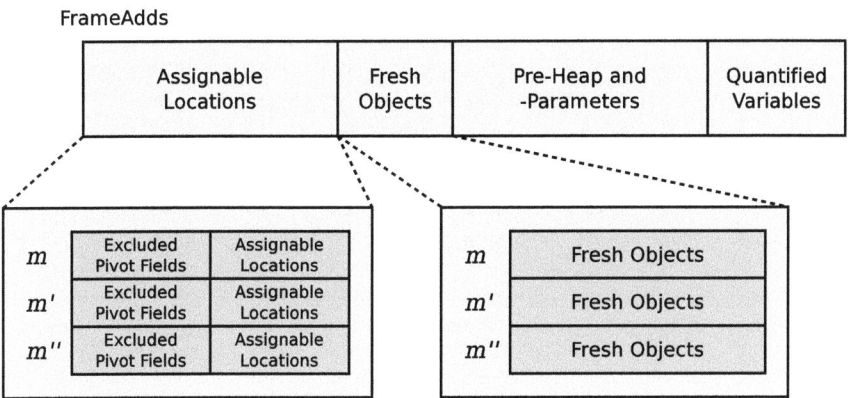

Figure 4.6: The auxiliary data structures FrameAdds of $\mathcal{S}_{\text{rac2}}$, in the situation $m'' \hookrightarrow m' \hookrightarrow m$

see that the excluded pivots are passed to a predicate FieldInDg_rac. The predicate holds, if field f is in data group dg, without using any pivot field from ep. So let's look at the definition of FieldInDg_rac to finally see the difference between $\mathcal{S}_{\text{rac1}}$ and $\mathcal{S}_{\text{rac2}}$.

```
Parameter UnfoldDatagroups_rac : Program →Heap.t →
                (* excluded pivots *) LocSet.t → (* data groups *) LocSet.t → LocSet.t.
Axiom UnfoldDatagroups_rac_def: ∀p h ep dgs f,
    f ∈ (UnfoldDatagroups_rac p h ep dgs)
    ↔
    ∃ dg, dg ∈ dgs ∧FieldInDg_rac p h ep f dg).
```

Listing 4.28: Axiomatized function to unfold data groups in the presence of excluded pivots.

Listing 4.29 shows the interesting constructor of the implementation of FieldInDg_rac. The definition closely resembles FieldInDg from listing 2.72 with except for ₆ the additional check that the pivot from directFieldInDg_ dynamic is not a member of the set of excluded pivots, ep.

```
Inductive FieldInDg_rac (p : Program) (h : Heap.t) (ep : LocSet.t):
                (* field *) Location → (* dg *) Location → Prop :=
  ...
  | FieldInDg_rac_dynamic : ∀ field  dg pivot ,
    direct_FieldInDg_dynamic p h field  dg pivot →
    pivot ∉ ep →
```

CHAPTER 4. CORRECTNESS PROOF OF THE RAC FOR ASSIGNABLE CLAUSES

```
7   FieldInDg_rac  p h ep  field  dg
8   ...
```

Listing 4.29: The predicate FieldInDg_rac.

Although the difference between the unfolding of data groups in $\mathcal{S}_{rac1}$ and $\mathcal{S}_{rac2}$ are small, we need quite some additional information to be able to show the correspondence between the two semantics. We prove a set of lemmas about UnfoldDatagroups_rac and FieldInDg_rac to facilitate the correctness proofs for the frame condition functions.

Facts about Data Group Unfolding and Membership

The following definitions and lemmas highlight the most prominent and interesting facts about the $\mathcal{S}_{rac2}$ implementation of data group unfolding and membership. We relate the new implementation to the original one of $\mathcal{S}_{sem}$, and also flesh out central properties of the new definitions.

Facts about definition FieldInDg_rac

Lemma 4.6. *The $\mathcal{S}_{rac2}$ implementation* FieldInDg_rac *is equivalent to* FieldInDg, *if the set of excluded pivots is empty.*

```
1   Lemma FieldInDg_rac_1:
2     ∀ p h f dg,
3     FieldInDg  p h f dg ↔ FieldInDg_rac  p h ∅ f dg.
```

Proof. Both directions of the full implication by structural induction over the shape of the inductive definition FieldInDg and FieldInDg_rac, respectively. As the set of excluded pivots is empty, the additional premise pivot ∉ ep in constructor FieldInDg_rac_dynamic always holds. □

Lemma 4.7. *Allocating a new object in the heap doesn't affect the predicate* FieldInDg_rac.

```
1   Lemma FieldInDg_rac_2:
2     ∀ p h h' lt obj pivots a dg,
3     Heap.new h p lt = Some (obj, h') →
4     ( FieldInDg_rac  p h pivots a dg ↔ FieldInDg_rac  p h' pivots a dg).
```

Proof. Both directions of the full implication by structural induction over FieldInDg_rac. We discuss only one direction as the proofs are fairly similar.

"→": The only constructor of FieldInDg_rac that leads to a non trivial proof obligation is FieldInDg_rac_dynamic. After some unfolding, besides another set of fairly simple goals, we end up in the following proof obligation:

4.6. SECOND REFINEMENT

```
H : Heap.new h p (ObjectObject cn um) = Some (obj, h')
H3 : pivot_loc = Heap.InstanceField pivot_obj pivot_fsig
H4 : Heap.get h pivot_loc = Some (Ref field_obj)
─────────────────────────────────────────────────────────
Heap.get h' pivot_loc = Some (Ref field_obj)
```

Listing 4.30: Proof excerpt

Hypothesis H is the premise of the original goal, the other hypotheses originate in premises of the definition of direct_FieldInDg_dynamic. The goal essentially reads as "If we allocate a new object in the heap, the value of field pivot_loc doesn't change. It is pretty obvious, but we do not have the information in any hypothesis that obj and pivot_obj are not equal, that is why our proof is a bit more indirect as one might think.

We first show pivot_obj ≠ obj. A non-equality a ≠ b can be simplified to a = b → False. Thus, after introduction, we get pivot_obj = obj as additional hypothesis and need to prove False.

```
H : Heap.new h p (Heap.ObjectObject c u) = Some (obj, h')
H3 : pivot_loc = Heap.InstanceField pivot_obj pivot_fsig
H4 : Heap.get h pivot_loc = Some (Ref field_obj)
H11 : pivot_obj = obj
─────────────────────────────────────────────────────────
False
```

Listing 4.31: Proof excerpt

We need to find a contradiction in the hypotheses to prove False. Indeed, we can find such a contradiction. On the one hand, we know from the heap model, that the newly created object obj cannot be allocated in heap h. On the other hand, we state in H4 that reading the field pivot_loc, yields a value. Thus, the field's object is obviously allocated in h, and according to H11, that object is obj.

With the information that pivot_obj ≠ obj, we can basically finish the proof by applying an axiom from the heap model. The axiom states: If we allocate object obj, the value of any field from any object except for obj doesn't change. □

Lemma 4.8. *If field* f *is in data group* dg *without using any pivots from the set* excluded ∪ {pivot}, *then* f *is also in* dg *if the set of excluded pivots is just* excluded.

```
1  Lemma FieldInDg_rac_pivots_1:
2    ∀ p h pivot excluded f dg,
3      FieldInDg_rac p h (excluded ∪ {pivot}) f dg →
```

155

```
4    FieldInDg_rac p h excluded f dg.
```

Listing 4.32: Lemma FieldInDg_rac_pivots_1

Proof. By structural induction over the premise without any non-trivial goals. □

Lemma 4.9. *If a field* f *is in data group* dg *in the presence of the excluded pivots* excluded, *and if* f *is not any more in* dg *if we add* pivot *to that set of excluded pivots, then there exists a path from* f *to some* dg1 *via* pivot *to some* dg' *to* dg.

```
1  Lemma FieldInDg_rac_pivots_2:
2    ∀ p h f dg excluded pivot,
3    FieldInDg_rac p h excluded f dg →
4    ¬ FieldInDg_rac p h (excluded ∪ {pivot}) f dg →
5    ∃ dg1,
6      FieldInDg_rac p h (excluded ∪ {pivot}) f dg1 ∧
7      ∃ dg',
8        direct_FieldInDg_dynamic p h dg1 dg' pivot ∧
9        FieldInDg_rac p h excluded dg' dg.
```

Listing 4.33: Lemma FieldInDg_rac_pivots_2

Proof. We prove the lemma by structural induction over the first premise. In any of the three base cases of FieldInDg_rac, it's easy to find the right witnesses for dg1 and dg. The challenging case is if f is not directly contained in dg, but transitively. We get the following goal.

```
pivots' := pivots ∪ {pivot}
H  : FieldInDg_rac p h pivots dg' dg
H1 : FieldInDg_rac p h pivots f dg'
H0 : ¬ FieldInDg_rac p h pivots' f dg
IHFieldInDg_rac1 : ¬ FieldInDg_rac p h pivots' dg' dg → ...
IHFieldInDg_rac2 : ¬ FieldInDg_rac p h pivots' f dg' → ...

∃ dg1 : Location,
FieldInDg_rac p h pivots' f dg1
∧ (∃ dg2 : Location,
    direct_FieldInDg_dynamic p h dg1 dg2 pivot
    ∧ FieldInDg_rac p h pivots dg2 dg)
```

Listing 4.34: Proof excerpt

By applying the step case FieldInDg_rac_step of the inductive definition FieldInDg_rac, we divide the path from f to dg into two paths, one from f to some data group dg' and one from dg' to dg. The field pivot must be in either of the two paths, otherwise we contradict H0. Thus, either the premise of the first or the second induction hypothesis holds. From the respective hypothesis, we get witnesses for both dg1 and dg2.

If we apply the first induction hypothesis, we still need to prove FieldInDg_rac p h pivots' f dg1. From the induction hypothesis, we get FieldInDg_rac p h pivots' dg' dg1. From the case split, we get that pivot is (only) in the path between dg' and dg, thus we know FieldInDg_rac p h pivots' f dg', thus, by applying the step rule, we can prove the goal.

If we apply the second induction hypothesis, we need to prove FieldInDg_rac p h pivots dg2 dg. From the induction hypothesis, we get FieldInDg_rac p h pivots dg2 dg', from H we get the second part of the path. Again, we can apply the step rule to prove the goal. □

Basic Facts about UnfoldDatagroups_rac

Lemma 4.10. *If the set of excluded sets is empty,* UnfoldDatagroups_rac *is equivalent to* UnfoldDatagroups.

```
Lemma UnfoldDatagroups_rac_1:
∀ p h dgs f,
f ∈ (UnfoldDatagroups p h dgs)
↔
f ∈ (UnfoldDatagroups_rac p h ∅ dgs).
```

Proof. By applying the axioms that define the two functions UnfoldDatagroups and UnfoldDatagroups_rac and by lemma 4.6. □

The outcome of unfolding data groups in S_{rac2} depends on three inputs: The heap, the excluded pivots, and of course the set of assignable locations that we want to unfold.

We defined in S_{sem} that an assignable clause is evaluated (including unfolding of data groups) in the pre state of the method. To achieve this, we access the pre-heap in S_{rac1} to unfold the data groups when necessary. Now, we do not have the pre-heap any more, but only the current heap, which can be different for each application of UnfoldDatagroups_rac. Thus, we need to define, under which circumstances the unfolding of data groups leads to the same set of locations.

First, while keeping the excluded pivots and the set of assignable locations fixed, we define which heaps we can consider equivalent for unfolding data groups. The predicate in listing 4.35 holds if all pivot fields that are not contained in the set of excluded pivots have the same value in the two heaps. Any other element in the heap can change arbitrarily.

```
Definition EquivAssignableHeap (p:Program) (h h':Heap.t) (excluded:LocSet.t): Prop :=
  ∀ loc,
    PivotField p loc →
    loc ∉ excluded →
    Heap.get h loc = Heap.get h' loc.
```

Listing 4.35: Equivalent Heaps for unfolding data groups

We prove the validity of our assessment of equivalent heaps by the following lemma.

Lemma 4.11. *If two heaps are equivalent according to* EquivAssignableHeap, *unfolding the same assignable clauses in both heaps yields equal sets.*

```
Lemma UnfoldDatagroups_rac_2:
  ∀ p h h' excluded assignables,
    EquivAssignableHeap p h h' excluded →
    UnfoldDatagroups_rac p h excluded assignables [=]
    UnfoldDatagroups_rac p h' excluded assignables.
```

Proof. By unfolding the definitions, applying UnfoldDatagroups_rac_def and discharging some trivial goals, we get to the essence of this lemma:

```
H : ∀ loc : Location,
      PivotField p loc →
      loc ∉ excluded →
      Heap.get h loc = Heap.get h' loc
H1 : FieldInDg_rac p h excluded f dg
―――――――――――――――――――――――――――――――
FieldInDg_rac p h' excluded f dg
```

Listing 4.36: Proof excerpt

This proof obligation shows only the "→" direction of the set-equality. We perform an induction on the structure of hypothesis H1. The only constructor of FieldInDg_rac that deals with the heap is FieldInDg_rac_dynamic. After unfolding of H1 in this case, We can instantiate the variable loc in H by the pivot specified by direct_FieldInDg_dynamic, see s listing 4.29 on page 153. We apply the same constructor to the goal, with the appropriate variables, and get the following goal.

```
H : PivotField p pivot_loc →
    pivot_loc ∉ pivots →
    Heap.get h pivot_loc = Heap.get h' pivot_loc
```

4.6. SECOND REFINEMENT

```
(* from FieldInDg_rac_dynamic *)
H1 : pivot_loc ∉ pivots
(* from unfolding of direct_FieldInDg_dynamic *)
H3 : pivot_loc = Heap.InstanceField pivot_obj pivot_fsig
H4 : Heap.get h pivot_loc = Some (Ref field_obj)
H5 : findField p pivot_fsig = Some pivot_f
H6 : dg ∈ (FIELD.dataGroups pivot_f)
H7 : DATA_GROUP.isDynamic dg = true
...
─────────────────────────────────────────────────────────
Heap.get h' pivot_loc = Some (Ref field_obj)
```

Listing 4.37: Proof excerpt

The goal is nearly identical to H4, except for the different heap variable. Hypothesis H would help, if we can proof its premises. The premises state that predicate PivotField needs to hold for pivot_loc, and that the location is not in the set of excluded pivots. Listing 4.38 shows the definition of PivotField. In the current context, the predicate obviously holds, as all its premises are hypotheses in the goal. We also know from H6 that pivot_loc is not in excluded. Thus, we can finish the proof by applying H. □

```
1  Inductive PivotField (p : Program) (loc : Location) : Prop :=
2  | PivotField_def : ∀ fsig obj f dg,
3      loc = Heap.InstanceField obj fsig →
4      findField p fsig = Some f →
5      dg ∈ (FIELD.dataGroups f) →
6      DATA_GROUP.isDynamic dg = true →
7      PivotField p loc.
```

Listing 4.38: The predicate PivotField

Lemma 4.12. *Allocating a new object in a heap has no influence in unfolding the data groups in an assignable clause.*

```
1  Lemma UnfoldDatagroups_rac_3:
2    ∀ p h h' lt obj pivots assignables,
3    Heap.new h p lt = Some (obj, h') →
4    UnfoldDatagroups_rac p h pivots assignables [=]
5    UnfoldDatagroups_rac p h' pivots assignables.
```

Proof. By unfolding the definitions, applying UnfoldDatagroups_rac_def and lemma 4.7 □

159

4.6.3 Lazy Unfolding of Data Groups

If we change the heap during method execution, we need to check if the resulting heap is still equivalent for a given element in the stack of assignable locations. Otherwise, we need to perform the lazy unfolding for that stack element and pivot.

Listing 4.39 shows the definition SavePreState that performs this task. The function gets the pivot field which will be updated, and an element of the assignable stack. ₃ If the pivot element is already contained in the set of excluded pivots, the pivot has already been changed earlier and the pre-state is already preserved. Nothing needs to be done. Otherwise, ₆ the function retrieves all fields that are directly dynamically contained in a data group via the pivot in question. ₇ It then adds the pivot to the set of excluded pivots, and the retrieved fields to the assignable locations.

```
1  Definition SavePreState (p : Program) (h : Heap.t) (pivot : Location)
2                  ( assignable : LocSet.t * LocSet.t ) : (LocSet.t * LocSet.t) :=
3  if  pivot ∈ (assignable)₁ then
4     assignable
5  else
6     let  fields := AssignablePivotTargets p h pivot assignable in
7     ( assignable )₁ ∪ {pivot}, (assignable)₂ ∪ fields.
```

Listing 4.39: The function SavePreState

Listing 4.40 shows the axiomatization of function AssignablePivotTargets. For a given pivot field and an element of the assignable stack, the function yields the fields that are assignable via a dynamic data group trough the pivot. The axiom is straight-forward: ₄ f is in the result, if ₆ it is directly contained in a data group via pivot and if ₇ that data group is assignable.

```
1  Parameter AssignablePivotTargets: Program →Heap.t → Location → (LocSet.t*LocSet.t)
2                                                               → LocSet.t .
3  Axiom AssignablePivotTargets_def: ∀ p h pivots aset pivot f,
4     f ∈ (AssignablePivotTargets p h pivot ( pivots, aset ))
5     ↔
6     ∃ dg', direct_FieldInDg_dynamic p h f dg' pivot ∧
7     ∃ dg , FieldInDg_rac p h pivots dg' dg ∧ dg ∈ aset .
```

Listing 4.40: The axiomatized function AssignablePivotTargets

We prove a set of lemmas on SavePreState. The first lemma ensures the most important property of SavePreState: It doesn't affect the unfolding of data groups.

4.6. SECOND REFINEMENT

Lemma 4.13. *Saving the pre-state for a pivot field preserves the outcome of unfolding data groups.*

```
Lemma SavePreState_1:
  ∀ p h pivot excluded assignable ,
  let a' := SavePreState p h pivot (excluded, assignable ) in
  UnfoldDatagroups_rac p h excluded assignable [=]
  UnfoldDatagroups_rac p h (a')₁ (a')₁.
```

Proof. Firstly, we perform a case split on pivot ∈ excluded. If the excluded set of pivots already contains pivot, SavePreState yields the unmodified input, and thus the goal is trivially true. If pivot is not contained in excluded we actually have to save the pre-state, and a' is the updated assignable stack element.

After some unfolding of definitions and some simplifications, we get the following goals for the two direction of the set-equality.

"→": If dg is in the set of assignable locations and field f is contained in the data group dg, then there exists a data group dg' in the updated set of assignable locations and f is contained in dg' without using the pivot field pivot.

```
H  : pivot ∉ excluded
H0 : dg ∈ assignable
H1 : FieldInDg_rac p h excluded f dg
─────────────────────────────────────
∃ dg' : LocSet.elt ,
  dg' ∈ assignable ∪ (AssignablePivotTargets p h pivot (excluded, assignable ))
  ∧
  FieldInDg_rac p h (excluded ∪ {pivot}) f dg'
```

Listing 4.41: Proof excerpt

We perform another case split on the question if f is still in dg if we add pivot to excluded. If so, we can use dg as witness for dg'. The ₆ first part of the goal can be proven because of H0, we know that dg is in assignable, so it's certainly in assignable ∪ •. The ₈ second part is trivially true as it is exactly the hypothesis for this case.

Interesting is the case if f is no more in dg if we add pivot to the excluded pivots. In this setting, we can apply lemma 4.9 to get the following goal, after using dg' from H3 as witness for the existential in the goal.

```
H  : pivot ∉ excluded
H0 : dg ∈ assignable
H1 : FieldInDg_rac p h excluded f dg
H3 : FieldInDg_rac p h (excluded ∪ {pivot}) f dg'
```

```
     ∧ (∃ dg'' : Location,
        direct_FieldInDg_dynamic p h dg' dg'' pivot
        ∧ FieldInDg_rac p h excluded dg'' dg)

 dg' ∈ assignable ∪ (AssignablePivotTargets p h pivot (excluded, assignable))
 ∧
 FieldInDg_rac p h (excluded ∪ {pivot}) f dg'
```
Listing 4.42: Proof excerpt

In this case, we do not know if dg' is in the set assignable, but we know for sure from H0 and the second part of 6,7 H3, that it is an assignable pivot target. The second part of the goal is exactly the 4 first part of H3. Hence, we can prove this goal.

"←": The proof backwards is similar but simpler. This time we know that f is assignable in the updated stack element.

```
H0 : dg' ∈ assignable∪(AssignablePivotTargets p h pivot (excluded, assignable))
   ∧
   FieldInDg_rac p h (excluded ∪ {pivot}) f dg'

∃ dg : LocSet.elt,
dg ∈ assignable ∧ FieldInDg_rac p h excluded f dg
```
Listing 4.43: Proof excerpt

If dg' is in the set assignable, we apply lemma 4.8 to 3 H0 and use dg' as witness for the existential. If dg' is an assignable pivot target, we use the definition of AssignablePivotTargets and some unfolding of definitions to end up in the following goal.

```
H  : pivot ∉ excluded
H0 : direct_FieldInDg_dynamic p h dg' dg'' pivot
dg : Location
H2 : FieldInDg_rac p h excluded dg'' dg
H3 : dg ∈ assignable
H1 : FieldInDg_rac p h (excluded ∪ {pivot}) f dg'

FieldInDg_rac p h pivots f dg
```
Listing 4.44: Proof excerpt

We can apply lemma 4.8 in H1. Thus, we define in the hypotheses a path from field f via dg' directly to dg. Applying twice the step rule of FieldInDg_rac and once the rule FieldInDg_rac_dynamic with the information in H, we prove this goal. □

4.6.4 Equivalence Relation on Assignable Clauses

We now look at the bigger picture and define under which circumstances two states express the same assignable locations. Listing 4.45 shows the predicate EquivAssignables and its helper EquivAssignables_ind. The predicate compares the two stack of assignable locations in the supplied states.

If one stack is larger than the other, we 15 truncate the larger stack to the size of the smaller stack before we compare the elements. 10,11 Two equally large stacks of assignable locations are equivalent, if all corresponding stack elements of the two stacks contain the same locations after unfolding.

```
1  Inductive EquivAssignables_ind (p : Program) (h h' : Heap.t)
2                                  (a a' : stack (LocSet.t * LocSet.t)) : Prop :=
3  | EquivAssignables_base :
4      a = [] → a' = [] →
5      EquivAssignables_ind p h h' a a'
6  | EquivAssignables_step :
7      ∀ head tail head' tail ',
8      a = head:: tail → a' = head':: tail ' → | tail | = | tail '| →
9      EquivAssignables_ind p h h' tail tail ' →
10     UnfoldDatagroups_rac p h  (head )₁ (head )₂ [=]
11     UnfoldDatagroups_rac p h' (head')₁ (head')₂ →
12     EquivAssignables_ind p h h' a a'.
13
14 Definition EquivAssignables (p : Program) (st st' : State.t) : Prop :=
15     let (a, a') := level st@fr@assignables st'@fr@assignables in
16     EquivAssignables_ind p st@h st'@h a a'.
```

Listing 4.45: The Relation EquivAssignables.

We define a set of properties on the equivalence relation over stacks assignable locations.

Lemma 4.14. *Performing a lazy unfolding for a pivot* loc *on a stack of assignable locations yields an equivalent stack of assignable locations.*

```
1  Lemma SavePreState_3:
2     ∀ p loc st v,
3     let (a, a') := level st@fr@assignables
4        (map (SavePreState p st @h loc) st@fr@assignables ) in
5     EquivAssignables_ind p st@h (Heap.update st@h loc v) a a'.
```

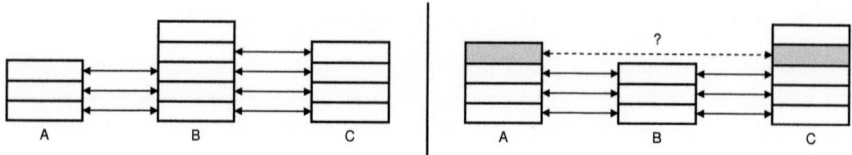

Figure 4.7: The problem with transitivity of EquivAssignables. The situation on the left is ok, but not the situation on the right. Boxes depict stack elements, solid arrows depict checked equivalence between elements. The gray elements are not checked to be equivalent.

Proof. We prove this fact by structural induction on the stack of assignable locations. To prove an individual stack element, we use lemmas 4.13 and 4.11 and quite some massaging of the proof term. □

We prove reflexivity, symmetry and transitivity for EquivAssignables. While the first two properties are straight-forward, we need to tweak a little on the transitivity, as it's not true in general. Because we ignore the additional stack elements if one stack is larger than the other, we do not have transitivity, if the stack in the middle is strictly smaller than one of the other stacks.

Fig. 4.7 shows the situation on the left side where transitivity applies, and the problematic situation on the right side. If the stack in the middle is at least as big as the other two, we can conclude from the equivalence between A and B, and the equivalence between B and C that A and C are equivalent. If, however, the stack in the middle is smaller than the two others, then we can still have a situation in which stack A and B are equivalent, concerning just the bottom three elements, and B and C are equivalent, also concerning only the bottom three elements, but A and C might not be equivalent, as we now check also the element on the fourth position (in gray). Thus, we restrict transitivity to only the situations on the left. This restriction will not pose a problem in the upcoming proofs, as during program execution, we can never encounter a situation as depicted on the right. The transitivity lemma gets a bit cumbersome, though.

Lemma 4.15. *If the stack of assignable location in states* st *and* st' *are equivalent, and the same is true for states* st' *and* st'', *and if the stack in* st' *is not smaller than the other two stacks, then the stacks of assignable locations of states* st *and* st'' *are equivalent.*

```
Lemma EquivAssignables_trans:
∀ p st st' st'',
let x := st@fr@assignables in
let x' := st'@fr@assignables in
let x'' := st''@fr@assignables in
EquivAssignables p st st' →
```

4.6. SECOND REFINEMENT

```
7  EquivAssignables p st' st'' →
8  min |x| |x''| ≤ |x'| →
9  EquivAssignables p st st''.
```

Proof. We split the goal into two subgoals. The smallest stack is either x or x''. Both proofs are obviously very symmetrical, let's say that x is smaller. By some rewriting and application of lemma level_le, see 4.12 on page 138, we get the following proof obligation.

```
H : EquivAssignables_ind p st@h st'@h x (truncate |x| x')
H0 : let (a, a') :=
         match nat_compare |x'| |x''| with
         | Eq ⇒ (x', x'')
         | Lt ⇒ (x', truncate |x'| x'')
         | Gt ⇒ (truncate |x''| x', x'')
         end in
     EquivAssignables_ind p st'@h st''@h a a'
H1 : |x| ≤ |x'|
H2 : |x| ≤ |x''|

EquivAssignables_ind p st@h st''@h x (truncate |x| x'')
```

Listing 4.46: Proof excerpt

We have three cases in H0. In all cases, we truncate a and a' to the size of x. Depending on the case, we get the situation that we truncate a stack twice. For instance, in the case Lt, we truncate x'' first to the size of x' and then to the size of x. As we know from H1 and H2 that x has the smallest size, we can apply lemma truncate_truncate to eliminate the first truncate. In all cases, we end up in a situation where we truncate both attributes x' and x'' of EquivAssignables_ind to the size of x.

H0 : EquivAssignables_ind p st'@h st''@h
        (truncate |x| x') (truncate |x| x'')

Now, we have two hypotheses that assume equivalence between x and x', as well as x' and x'', all truncated to the size of x, and we want to show that x is equivalent to x'', truncated to the size of x. We can prove this goal by structural induction on any of the stacks, in a lengthy, but straight-forward proof. □

4.6.5 The Bisimulation Relation

Listing 4.47 shows the only interesting aspect of the bisimulation relation $\mathcal{R}_{rac2}^{rac1}$ between $\mathcal{S}_{rac1}$ and $\mathcal{S}_{rac2}$. The stacks of assignable locations in $\mathcal{S}_{rac1}$ and $\mathcal{S}_{rac2}$ correspond, if they have the same size and if unfolding the data groups in the elements at the same position in both stacks leads to equal sets.

```
1  Inductive CorrespondingAssignables (p : Program) (h : Heap.t)
2                                     (rac : stack (Heap.t * LocSet.t))
3                                     (rac2: stack (LocSet.t * LocSet.t)):=
4  CorrespondingAssignables_def :
5    length rac = length rac2 →
6    (∀ n,
7      UnfoldDatagroups p (nth n  rac (InitHeap, ∅))₁ (nth n rac (InitHeap, ∅))₂ [=]
8      UnfoldDatagroups_rac p h (nth n  rac2 (∅,∅))₁ (nth n rac2 (∅,∅))₂) →
9    CorrespondingAssignables p h rac rac2.
```

Listing 4.47: The definition CorrespondingAssignables

4.6.6 Implementation of the Frame Conditions Interface

From the five functions in the frame condition interface, we implement four of them different to S_{rac1}. The first is FieldUpdateCheck, see listing 4.48, which uses the predicate FieldInDg_rac which we just introduced. The second is MethodCallAction, see listing 4.49, which stores an empty set of excluded pivots in the top most element of the assignable stack, rather than the pre-heap of the method. The third is MethodReturnAction, which cannot reuse the stack of assignable locations from the caller any more. The fourth is FieldUpdateAction, which performs the lazy unfolding.

```
1  Definition FieldUpdateCheck (p : Program) (loc : Location) (st : State.t) : Prop :=
2  ∀ n,
3    n < |st@fr@assignables| →
4    (∃ m,
5      m ≤ n ∧ m < |st@fr@fresh| ∧ loc ∈ ObjSet2LocSet (nth m st@fr@fresh ∅))
6    ∨
7    ∃ dg, dg ∈ (nth n st@fr@assignables (∅,∅))₁ ∧
8      FieldInDg_rac p st@h (nth n  st@fr@assignables (∅,∅))₂ loc dg.
```

Listing 4.48: The S_{rac2} implementation of FieldUpdateCheck.

```
1  Definition MethodCallAction (p:Program) (c:Class) (m:Method) (st:State.t) : State.t :=
2  let locs := EvalAssignableClause p c m st in
3  st [ fr:=st@fr[ assignables :+ (∅, locs)]].
```

Listing 4.49: The S_{rac2} implementation of MethodCallAction.

Listing 4.50 shows the definition of FieldUpdateAction. ₃ It checks if the field we are about to update is a pivot field. If so, ₄ it performs a lazy unfolding of all data groups defined over pivot. This needs to be performed per stack element, because the situation can be different in each stack element. Here is an example: suppose we have three methods in the call stack, $m'' \hookrightarrow m' \hookrightarrow m$. Let's say we update a field pivot in m'' and in m. For the update in m'', there is only one element on the stack, the assignable locations for m''. We save the pre-state for pivot in the single stack element, representing the assignable clause of m''. Now we call m', and finally m, and again assign a new value to pivot. this time, it should save the pre-state of the stack element for m', and m. However, it should not change the assignable locations for m''. As we have seen on page 160, the definition of SavePreState takes care of not overwriting an already saved pre-state.

```
1  Definition FieldUpdateAction (p : Program) (pivot : Location) (new_loc : Value)
2                                            (st : State.t) : State.t :=
3    if ( isPivot p pivot ) then
4      st [ fr:=st@fr[ assignables := map (SavePreState p st@h pivot) st@fr@assignables ]]
5    else
6      st .
```

Listing 4.50: The $\mathcal{S}_{rac2}$ implementation of FieldUpdateAction.

Listing 4.51 shows the definition of MethodReturnAction in $\mathcal{S}_{rac2}$. In addition to updating the newly allocated objects in the stack of fresh objects, we use the stack of assignable locations form the callee as the stack of assignable locations of the caller, after removing the top most element, which corresponds to the assignable clause of the callee. As we have just seen, updating a pivot field may possibly change all elements of the assignable stack. This is why we need to proceed with the most current stack of assignable locations.

```
1  Definition MethodReturnAction (p:Program) (st_c:State.t) (st:State.t) : State.t :=
2    st_c [ fr:=st@fr[ fresh :∪(peekd st_c@fr@fresh ∅)][assignables:=pop st_c@fr@assignables ]].
```

Listing 4.51: The $\mathcal{S}_{rac2}$ implementation of MethodReturnAction.

4.6.7 Proof of the Second Refinement

We present the proof of the second refinement as follows: firstly, we show for each function of the frame conditions interface which yields a new state, that the stack of assignable locations is equivalent to the stack from the input state. We then prove a theorem that states that performing any possible step in $\mathcal{S}_{rac2}$ preserves the equivalence of stacks of assignable locations. Secondly, we show that the $\mathcal{S}_{rac2}$ implementations of the frame conditions interface preserve correspondence between states from $\mathcal{S}_{rac1}$ and $\mathcal{S}_{rac2}$. Finally, we prove the main theorem for this refinement that states that the semantics $\mathcal{S}_{rac1}$ and $\mathcal{S}_{rac2}$ are in fact bisimilar.

Proof of Preservation of Equivalent Assignable Clauses

Before we can prove that the stacks of assignable locations stay equivalent for any possible step in our semantics, let's think about the size of the stacks. It is a fact that in each step of the semantics, the size of the stack in the input state is equal to the size of the stack in the output state. This may surprise at first, but becomes clear, considering the big-step semantics. The only operation that changes the stack size is the method call step. Upon the call, we increase the stack size by one. In a big step semantics, the step includes returning to the caller after the method execution has terminated. Thus, we remove again the top most element and end up in the same stack size again. We prove this fact in our formalization by mutual induction. With this in mind, let's prove the theorem on equivalent stacks.

Theorem 4.16. Equivalent Stacks of Assignable Clauses

Any possible step of the operational semantics S_{rac2} results in a state, whose stack of assignable locations is equivalent to the stack from the input state.

Proof. We prove the theorem as usual by mutual induction. All the hard work has already been done in the lemmas, we basically need to apply the right lemmas to prove the theorem. We only present the case of method call, all other cases are similar but simpler.

Case Method Call: We are confronted with the following proof obligation. ₂₋₇ The first two hypotheses come from the fact described above that stack sizes are equal at the begin and the end of a step. ₁₀₋₁₇ The hypotheses H4 to H21 are the premises of the method call rule, and ₁₉₋₂₁ the hypotheses H5, H10, and H19 are the induction hypotheses for the steps in H4, H9, and H18.

```
1   (* Hypotheses about the size of stacks *)
2   H  : ∀ e st st' r, OpRac2.ExpressionStep p e st st' r →
3          | st@fr@assignables | = | st'@fr@assignables |
4   H0 : ∀ l st st' r, OpRac2.ListSteps p l st st' r →
5          | st@fr@assignables | = | st'@fr@assignables |
6   H2 : ∀ m b st st' r, OpRac2.BlockStep p m b st st' r →
7          | st@fr@assignables | = | st'@fr@assignables |
8
9   (* Hypotheses from the method call rule *)
10  H4  : OpRac2.ExpressionStep p o st st1 (normal_step_v (Ref this ))
11  H9  : OpRac2.ListSteps p ps st1 st2 psnv
12  H13 : fr_c1 = NewFrame m' (lv2params m' (Ref this :: psv)) st2
13  H14 : st3 = st2 [ fr := fr_c1 ]
14  H15 : MethodCallAction p c' m' st3 = st_c
15  H18 : OpRac2.BlockStep p m' b st_c st_c' normal_step
16  H21 : MethodReturnAction p st_c' st2 = st'
```

4.6. SECOND REFINEMENT

```
17  ...
18  (* Induction hypotheses *)
19  H5 : EquivAssignables p st st1
20  H10 : EquivAssignables p st1 st2
21  H19 : EquivAssignables p st_c st_c'
22  ─────────────────────────────────────
23  EquivAssignables p st st'
```

Listing 4.52: Proof excerpt

We use the transitivity of EquivAssignables (lemma 4.15) to solve the goal. The induction hypotheses are a good starting point, but we need to prove additional equivalences of stacks of assignable locations, to fill the gaps.

We create a new method frame in st2 and evaluate the assignable clause of the method, which results in state st_c. Thus, we can assert EquivAssignables st2 st_c because NewFrame pushes an element onto the assignable stack, leaving the existing content unchanged, and the function MethodCallAction changes only the element on top. Furthermore, we can assert the equivalence between st_c' and st' because MethodReturnAction takes the assignable stack from st_c', removes the top most element and stores the resulting stack in st'.

Now we get the whole chain of equivalent stacks of assignable locations, and we apply the transitivity lemma 4.15 several times to prove the goal. In the process of applying the transitivity lemma, we need to prove for each application of the lemma, that the size of the stack in the middle is not strictly smaller than the other two stacks. We can prove this with hypothesis H, H0, and H2 for the recursive steps, and by unfolding the definitions of the frame condition interface in the other cases. □

Correctness Proof of the Frame Condition Implementation

Lemma 4.17. Correct Field Update Check

The field update checks of the semantics S_{rac1} and S_{rac2} are equivalent for corresponding states.

```
1  Lemma FieldUpdateCheck_Correct:
2    ∀ loc p st_rac1 st_rac2 ,
3    CorrespondingState p st_rac1 st_rac2 →
4    ( Rac1.Assignables.FieldUpdateCheck p loc st_rac1
5    ↔
6      Rac2.Assignables.FieldUpdateCheck p loc st_rac2 ).
```

Proof. By unfolding all involved definitions, we get to the following proof obligation for the forward direction of the proof. The hypotheses H0 to H3 originate in the correspondence relation. H4 and the goal are the unfolded FieldUpdateCheck definitions. H5 is the premise of the goal introduced as hypothesis. We omit to discuss the backwards direction, which is symmetrical.

```
H0 : | st_rac1@fr@assignables | = | st_rac2@fr@assignables |
H1 : ∀ (n:nat),
       UnfoldDatagroups p
         (nth n st_rac1@fr@assignables (InitHeap, ∅))₁
         (nth n st_rac1@fr@assignables (InitHeap, ∅))₂ [=]
       UnfoldDatagroups_rac p st_rac2@h
         (nth n st_rac2@fr@assignables (∅, ∅))₁
         (nth n st_rac2@fr@assignables (∅, ∅))₂
H2 : | st_rac1@fr@fresh | = | st_rac2@fr@fresh |
H3 : ∀ (n : nat) (d : ObjSet.t),
       nth n st_rac1@fr@fresh d [=] nth n st_rac2@fr@fresh d
H4 : ∀ n : nat,
       n < | st_rac1@fr@assignables | →
       (∃ m : nat,
          (m ≤ n ∧ m < |st_rac1@fr@fresh |) ∧
          loc ∈ (ObjSet2LocSet (nth m st_rac1@fr@fresh ∅))) ∨
       (∃ dg : Location,
          dg ∈ (nth n st_rac1@fr@assignables (InitHeap, ∅))₂ ∧
          FieldInDg p (nth n st_rac1@fr@assignables (InitHeap, ∅))₁ loc dg)
n : nat
H5 : n < |st_rac2 @fr @assignables |
───────────────────────────────────────────────
(∃ m : nat,
   (m ≤ n ∧ m < |st_rac2@fr@fresh |) ∧
   loc ∈ ObjSet2LocSet (nth m st_rac2@fr@fresh ∅)) ∨
(∃ dg : Location,
   dg ∈ (nth n st_rac2@fr@assignables (∅, ∅))₂ ∧
   FieldInDg_rac p st_rac2@h (nth n st_rac2@fr@assignables (∅,∅))₁ loc dg)
```

Listing 4.53: Proof excerpt

We take the following route from here. The goal and H4 are already nearly identical. The only difference is the use of different stacks of fresh objects, however, H2 and H3 state that both stacks are equivalent. Furthermore, H4 uses FieldInDg to compute if loc is contained in the data group dg, whereas the goal uses FieldInDg_rac. With the information from H1 and the definition of UnfoldDatagroups and UnfoldDatagroups_rac, we can prove the goal. □

Lemma 4.18. Correct Method Call Action

Starting from corresponding states, applying MethodCallAction *in semantics* S_{rac1} *and* S_{rac2} *leads to corresponding states.*

```
1  Lemma MethodCallAction_Correct:
2    ∀ p c m st_rac1 st_rac1' st_rac2 st_rac2',
3    CorrespondingState p st_rac1 st_rac2 →
4    Rac1.Assignables.MethodCallAction p c m st_rac1 = st_rac1' →
5    Rac2.Assignables.MethodCallAction p c m st_rac2 = st_rac2' →
6    CorrespondingState p st_rac1' st_rac2'.
```

Proof. The only part of the state that is affected by MethodCallAction, is the stack of assignable locations. Thus, the interesting subgoal is the equivalence between stack of assignable locations, after applying MethodCallAction on the states. After some unfolding and simplifications, we get the following proof obligation.

```
...

UnfoldDatagroups p
  ( nth n
    ( replace_top
        (st_rac1@h, EvalAssignableClause p c m st_rac1)
        st_rac1@fr@assignables ) (InitHeap, ∅))₁
  ( nth n
    ( replace_top
        (st_rac1@h, EvalAssignableClause p c m st_rac1)
        st_rac1@fr@assignables ) (InitHeap, ∅))₂
[=]
UnfoldDatagroups_rac p st_rac2@h
  ( nth n
    ( replace_top
        (∅, EvalAssignableClause p c m st_rac2)
        st_rac2@fr@assignables ) (∅, ∅))₁
  ( nth n
    ( replace_top
        (∅, EvalAssignableClause p c m st_rac2)
        st_rac2@fr@assignables ) (∅, ∅))₂
```

Listing 4.54: Proof excerpt

The proof follows the usual pattern. We perform a case split on n. If n = 0, we get the following goal:

```
...
─────────────────────────────────────────
UnfoldDatagroups p st_rac1@h
  (EvalAssignableClause p c m st_rac1)
[=]
UnfoldDatagroups_rac p st_rac2@h ∅
  (EvalAssignableClause p c m st_rac2)
```

Listing 4.55: Proof excerpt

As we know from the correspondence between st_rac1 and st_rac2, both heaps are the same. Furthermore, the sets yielded by EvalAssignableClause are equal in corresponding states. By apply lemma 4.10 we can solve the goal.

If $n > 0$, we can directly use the correspondence relation of st_rac1 and st_rac2 to prove the goal, as only the first elements of the stacks get changed by MethodCallAction. □

Lemma 4.19. Correct Method Return Action

If the input states to the S_{rac1} and S_{rac2} implementation of MethodReturnActions correspond, and if the stack of assignable locations of the state yielded by the callee in S_{rac2} is equivalent to the stack from the caller but contains one more element, then the states yielded by both implementations correspond.

```
1  Lemma MethodReturnAction_Correct:
2    ∀ p st_rac1 st_rac1_c st_rac1_c' st_rac2 st_rac2_c st_rac2_c',
3    CorrespondingState p st_rac1_c st_rac2_c →
4    CorrespondingState p st_rac1 st_rac2 →
5    Rac1.Assignables.MethodReturnAction p st_rac1_c st_rac1 = st_rac1_c' →
6    Rac2.Assignables.MethodReturnAction p st_rac2_c st_rac2 = st_rac2_c' →
7    EquivAssignables p st_rac2 st_rac2_c →
8    | st_rac2@fr@assignables | + 1 = | st_rac2_c@fr@assignables | →
9    CorrespondingState p st_rac1_c' st_rac2_c'.
```

Proof. Again, we only focus on the correspondence of the stack of assignable locations. We get the following goal to prove, after some massaging. The left hand side of the set equivalence originates in the unfolding of the S_{rac1} implementation of MethodReturnAction, whereas the right hand side of the equivalence originates in the S_{rac2} implementation.

```
...
─────────────────────────────────────────
UnfoldDatagroups p
  (nth n st_rac1@fr@assignables (InitHeap, ∅))₁
```

```
(nth n st_rac1@fr@assignables (InitHeap, ∅))₂
[=]
UnfoldDatagroups_rac p st_rac2_c@h
  (nth n (pop st_rac2_c@fr@assignables ) (∅, ∅))₁
  (nth n (pop st_rac2_c@fr@assignables ) (∅, ∅))₂
```

Listing 4.56: Proof excerpt

From the correspondence relation between st_rac1 and st_rac2, we learn that we can replace st_rac1@fr@assignables by st_rac2@fr@assignables on the left side of the equivalence. We need to prove the equivalence of two stacks of assignable locations in $\mathcal{S}_{rac2}$, for which we assumed equivalence in a premise of the lemma. Furthermore, we assume in the lemma that st_rac2_c contains one more element, which is the one we pop from the stack on the right hand side of the equivalence. Thus, by unfolding the definition of EquivAssignables and applying lemma truncate_pop, we can prove that the two resulting sets are indeed equivalent. □

Lemma 4.20. Correct Field Update Action

The $\mathcal{S}_{rac2}$ implementation of FieldUpdateAction preserves the correspondence relation between states, after the field has been updated with the new value.

```
1  Lemma FieldUpdateAction_Correct:
2    ∀ p loc st_rac1 v st_rac1 ' st_rac2 st_rac2 ',
3    CorrespondingState p st_rac1 st_rac2 →
4    Rac1.Assignables.FieldUpdateAction p loc v st_rac1 = st_rac1' →
5    Rac2.Assingables.FieldUpdateAction p loc v st_rac2 = st_rac2' →
6    CorrespondingState p
7      st_rac1 '[h:=Heap.update st_rac1@h loc v]
8      st_rac2 '[h:=Heap.update st_rac2@h loc v].
```

Proof. The implementation of FieldUpdateAction in $\mathcal{S}_{rac2}$ distinguishes between loc being a pivot or not. If loc is a pivot, we get the following proof obligation, which states the correspondence of the stacks of assignable locations in both resulting states

```
UnfoldDatagroups p
  (nth n st_rac1@fr@assignables (InitHeap, ∅))₁
  (nth n st_rac1@fr@assignables (InitHeap, ∅))₂
[=]
UnfoldDatagroups_rac p (Heap.update st_rac2@h loc v)
  (nth n (map (SavePreState p st_rac2@h loc) st_rac2@fr@assignables ) (∅, ∅))₁
```

```
(nth n (map (SavePreState p st_rac2@h loc) st_rac2@fr@assignables ) (∅, ∅))₂
```
Listing 4.57: Proof excerpt

We can prove equivalence between each set in the stack, and thus conclude that the intersection over the stack of sets is equivalent. Lemma 4.13 states that saving the pre-state for a pivot field does not affect the unfolding of a set of locations. Furthermore, lemma 4.11 states that we can change the value of loc without affecting the unfolding, because loc has been put into the set of excluded pivots by SavePreState.

If loc is not a pivot, changing its value does not affect the unfolding of data groups. We can directly apply lemma 4.11. □

Proof of the Bisimulation Property

Theorem 4.21. Correctness of the Second Refinement

If one starts in a state st_{rac1} and performs a step in the semantics to get state st'_{rac1}, and given a state st_{rac2} that corresponds to state st_{rac1}, then there exists a state st'_{rac2} that one gets by applying the same step in the runtime assertion checker and that corresponds to st'_{rac1}.

Moreover, if one can perform a step in the runtime assertion checker from st_{rac2} to st'_{rac2}, and st_{rac1} corresponds to st_{rac2}, then there exists a corresponding st'_{rac1} which one gets by performing the same step in the semantics:

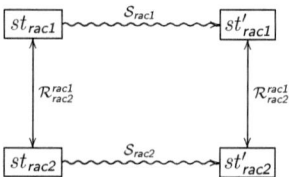

Proof. The proof of the main theorem of the second refinement follows the same reasoning than the proof of theorem 4.5. Thus, we do not show the proof again in details. We perform a mutual induction on the the four inductive definitions of steps. We use the induction hypotheses to reason about the mutual applications of steps, and the correctness lemmas of the S_{rac2} implementation of the frame condition interface to reason about the application of these functions. □

4.7 Third Refinement

"THERE IS NO MAGIC ANY MORE."

In the third refinement, our goal is to concretize the dynamic data group inclusion by introducing back-links as part of the program state. By building up data structures using these back-links, we can replace the axiomatically defined functions UnfoldDatagroups_rac and AssignablePivotTargets with concrete implementations. Effectively, we eliminate the last bit of "magic" in the formalization of the runtime assertion checker.

This refinement defines the semantics $\mathcal{S}_{rac3}$, which is reasonably close to the implementation of the RAC for assignable clauses in OpenJML. The algorithms are identical and the auxiliary data structures in the program state can directly be mapped to Java constructs used in the RAC implementation. From $\mathcal{S}_{rac3}$ we can conclude that the algorithm presented in chapter 3 is correct, that is, checks the frame conditions as described in the semantics.

There is one thing that might deserve another refinement: caches. For most data structures and applications, caches improve the performance of the checker dramatically. However, the logic behind caches is reasonably simple: for each set of assignable locations in the stack, we store the set of locations that have been determined to be assignable. As assignable locations do not change over time for a given stack element, caches do not need to be cleverly updated or invalidated. Thus, we can safely assume that introducing caches doesn't change the behavior of the RAC.

4.7.1 Additions to the Program State

We add a global auxiliary data structure to store back-links. All other data structures stay unchanged compared to $\mathcal{S}_{rac2}$. Fig. 4.8 presents the complete picture of the data structures used to model the state of the runtime assertion checker for assignable clauses.

Listing 4.58 introduces the data structures to store back-links in the program state. We declare two dictionaries: LocDict is a dictionary from a location to a set of locations, and Backlinks is a dictionary from locations to a LocDict dictionary. The key of an entry in Backlinks refers to a field, the keys in LocDict are pivots, and the set of locations in LocDict refer to the data groups that contain the field via the corresponding pivot. Thus, for each field that is dynamically contained in a data group, the back-links data structure reveals which are these data groups and via which pivot field they are making the connection.

```
1  Declare Module LocDict: DICT
2    with Definition Key := (* pivot *) Location
3    with Definition Val := (* data groups *) LocSet.t.
4
5  Declare Module Backlinks : DICT
6    with Definition Key := (* field *) Location
7    with Definition Val := LocDict.t.
8
9  Module Adds <: ADDS.
10   Record t_rec : Type := make {
11     backlinks : Backlinks.t
```

CHAPTER 4. CORRECTNESS PROOF OF THE RAC FOR ASSIGNABLE CLAUSES

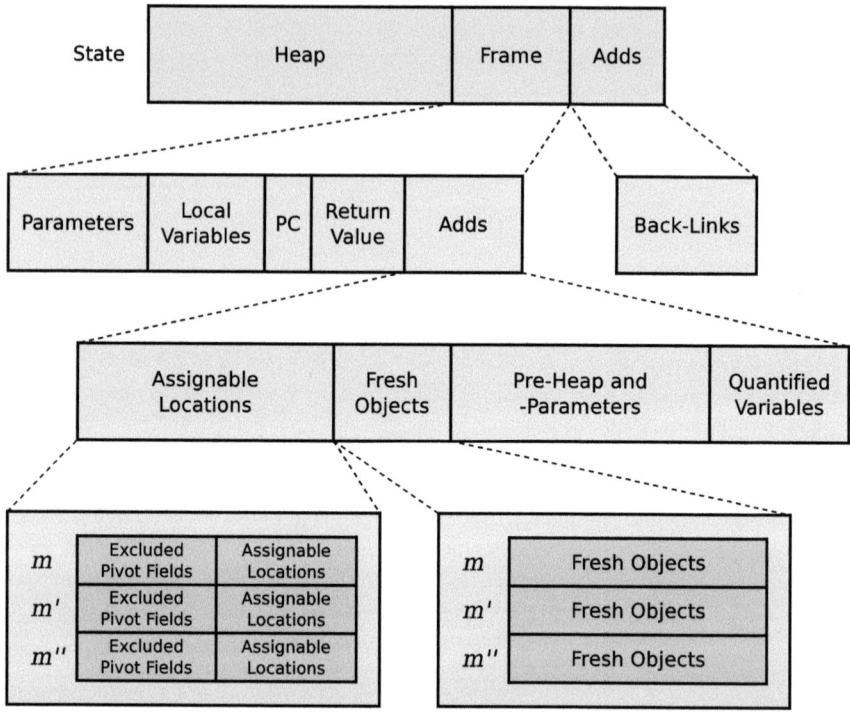

Figure 4.8: The complete state data structure in $\mathcal{S}_{rac3}$, in the situation $m'' \hookrightarrow m' \hookrightarrow m$. We add a back-link dictionary as global auxiliary data structure.

```
12      }.
13    Definition t := t_rec .
14    End Adds.
```

Listing 4.58: The data structure for back-links, and the implementation of the module Adds in type State.t

For easier handling, we introduce three functions set_backlink, remove_ backlink, and get_backlinks. The functions take care of special cases which an application of the data structure should not care about: if we set the first back-link for a field, the dictionary Backlinks doesn't contain an entry for this field yet, and we need to create a LocSet.t dictionary, before we can store the back-link. Similarly, the implementation for removing back-links from the data structure depends on the presence of a LocSet.t for the given field. get_backlinks yields the LocDict dictionary for a given field f, if it is present, or an empty dictionary otherwise.

Listing 4.59 shows the predicates CorrectBacklink and CorrectBacklinks. The former holds if ₄ there exists a back-link from f to dg via pivot if and only if ₂ f is directly contained in the data group dg via pivot. The latter property quantifies over all fields, pivots, and data groups and therefore relates the whole auxiliary data structure for back-links to the actual situation in the heap.

```
1   Definition CorrectBacklink (p:Program) (st:State.t) (f dg pivot:Location) : Prop :=
2   direct_FieldInDg_dynamic p st@h f dg pivot
3   ↔
4   ∃ dgs,  LocDict.get (Backlinks_get st@bl f) pivot = Some dgs ∧ dg ∈ dgs.
5
6
7   Definition CorrectBacklinks (p : Program) (st : State.t) : Prop :=
8   ∀ f dg pivot , CorrectBacklink p st f dg pivot.
```

Listing 4.59: Correctness condition for back-links

4.7.2 Implementation of Data Group Relations

Prior to this refinement, we provided two inductive predicates for static and dynamic data group inclusion, direct_FieldInDg_static and direct_FieldInDg_ dynamic, respectively, see the paragraph on data group membership on page 94. Now, we implement several functions to cover different aspects of static and dynamic data group membership and prove their correctness. We present two dynamic data group membership aspects and omit static data group inclusion in this description, as they are very similar, but simpler.

The first function, DynamicDGs is shown in 4.60. The function yields a list of data groups that contain a given field via a given pivot.

As opposed to the predicate direct_FieldInDg_dynamic, DynamicDGs just takes the signature of the target field. The pivot field together with the signature of the target field is all it needs to compute the list of data groups. The reason why we use a field in the predicate is because the predicate is more general than this function.

Let's have a closer look at the definition. ₄ If pivot is an instance field, we ₇,₈ extract the dynamic data groups and ₉₋₁₇ keep the data group declarations that mention f_sig as pivot target. We use ₁₄ the decidable equality FsigDec.eq_dec to compare field signatures. Finally, ₁₈,₁₉ we retrieve the lists of data groups from the remaining data group declarations and chain them together.

```
Definition DynamicDGs (p : Program) (f_fsig : FieldSignature) (pivot : Location) :
                                                               list Location :=
  match pivot with
  | Heap.InstanceField pivot_obj pivot_fsig ⇒
    match findField p pivot_fsig with
    | Some pivot_f ⇒
      let dgs_dyn := filter (fun dg ⇒ DATA_GROUP.isDynamic dg)
                            (FIELD.dataGroups pivot_f) in
      let dgs_f_target :=
        filter
          (fun dg ⇒
            match DATA_GROUP.pivotTarget dg with
            | Some (FieldDg fsig) ⇒
              if FsigDec.eq_dec fsig f_fsig then true else false
            | _ ⇒ false
            end)
          dgs_dyn in
      let dg_fsig := flat_map DATA_GROUP.dataGroups dgs_f_target in
      map (Heap.InstanceField pivot_obj) dg_fsig
    | _ ⇒ []
    end
  | _ ⇒ []
  end.
```

Listing 4.60: An implementation of a dynamic data group lookup

Beside the more general applications, we can see why we prefer the inductive definition direct_FieldInDg_dynamic over such functions: it's a bit of a pain to read and understand the meaning of such a function compared to the simple and straight-forward inductive predicate. However, we now actually *built* a function instead of just describing its behavior. In order to be useful in proofs, and to settle our doubts about this implementation, we show that the function DynamicDGs behaves as specified by direct_FieldInDg_dynamic.

Lemma 4.22. *The list of locations yielded by* DynamicDGs p fsig pivot *contains exactly the data groups that contain the field with signature* fsig *via* pivot.

---
1 **Lemma** DynamicDGs_Correct:
2 ∀ p h f_obj f_fsig pivot dg,
3 Heap.get h pivot = Some (Ref f_obj) →
4 dg ∈ (DynamicDGs p f_fsig pivot)
5 ↔
6 direct_FieldInDg_dynamic p h (Heap.InstanceField f_obj f_fsig) dg pivot.

Proof. "→": In this direction, we assume the function DynamicDGs with arbitrary inputs and need to show that direct_FieldInDg_dynamic holds. We introduce a case split on each term over which the function performs a matching. If we pick invalid cases, DynamicDGs yields the empty list, and thus, we get a hypothesis dg ∈ [] which is obviously false and the case is trivially discharged. In valid cases, we get an additional hypothesis from the case distinction which we use to prove the goal. For functions on lists such as map and filter , the standard library provides the lemmas which, applied in the right way, allows us to discharge the proof obligation.

"←": If we assume the predicate direct_FieldInDg_dynamic and need to show that the function yields the right list of data groups, we unfold the predicate and get a set of hypotheses that describe the dynamic data group membership. We eliminate the pattern matchings in the goal by applying the corresponding hypothesis which describes what cases can occur. For instance, the ₃ pattern matching on variable pivot can be removed in the goal as we get a hypothesis from the predicate which states that pivot is an instance field. The remainder of the proof is straight-forward by applying standard library lemmas for the list manipulation functions. □

We define a second function whose behavior can be described with the predicate direct_FieldInDg_dynamic. The function PivotTargets : Program → *(∗ pivot ∗)* Location → list FieldSignature yields a list of field signatures that are targets of dynamic data group definition for a given pivot field. We prove the following lemma about this function.

Lemma 4.23. *The list of field signatures yielded by* PivotTargets p pivot *contains exactly the fields that are dynamically contained in a data group via pivot.*

---
1 **Lemma** PivotTargets_Correct:
2 ∀ p h f_fsig f_obj pivot,
3 Heap.get h pivot = Some (Ref f_obj) →
4 In f_fsig (PivotTargets p pivot)

CHAPTER 4. CORRECTNESS PROOF OF THE RAC FOR ASSIGNABLE CLAUSES

```
5       ↔
6       ∃ dg, direct_FieldInDg_dynamic p h (Heap.InstanceField f_obj  f_fsig ) dg pivot .
```

Proof. We prove this lemma similar to the proof of DynamicDGs_Correct. □

4.7.3   Operations on Back-Links

We define two high level operations on back-links, see listings 4.61 and 4.62. The first is SetBacklinks. It updates the back-link dictionary for a given pivot field. Firstly, the implementation ₉ retrieves a list of all field signatures that are directly contained in a data group via the pivot field. For each field ₆ composed from the field signature in the list and the object pivot points to, SetBacklinks ₆,₇ adds an entry to the LocDict of the back-link data structure with key pivot and the set of data groups that directly contain f via pivot as value.

```
1   Definition SetBacklinks (p:Program) (pivot:Location) (v:Value) (bl:Backlinks.t) :
2                                                                   Backlinks.t :=
3   match v with
4   | Ref obj ⇒
5       fold_right
6         (fun f bl' ⇒ set_backlink bl' (Heap.InstanceField obj f) pivot
7                                       ( list2LocSet  (DynamicDGs p f pivot)))
8         bl
9         (PivotTargets p pivot)
10
11  | _ ⇒ bl
12  end.
```

Listing 4.61: The operation SetBacklinks

The second operation is RemoveBacklinks. It deletes all back-links from the data structure that are defined over a given field pivot. Similar to the latter operation, RemoveBacklinks ₈ retrieves a list of all field signatures that are pivot targets. For each field composed of the object referred by pivot and a field signature from the list, the function ₆ removes all data groups that use pivot by removing the entry with key pivot from the LocDict dictionary for the pivot field.

```
1   Definition RemoveBacklinks (p : Program) (pivot : Location) (st : State.t) :
2                                                                   Backlinks.t :=
3   match Heap.get st@h pivot with
4   | Some (Ref obj) ⇒
```

```
5     fold_right
6       (fun f bl ⇒ remove_backlink bl (Heap.InstanceField obj f) pivot)
7       st@bl
8       (PivotTargets p pivot)
9     | _ ⇒ st@bl
10    end.
```

Listing 4.62: The operation RemoveBacklinks

The following lemma states the desired behavior of the two operations. It relies on a couple of other lemmas that we omit in this description.

Lemma 4.24. Correctness of Back-Link Operations

Given that loc *refers to a pivot field and* v *a value that can be assigned to* loc. *If the back-link data structure correctly reflects the situation in the heap before the update, removing all back-links that use* loc *as pivot and adding new back-links for all pivot targets of* loc *in object* v *leads to a back-link data structure that correctly reflects the heap in which we update* loc *by* v.

```
1   Lemma SetRemoveBacklinks_Correct:
2     ∀ p loc st st' f dg pivot v cn um loc_obj loc_fsig ,
3     (* Specification of 'loc' *)
4     PivotField p loc →
5     loc = Heap.InstanceField loc_obj loc_fsig →
6     Heap.typeof st@h loc_obj = Some (Heap.ObjectObject cn um) →
7     defined_field p cn loc_fsig →
8     assign_compatible p st@h v (FIELDSIGNATURE.type (loc_fsig)₂) →
9     (* Correctness of back−link update *)
10    st' = st[h := (Heap.update st@h loc v)]
11         [bl := (SetBacklinks p loc v (RemoveBacklinks p loc st ))] →
12    CorrectBacklink p st f dg pivot →
13    CorrectBacklink p st' f dg pivot.
```

Proof. Upon introduction of all quantified variables and the premises as hypotheses, we unfold CorrectBacklink and are confronted with a full implication.

"→": If f is directly contained in data group dg via the field pivot in the updated heap, there exists a back-link from f to dg via pivot in the updated back-link data structure:

```
... (* Other Hypotheses from premises *)
H4 : direct_FieldInDg_dynamic p st@h f dg pivot ↔
       (∃ dgs : LocDict.Val,
         LocDict.get ( get_backlinks st@bl f) pivot = Some dgs ∧dg ∈ dgs)
```

H5 : direct_FieldInDg_dynamic p (Heap.update st@h loc v) f dg pivot

∃ dgs : LocDict.Val,
  LocDict.get
    (get_backlinks (SetBacklinks p loc v (RemoveBacklinks p loc st)) f)
    pivot = Some dgs ∧dg ∈ dgs

Listing 4.63: Proof excerpt

Hypothesis H4 states that the back-link data structure is correct before update.

We distinguish between the cases loc = pivot and loc ≠ pivot.

Case loc = pivot: We can guess the correct witness for the existentially quantified variable dgs. We use list2LocSet (DynamicDGs p field_fsig pivot), where field_fsig is the field signature of f. For this witness, we need to be able to prove the right part of the conjunction, which states that dg is in dgs. We can deduce this from H5 and lemma 4.22. Furthermore, as loc is pivot we know from lemma Heap.get_update_same and the definition of direct_FieldInDg_dynamic, that v must be the object in which f is defined.

We use lemma 4.23 to introduce the list of pivot targets for pivot. By structural induction on the list, we prove the left hand side of the conjunction, that is, that we create the correct back-link for all pivot targets of loc.

The base case is trivial as the assumption that the pivot targets are empty contradicts with H5. In the step case, we distinguish the cases if field_fsig is the field signature added in the inductive step or if it is already in the tail of the list of pivot targets.

In the earlier case, we update exactly these elements in the back-link data structure that we read subsequently. Thus, we apply the lemma get_update_same for both involved dictionaries: Backlink and LocDec. In the latter case, we update different elements in the back-link data structure than we read. Thus, we can apply the lemma get_update_old from the dictionary formalization, which removes the update operation. Now we can apply the induction hypothesis.

Case loc ≠ pivot: Using lemma Heap.get_update_old, we can remove the update on the heap in H5 as we are reading a different location than we update. Thus, we know that the right hand side of the full implication in H4 holds. In two lemmas that we omit in this description, we prove that we can remove the application of SetBacklinks in the current goal, as we do not read the same elements from the back-link data structure than we update. For the same reasons, we can remove the application of RemoveBacklinks from the goal. Thus, the goal states the same than the right hand side of H4, which holds.

"←": If there exists a back-link from f via pivot to dg in the updated back-link data structure, f is directly contained in data group dg via pivot:

H4 : direct_FieldInDg_dynamic p st@h f dg pivot ↔
    (∃ dgs : LocDict.Val,
      LocDict.get (get_backlinks st@bl f) pivot = Some dgs ∧dg ∈ dgs)

```
H5 : ∃ dgs : LocDict.Val,
     LocDict.get
       ( get_backlinks (SetBacklinks p loc v (RemoveBacklinks p loc st)) f)
     pivot = Some dgs ∧dg ∈ dgs
```

```
direct_FieldInDg_dynamic p (Heap.update st@h loc v) f dg pivot
```

Listing 4.64: Proof excerpt

Case loc = pivot: We either assign `null` to loc, an object, or an array. In the first case, SetBacklinks doesn't update the back-links and we can remove the application of SetBacklinks in H5. We now claim in hypothesis H5 that we retrieve some set of data groups for field f via pivot, although we just removed all back-links via pivot loc, which is in this case pivot. In a separate lemma, we show that this can never holds. In the second and third case, that is, if we update loc with a reference type, we distinguish between the cases that f is defined in that reference type or not.

If f is a field of the reference type assigned to loc, we need to perform another case split on the question if the signature of f is in the list of pivot targets or not. If yes, we solve the goal by structural induction on that list. Similar to the forward direction, the base case is trivial, and we perform another case split in the step case to distinguish if the signature of f has been added in the induction step or if it was already in the tail of the list. We solve both cases analogously to the forward direction.

If f is not a pivot target, we can remove of SetBacklinks and RemoveBacklinks from H5 as they can not influence the non-existent back-links on f. We can use the rewritten H5 to show that the left hand side of H4 holds, which is not possible if f is not a pivot target.

If f is not defined in the reference type that gets assigned to loc, we again know that updating the back-link data structure for pivot loc cannot influence the back-links on f. *Case* loc ≠ pivot: We prove this case analogously to this case in the forward direction. □

4.7.4 A Tree of Back-Links

As introduced in section 3.5, the runtime assertion checker builds a tree of data groups using the back-links in the process of checking `assignable` clauses. Listing 4.65 shows the inductive definition of that tree. A node in the tree contains a location l and a (possibly empty) list of children dgs, and each child is again a tree. The tree allows us to write constructive implementations of operations that we had to define axiomatically in the last refinement.

```
1  Inductive DGTree := DGNode (l : Location) (dgs: list DGTree).
```

Listing 4.65: The data type of the tree of back-links

As natural as this definition is, as useless the automatically generated induction principle used by the tactics induction is. Thus, we need to define our own induction principle "by hand". The following tutorial describes the problem and a decent solution.

─────────── A MADE-TO-MEASURE COQ TUTORIAL ───────────

Part 14   Creating Custom Induction Principle

In the inductive definition above, we define the type DGTree, which has a mutual dependency with type list DGTree. When generating the induction principle for DGTree, Coq doesn't realize the mutual induction and produces the following principle:

```
1  DGTree_ind
2      : ∀ P : DGTree →Prop,
3        (∀ (l : Location) (dgs : list DGTree),
4           P (DGNode am dgs)) →
5        ∀ t : DGTree, P t
```

It reads as follows: ₅ In order to prove a property P for a tree t, we need to prove that ₃,₄ the property holds for a node with an arbitrary location l and an arbitrary list of children dgs.

To get the idea how the induction principle should look like, let's introduce a binary tree with the children left and right, and two kind of nodes: Leafs and Branches.

Inductive DGBinaryTree :=
| Leaf
| Branch (l : Location) (left : DGBinaryTree) (right : DGBinaryTree).

In this case, Coq correctly generates the necessary induction hypotheses:

```
1  DGBinaryTree_ind
2      : ∀ P : DGBinaryTree →Prop,
3        P Leaf →
4        (∀ (l : Location) (left : DGBinaryTree),
5           P left →
6           ∀ right : DGBinaryTree,
7           P right →
8           P (Branch l left right)) →
9        ∀ t : DGBinaryTree, P t
```

It reads as follows: ₉ In order to prove a property P for a binary tree t, we need to prove that ₃ the property holds for leafs, and, given that the property holds ₅ for the left and ₇ the right child, ₈ the property holds for a branch with an arbitrary location l. — Much better.

So, how can we convince Coq to generate an induction principle that doesn't overlook the mutual dependency in DGTree? It turns out we cannot. In tutorial 12, we learned how to use the **Scheme** command to generate induction principles for mutually inductive definitions. This approach fails because we do not mutually define two inductive data types, using the with construct, but the mutual dependency only arises from the parameter A of list A, which we set to the enclosing type DGTree.

The only way to get a usable induction principle is to build it completely manually, which also involves manually applying it in proofs. Chapter 14.3.3 of [7] describes exactly this issue. In a very non-trivial manner, they construct an induction principle, with the following type:

```
1  DGTree_ind2
2    : ∀ (P : DGTree →Prop) (Q : list DGTree →Prop),
3      (∀ (a : Location) (l : list DGTree),
4         Q l → P (DGNode a l)) →
5      Q [] →
6      (∀ t : DGTree,
7         P t →
8         ∀ l : list DGTree,
9         Q l →
10        Q (t :: l)) →
11     ∀ t : DGTree, P t
```

Let's again read this. Firstly, besides the property P, which we are interested in, there is a second property Q. It basically states the same as P but for a list of trees instead for a single tree. It's part of the proving effort to come up with the correct Q. Once we have Q that corresponds to P, applying the induction principle gives us three proof obligations:

- 3,4 If Q holds for the children of a node, then P needs to hold for that node with any location l.

- 5 Property Q needs to hold for the empty list.

- 6-10 If property P holds for an individual tree t and Q holds for a list of trees l then Q needs to hold for the list t :: l.

This is an inductive principle that we can actually use. We'll see it in action in proofs below.

Listing 4.66 shows the definition of the function BuildDGTree, which build the tree of data groups for a given location. Although this refinement is all about getting rid of the "magic", we cannot directly implement the function, but need to axiomatize it. The reason is that Coq requires us to define recursive functions that operate on a structurally-decreasing argument, in order to ensure that the recursion is well-founded. We cannot provide this, as the underlying data structure is not an inductive type. One alternative is to use a Program **Fixpoint** instead of a **Fixpoint**, for which we can specify any kind of termination measure. However, dealing with the experimental Program commands introduced a lot of extra-complexity and leads to more fragile Coq code. Therefore we decide to axiomatize BuildDGTree and prove that the axiom cannot introduce an inconsistency.

```
1   Inductive ValidDGTree (p:Program) (bl:Backlinks.t) (excluded:LocSet.t)
2                         (f : Location) ( available : LocSet.t) : DGTree →Prop :=
3   | ValidDGTree_def:
4     ∀ dg dgs flist ,
5     filter
6       (fun f' ⇒ f' ∈ available)
7       (LocSet.elements
8         ( fold_right
9           LocSet.union
10          ∅
11          (LocDict. filter
12            ( Backlinks_get bl f)
13            (fun pivot ⇒ pivot ∉ excluded))))
14    ++ (StaticDGs p f) = flist →
15    length dgs = length flist →
16    (∀ n f '' f' dgs',
17      n < length dgs →
18      nth n flist f '' = f' →
19      nth n dgs (DGNode f'' []) = dgs' →
20      ValidDGTree p bl ep f' ( available \ {f'} dgs') →
21      dg = DGNode f dgs →
22    ValidDGTree p bl excluded f available dg.
23
24  Parameter BuildDGTree: Program →Backlinks.t →(∗excluded∗) LocSet.t →
25                         (∗ field ∗) Location → (∗ available ∗) LocSet.t → DGTree.
26
27  Axiom BuildDGTree_def: ∀p bl excluded f tree available ,
28    ValidDGTree p bl excluded f available tree
29      ↔
30    BuildDGTree p bl excluded f available = tree.
```

Listing 4.66: The axiomatized function BuildDGTree

Let's have a detailed look at the definitions above.

24,25 We declare a function BuildDGTree which takes an environment consisting of the current program and the back-links data structure, a set of excluded pivots, the field that becomes the root of the tree and a set of locations that have not yet been added to the tree. This set of *available* locations needs to be initialized with all locations in the heap[1]. We use this set to detect cycles in data group relations.

~27-30~ The axiom BuildDGTree_def states, that BuildDGTree yields a tree for which the inductive predicate ValidDGTree holds.

~1-22~ The predicate ValidDGTree specifies how such a tree looks like. As opposed to inductive predicates in the previous refinement, we define it in terms of constructed instead of described data structures, as we want to be as close as possible to the implementation.

~7-13~ We construct a list of data groups that directly contain f dynamically via a pivot that is not in the set of excluded pivots. ~11~ LocDict. filter yields the set of values whose keys pass the filter. The a value itself is a set of locations, thus, we ~8,9~ fold the set of set of locations into a flat set. Finally, ~7~ we transform the set into a list. ~5,6~ From this list, we remove the data groups that are not in the set of available locations and ~14~ add the locations that statically contain f. Of course, we could also change the order of the last two operations.

Next, we specify the list of subtrees dgs of the current node. For each data group in the list flist we have a corresponding subtree in dgs. Thus, we know that ~15~ there are as many subtrees in the node as data groups in flist , ~17-19~ the root node of each subtree in dgs contains the location which is stored at the same position in flist , and ~20~ each subtree is again a valid subtree. The function 'nth *pos list d*' yields the element at position *pos* in *list*, or the default value *d*, if *pos* is too big.

For each subtree, we remove the location of its root node from the set of available locations to avoid cycles.

In tutorial 11, we show how we can safely axiomatize a function like BuildDGTree. We need to prove that there exists exactly one tree for which the predicate ValidDGTree holds in a given situation. The following two lemmas ensure this property.

Lemma 4.25. *There is only one possible tree for which the predicate* ValidDGTree *holds in a given situation.*

```
1  Lemma ValidDGTree_func: ∀p bl excluded tree f  available ,
2  ValidDGTree p bl excluded f  available tree →
3  ∀ tree ',
4  ValidDGTree p bl excluded f  available tree' →
5  tree = tree'.
```

Proof. We prove this lemma by structural induction on tree. We apply the home brewed induction principle BGTree_ind2 as follows:

---

[1]The heap is finite.

```
elim tree using
DGTree_ind2
  with
  (Q := fun dgs ⇒
      ∀ t f available ,
      In t dgs →
      ValidDGTree p bl excluded f ( available \ {f}) t →
      ∀ t',
      ValidDGTree p bl excluded f ( available \ {f}) t' → t = t').
```

Listing 4.67: Proof excerpt

We need to define Q, as explained in tutorial 14. It states the property that needs to hold for the children of a node in order to prove the lemma for the node. It expresses that each subtree in the list is the only possible one. Naturally, the property is very similar to the lemma itself. By applying the induction principle, we get tree subgoals.

The first subgoal is the most challenging one: If we know that Q holds for the children of a node, then P holds for the node. After unfolding the predicates ValidDGTree for both tree and tree' and writing tree as DGNode f dgs and tree' as DGNode f dgs', and some heavy rewriting, we need to prove the following subgoal.

```
H :    ∀ (t : DGTree) (f : Location) ( available : LocSet.t),
       t ∈ dgs →
       ValidDGTree p bl excluded f ( available \ {f}) t →
       ∀ t' : DGTree,
       ValidDGTree p bl excluded f ( available \ {f}) t' → t = t'
H7 :   ∀ (n : nat) (f'' f' : Location) (t' : DGTree),
       n < (length dgs) →
       (nth n flist f'') = f' →
       (nth n dgs (DGNode f'' nil )) = t' →
       ValidDGTree p bl excluded f' ( available \ {f'}) t'
H13 : |dgs| = |dgs'|
H14 : ∀ (n : nat) (f'' f' : Location) (t' : DGTree),
       n < (length dgs') →
       (nth n flist f'') = f' →
       (nth n dgs' (DGNode f'' nil )) = t' →
       ValidDGTree p bl excluded f' ( available \ {f'}) t'
────────────────────────────────────────
dgs = dgs'
```

Listing 4.68: Proof excerpt

4.7. THIRD REFINEMENT

Hypothesis H originates in Q, H7 originates in ValidDGTree for tree, we get H13 from the fact that dgs as well as dgs' have the same length than flist, and H14 originates in ValidDGTree for tree'. The proof is now a matter of sedulity. We want to show that both lists of children are identical.

From hypothesis H, we learn that if a tree is in dgs, and if it is valid, then this is the only possible valid tree. So we introduce an assertion that states that for any position in dgs, the tree is identical to the tree at the same position in dgs'. We apply H and set the quantified variable f in H to the location at the same position in flist. We now need to show that both trees are in fact valid trees. We can apply H7 and H14 to prove this. From the fact that we have cleverly chosen f, and because we compare trees at the same positions of dgs and dgs', we can discharge the premises of the hypotheses. With the above assertion, we can prove by induction over the length of dgs, that both lists are identical.

The second goal can trivially be discharged, because Q applied to the empty list results in the false hypothesis t∈[].

The third goal can also be discharged in a relatively simple way. We get the following proof obligation:

```
H  : ∀ (f : Location) ( available : LocSet.t ),
       ValidDGTree p bl excluded f available tree →
       ∀ tree' : DGTree, ValidDGTree p bl excluded f available tree' →
       tree = tree'
H0 : ∀ (t : DGTree) (f : Location) ( available : LocSet.t ),
       t ∈ tail →
       ValidDGTree p bl excluded f ( available \{f}) t →
       ∀ t' : DGTree,
       ValidDGTree p bl excluded f ( available \{f}) t' → t = t'
H1 : t ∈ (tree:: tail )
H2 : ValidDGTree p bl excluded f ( available \{f}) t
H3 : ValidDGTree p bl excluded f ( available \{f}) t'
―――――――――――――――――――――――――――――――――――――――――――――――
t = t'
```

Listing 4.69: Proof excerpt

We can split H1 into two cases. Either t = tree or t is in tail. In the former case, we can rewrite t to tree and apply H. In the latter case, we can directly apply H0, because we know that t is in the tail of the list. □

Lemma 4.26. *There always exists a tree for which the predicate* ValidDGTree *holds.*

```
1  Lemma ValidDGTree_∃: ∀p bl excluded available,
2  ∀ f, ∃ dg, ValidDGTree p bl excluded f available dg.
```

Proof. We prove this lemma by induction on the cardinality of the set of available locations.
Case | available | = 0: For any field f, the valid tree of data groups is DGNode f [] if the set of available locations is empty. In the definition of ValidDGTree we filter the list of data groups that directly contain f by available locations. As no location is available, the resulting list of subtrees is empty. We prove this fact by induction over the list of data groups.
Case | available | = n+1: In the induction step, we need to prove the following goal.

```
IHn :  ∀  available  :  LocSet.t,
          n = | available | →
          ∀ f : Location,
          ∃ dg : DGTree, ValidDGTree p bl excluded f available dg
H   :  n+1 = |available|
─────────────────────────────────────────────
∃ dg : DGTree, ValidDGTree p bl excluded f available  dg
```

Listing 4.70: Proof excerpt

IHn is the induction hypothesis from the induction over the cardinality. H states that the cardinality of available contains one more location than any set of available locations in IHn.

We know there exists a valid tree for a given set of available locations. We now need to show that there also exists a valid tree if we add one more location to the set. The prove is not obvious, as we do not know what location we add to the set. It may or may not influence the shape of the tree. If it influences the tree, we do not know where and how the tree changes.

As we would not be able to actually build a witness for the existentially quantified variable dg, we choose an indirect approach to solve this goal and switch to classical logic for a while. This doesn't hurt as we do not plan to extract programs from our proofs.

If we know that there exists a list of subtrees such that ValidDGTree holds for dg, we're fine. In classical logic, we can turn around the thought and prove that it is not true that there is no such list of subtrees which satisfies ValidDGTree. And twisting the thought around once more, if it were true that there is no such list of subtrees, we could prove False. So let's prove False in the following setting, where we omitted the two hypotheses IHn and H.

```
1 subgoal
... (∗ IHn, H ∗)
```

4.7. THIRD REFINEMENT

```
flist ' := LocSet.elements
            ( fold_right LocSet.union ∅
               (LocDict. filter ( Backlinks_get bl f)
                  (fun f'' ⇒ f'' ∉ excluded)))
         ++
         StaticDGs p f
flist := filter (fun f'' ⇒ f'' ∈ available) flist '
H1 : ∀ dgs : list DGTree,
    (|dgs| = | flist | ∧
    (∀ (n : nat) (f'' f' : Location) (t' : DGTree),
     n < |dgs| →
     nth n flist f'' = f' →
     nth n dgs (DGNode f'' []) = t' →
     ValidDGTree p bl excluded f' ( available \ {f'}) t')) → False
```
```
False
```

Listing 4.71: Proof excerpt

flist ' is the list of data groups that directly contain f, before filtering out the locations that are not in m. flist is the outcome of the filtering. H1 states the (wrong) claim that any list of trees doesn't satisfy the property which is necessary to make ValidDGTree hold for a DGNode that uses this list as children. The property corresponds to one of the premises of ValidDGTree, see 16-20 listing 4.66 on page 186.

We prove this goal by induction on the list flist '. In case of the empty list, we instantiate dgs in H1 with the empty list. We apply H1 to the goal and need to prove that dgs has the same size than flist, which is trivial as both lists are empty, and we need to prove the right part of the conjunction, which describes dgs. This is also trivially true, as the premise n < |dgs| is false if dgs is empty.

In the step case of the induction on flist ', we get the following proof obligation after applying the induction hypothesis and some rewriting. The induction step adds the location a to the unfiltered list of data groups.

```
IHn : ∀ available : LocSet.t,
       n = | available | →
       ∀ f : Location,
       ∃ dg : DGTree, ValidDGTree p bl excluded f available dg
H   : n+1 = |available|
flist := filter (fun f'' ⇒ f'' ∈ available) (a :: flist ')
H1 : ∀ dgs : list DGTree,
    (|dgs| = | flist | ∧
    (∀ (n : nat) (f'' f' : Location) (t' : DGTree),
```

```
            n < |dgs| →
            nth n flist  f'' = f' →
            nth n dgs (DGNode f'' []) = t' →
            ValidDGTree p bl excluded f' ( available \ {f'}) t')) → False
  flist0 := filter (fun f'' ⇒ f'' ∈ available) flist '
  H0 : |dgs0| = | flist0 | ∧
       (∀ (n : nat) (f'' f' : Location) (t' : DGTree),
       n < |dgs0| →
       nth n flist0  f'' = f' →
       nth n dgs0 (DGNode f'' []) = t' →
       ValidDGTree p bl excluded f' ( available \ {f'}) t')

False
```

Listing 4.72: Proof excerpt

We get flist0 and H0 that originate in the induction hypothesis. H0 says that there exists the list of trees dgs0 with the desired property.

We perform a case split on the check if a∈m which happens during construction of the list flist. If a is not in m, the two lists flist and flist0 are identical and we instantiate the universally quantified variable dgs in H1 by dgs0. We then apply H1 to the goal. As a result, we need to prove the premise of H1, which is identical to H0.

If a is in the set of available locations m, we instantiate dgs in H1 with dg':: dgs0 where dg' is a valid tree for location a that we get from the first induction hypothesis IHn. We can use this induction hypothesis because we remove location a from the set of available locations m and thus reduce the cardinality of m by one. Again, we then apply H1 to the goal and finish the proof in a straight-forward way. □

4.7.5 Implementation of FieldInDg

We provide a function FieldInDg_rac3, see listing 4.73, which yields true if field f is in data group dg, ignoring pivots from the set excluded, and false otherwise. The function needs access to the program p and to the back-link data structure bl.

The function computes the result by building up a tree of data groups for f, starting with field f as root. The direct children in the tree are the data groups that directly contain f, their children are the data groups that contain the direct data groups and so forth. Once the tree of data groups is built, the function searches for the data group dg in the tree. In the Java implementation, we stop building up the tree as soon as dg has been found and we use caches to avoid building up the three in the first place. Beside this difference, the algorithm is identical.

4.7. THIRD REFINEMENT

```
1  Definition FieldInDg_rac3 (p : Program) (bl : Backlinks.t) (excluded : LocSet.t)
2                              (f : Location) (dg : Location) : bool :=
3    InDGTree dg (BuildDGTree p bl excluded f (LocSetAll \ {f})).
```

Listing 4.73: The function FieldInDg_rac3

As mentioned earlier, we instantiate the set of available locations with a set that contains all heap locations, LocSetAll. We describe the set with the following axiom: $\forall$ loc, loc $\in$ LocSetAll.

Listing 4.74 shows the implementation of the function InDGTree. If dg is the stored in the current node, the function yields true, otherwise, the function applies itself to all subtrees and yields the disjunction of all answers. That is, at least one subtree needs to contain dg in order to make the disjunction true. If there is a path from f to dg in FieldInDg_rac there is also a path in the intermediate definition, but without possible loops.

```
1  Fixpoint InDGTree (dg : Location) (tree : DGTree) : bool :=
2    match tree with
3    | DGNode f dgs ⇒
4      if dg = f then true
5      else fold_right (fun tree' ⇒ (orb (InDGTree dg tree'))) false dgs
6    end.
```

Listing 4.74: Implementation of the function InDGTree, where orb is the boolean or function

For better handling in proofs, we also introduce a predicate InDG, listing 4.75, which states the same as InDGTree but in form of an inductive predicate with two constructors: either the data group dg is the root of the current tree or it is in one of the subtrees.

```
1   Inductive InDG (dg : Location) (tree : DGTree) : Prop :=
2   | InDG_base:
3     ∀ dgs,
4     tree = (DGNode dg dgs) →
5     InDG dg tree
6   | InDG_step:
7     ∀ dgs f tree ',
8     tree = (DGNode f kids) →
9     dg ≠ f →
10    In tree' dgs →
11    InDG dg tree' →
```

193

CHAPTER 4. CORRECTNESS PROOF OF THE RAC FOR ASSIGNABLE CLAUSES

```
12   InDG dg tree.
```

Listing 4.75: Predicate InDG

Lemma 4.27. *The predicate* InDg dg tree *holds if and only if the function* InDgTree *finds location* dg *in the tree* tree.

```
1  Lemma InDGTree_Correct:
2    ∀ tree dg,
3      InDG dg tree ↔ InDGTree dg tree = true.
```

Proof. "→": We prove the forward direction by induction on the term InDG dg tree. In the base case, we compute one step of the definition InDGTree and directly find the location dg. In the step case, we get the following proof obligation by unfolding InDGTree once.

```
H : tree = DGNode f dgs
H0 : dg ≠ f
H1 : tree' ∈ dgs
IHInDG : InDGTree dg tree' = true
─────────────────────────────────────────────
fold_right (fun t' ⇒ orb (InDGTree dg t')) false dgs = true
```

Listing 4.76: Proof excerpt

We need to prove that the disjunction of InDGTree applied to all subtrees is true, which is the case if the function is true for at least one subtree. From the hypotheses H1 and IHInDG, we know that there exists a tree tree' which is a subtree and for which the function yields true.

"←": We prove the backward direction by induction on the tree, that is, we need to apply our custom built induction principle and manually come up with the property Q that needs to hold for the children of a node, see tutorial 14 on page 184.

```
elim tree using
  DGTree_ind2
  with
    (Q := fun dgs ⇒
        ∀ dg tree', tree' ∈ dgs →InDGTree dg tree' = true → InDG dg tree').
```

Listing 4.77: Proof excerpt

The three resulting subgoals require similar solving strategies than the recursive case above. □

4.7. THIRD REFINEMENT

Correctness proof of FieldInDg_rac3. We prove that FieldInDg_rac3 is equivalent to predicate FieldInDg_rac from the second refinement by introducing an intermediate predicate FieldInDg_rac2, see listing 4.78. The intermediate form is very similar to FieldInDg_rac, but introduces a set of visited locations, which is used to disallow cycles in the search paths. It is obvious that the intermediate form is equivalent to the second refinement.

```
1  Inductive FieldInDg_rac2 (p : Program) (h : Heap.t) (excluded : LocSet.t)
2               ( visited  : LocSet.t ): (* field *) Location → (* dg *) Location → Prop :=
3   | FieldInDg_rac2_static  : ∀ f dg dg',
4       direct_FieldInDg_static  p f dg' →
5       dg' ∉ visited →
6       FieldInDg_rac2 p h excluded ( visited ∪ {dg'}) dg' dg →
7       FieldInDg_rac2 p h excluded visited  f dg
8   | FieldInDg_rac2_dynamic : ∀ f dg pivot dg',
9       direct_FieldInDg_dynamic p h f dg' pivot →
10      pivot ∉ excluded →
11      dg' ∉ visited →
12      FieldInDg_rac2 p h excluded ( visited ∪ {dg'}) dg' dg →
13      FieldInDg_rac2 p h excluded visited  f dg
14  | FieldInDg_rac2_base : ∀ f dg,
15      f = dg →
16      FieldInDg_rac2 p h excluded visited  f dg.
```

Listing 4.78: The intermediate form of predicate FieldInDg, introducing a measure to guarantee termination.

In the following, we present the proof of correspondence of the intermediate form and the implementation FieldInDg_rac3.

Lemma 4.28. *In an environment with a back-link data structure that correctly represents the data group relations,* FieldInDg_rac3 *yields true if and only if its counterpart* FieldInDg_rac2 *holds.*

```
1  Lemma FieldInDg_rac3_Correct:
2  ∀ p excluded st f dg ,
3  CorrectBacklinks p st →
4  (FieldInDg_rac2 p st@h excluded {f} f dg
5  ↔
6  FieldInDg_rac3 p st@bl excluded f dg = true).
```

195

Proof. "→": We prove the forward direction by structural induction over FieldInDg_rac2. We only discuss the most interesting case, which is the constructor FieldInDg_rac2_dynamic. In the proof obligation below, we have already introduced the variable tree and hypothesis H4 by lemma 4.26 and replaced the goal by InDG dg tree using axiom BuildDGTree_def and lemma 4.27. Hypotheses H to H3 originate in the definition of FieldInDg_rac2, IH-FieldInDg_rac2 is the generated induction hypothesis.

```
H  : CorrectBacklinks p st
H0 : direct_FieldInDg_dynamic p st@h f dg' pivot
H1 : pivot ∉ exluded
H2 : dg' ∉ visited
H3 : FieldInDg_rac2 p st@h excluded ( visited ∪ {dg'}) dg' dg
IHFieldInDg_rac2 : InDG dg
                    (BuildDGTree p st@bl excluded dg'
                      (LocSetAll \ ( visited ∪ {dg'})))
tree : DGTree
H4 : ValidDGTree p st@bl excluded f (LocSetAll \ visited ) tree
─────────────────────────────────────────────────────────────
InDG dg tree
```

Listing 4.79: Proof excerpt

The idea of the proof goes as follows: The induction hypothesis tells us that we can build a tree with location dg' in its root, that contains dg. We have to show, that this tree is one of the subtrees of tree. Therefore, we need to unfold the definition of ValidDGTree in H4 to continue reasoning. The following proof excerpt only shows the additional hypotheses from the unfolded H4.

```
...
H5 : tree = DGNode f dgs
H7 : LocSet.elements
        ( fold_right LocSet.union ∅
          (LocDict. filter ( Backlinks_get st@bl f)
            (fun f'' : LocDict.Key ⇒ f'' ∉ excluded)))
     ++ StaticDGs p f = flist'
H8 : filter (fun f'' ⇒ f'' ∈ (LocSetAll \ visited )) flist' = flist
H9 : |dgs| = | flist |
H10 : ∀ (n : nat) (f'' f' : Location) (t' : DGTree),
        n < |dgs| →
        nth n flist f'' = f' →
        nth n dgs (DGNode f'' []) = t' →
        ValidDGTree p st@bl excluded f' ((LocSetAll \ visited ) \ {f'}) t'
```

...

Listing 4.80: Proof excerpt

We prove an assertion that dg' is in the list flist '. From H0, we know that dg' is a data group that directly contains f. From hypothesis H we know that the back-link data structure st@bl reflects the current situation in the heap, and from H7 we see that flist ' is built up such that it contains all data groups that directly contain f. Thus, this assertion holds. Furthermore, we can show that dg is also contained in the list flist , as H2 states that dg' is not in the set of already visited locations.

As dg' is in the list flist , we learn from H10 that there exists a valid subtree of tree with location dg' in its root. Using the axiom BuildDGTree_def once more, and the induction hypothesis, we conclude that dg is indeed in tree.

"←": For the backward proof, we assume that the tree of back-links for field f contains dg and want to prove that FieldInDg_rac2 holds in this situation.

We can unfold FieldInDg_rac3, apply lemma 4.27 and axiom BuildDGTree_def to get the following proof obligation.

```
H : CorrectBacklinks p st
H0 : InDG dg tree
H1 : ValidDGTree p st@bl excluded f (LocSetAll \ {f}) tree

FieldInDg_rac2 p st@h excluded {f} f dg
```

Listing 4.81: Proof excerpt

We prove the goal by structural induction on InDG dg tree. We skip the base case and focus on the step case. After unfolding ValidDGTree and some rewriting, we get:

```
H : CorrectBacklinks p st
(* Step case of InDG *)
H0 : tree = DGNode f dgs
H8 : dg ≠ f
H9 : tree' ∈ dgs
H10 : InDG dg tree'
(* Unfolding of ValidDGTree *)
...
(* Induction hypothesis *)
IH : ∀ (n : nat) (f'' f' : Location) (dgs' : DGTree),
     n < |dgs| →
     nth n flist f'' = f' →
     nth n dgs (DGNode f'' []) = dgs' →
     InDG dg dgs' →
```

FieldInDg_rac2 p st@h excluded (LocSetAll\(available \{f'\})) f' dg
FieldInDg_rac2 p st@h excluded (LocSetAll \ available) f dg

Listing 4.82: Proof excerpt

From the step case of InDG, we get a subtree tree' that contains the location dg. The location in the root of the tree, let's call it f', is a data group that directly contains f. If it is a dynamic data group inclusion, we apply FieldInDg_rac2_dynamic. From ValidDGTree in the hypothesis, we can conclude that the pivot connecting f and f' is not excluded, and that f' is not in the set of already visited locations. We are left with proving that FieldInDg_rac2 holds for field f' and data group dg. By applying the induction hypothesis IH, we complete the proof for the dynamic case. The proof for the case that f is statically contained in f' is analogous. □

4.7.6 Implementation of Lazy Unfolding Operations

The main operation of the lazy unfolding is SavePreState, which adds a pivot to the list of excluded pivots and puts the fields that are assignable through a dynamic data group over the pivot field to the set of assignable locations. The implementation of SavePreState relies on the axiomatized function AssignablePivotTargets for which we provide an implementation in this refinement, based on the back-link data structure, see listing 4.83.

AssignablePivotTargets $_{12}$ retrieves the list of fields that contain back-links. We filter this list by a $_{5\text{-}11}$ function that yields true, if $_{8,9}$ there exists a back-link via pivot to a data group that is assignable in the supplied assignable stack element a and false otherwise. Finally, $_4$ list2LocSet transforms the list of Location into a LocSet.

```
1  Definition AssignablePivotTargets ( p : Program) (bl : Backlinks.t) ( pivot : Location)
2                                      (a : LocSet.t * LocSet.t) : LocSet.t :=
3    list2LocSet (
4      filter
5      (fun f ⇒
6        match LocDict.get ( Backlinks_get bl f) pivot with
7        | Some dgs ⇒
8          if LocSet. fold (fun dg b ⇒ (Assignable p bl dg a) || b) dgs false
9          then true else false
10       | None ⇒ false
11     end)
12     ( Backlinks. keys bl )).
```

Listing 4.83: Implementation of the function AssignablePivotTargets

The definition of the function Assignable is straight-forward, see listing 4.84. We remember that the first part of the tuple a is the set of excluded pivots, and the second part is the set of assignable locations declared in a given method. f is assignable if there exists at least one location dg in $(a)_2$ such that there is a path from f to dg without using any pivot mentioned in $(a)_1$.

```
Definition Assignable (p:Program) (bl:Backlinks.t) (f:Location) (a:LocSet.t*LocSet.t):
                                                                              bool :=
  LocSet.fold (fun dg b ⇒ (FieldInDg_rac3 p bl (a)₁ f dg) || b) (a)₂ false.
```

Listing 4.84: The function Assignable

Lemma 4.29. Correctness of AssignablePivotTargets

In an environment with correct back-links and two equal assignable stack elements, the set of assignable pivot targets is equal in S_{rac2} and S_{rac3}.

```
Lemma AssignablePivotTargets_Correct:
  ∀ p st a1 a2 pivot,
  CorrectBacklinks p st →
  (a1)₁ [=] (a2)₁ →
  (a1)₂ [=] (a2)₂ →
  Rac2.AssignablePivotTargets p st@h pivot a1
  [=]
  Rac3.AssignablePivotTargets p st@bl pivot a2.
```

Proof. We prove this lemma by unfolding the definitions of CorrectBacklinks and both AssignablePivotTargets and applying standard library lemmas for the involved list and set operations. Finally we apply lemma 4.28 to relate FieldInDg_rac3 which is used in the definition of Assignable to FieldInDg_rac, used in S_{rac2}.

In the implementation of AssignablePivotTargets as well as Assignable, we use the term LocSet.fold (fun l b ⇒ (f l) || b) s false, where f is a function from Location to bool, and s is the set that we fold with boolean or, beginning with false. By induction over the list, we can prove once and for all, that such a folding expresses the proposition $\exists\, l,\; l \in s \land (f\, l) = true$ □

4.7.7 The Bisimulation Relation

Listing 4.85 shows the interesting aspect of the bisimulation relation [16] $\mathcal{R}^{rac2}_{rac3}$ between $\mathcal{S}_{rac2}$ and $\mathcal{S}_{rac3}$. Two states correspond, if [19,20] all fields are equal and [21] the back-link data structure of the state in $\mathcal{S}_{rac3}$ reflects the actual situation in the heap.

CHAPTER 4. CORRECTNESS PROOF OF THE RAC FOR ASSIGNABLE CLAUSES

The predicate ₁ EqualAssignables defines equal stacks of assignable locations. Two stacks are considered equal, if ₃ they have the same size and if ₄₋₆ each set from one state is equal to the set at the same position in the other state.

```
1  Inductive EqualAssignables (a1 a2: list (LocSet.t * LocSet.t)) :=
2  | EqualAssignables_def :
3    |a1| = |a2| →
4    (∀ n a,
5      (nth n  a1 a)₁ [=] (nth n  a2 a)₁ ∧
6      (nth n  a1 a)₂ [=] (nth n  a2 a)₂) →
7    EqualAssignables a1 a2.
8
9  Inductive CorrespondingFrame : Rac2.Frame.t → Frame.t → Prop :=
10 | CorrespondingFrame_def:
11   ∀ fr_rac2 fr_rac3 ,
12   ... (* all fields are identical *)
13   EqualAssignables fr_rac2@assignables  fr_rac3@assignables →
14   CorrespondingFrame fr_rac2  fr_rac3 .
15
16 Inductive CorrespondingState (p : Program) : Rac2.State.t → State.t → Prop :=
17 | CorrespondingState_def :
18   ∀ st_rac2 st_rac3 ,
19   CorrespondingFrame st_rac2@fr st_rac3@fr →
20   st_rac2@h = st_rac3@h →
21   CorrectBacklinks p st_rac3 →
22   CorrespondingState p st_rac2 st_rac3 .
```

Listing 4.85: Excerpt of the definition CorrespondingState, which describes the bisimulation relation between $\mathcal{S}_{rac1}$ and $\mathcal{S}_{rac2}$.

4.7.8 Implementation of the Frame Conditions Interface

The two function FieldUpdateCheck and FieldUpdateAction are directly affected by the changes in this refinement, whereas the other functions are implemented the same way as in the second refinement. Thus, we only concentrate on the first two functions here and in the correctness proof section below. Naturally, we implement all functions of the frame condition interface in the Coq formalization and prove the correspondence to the second refinement for each function.

The $\mathcal{S}_{rac3}$ version of FieldUpdateCheck shown in listing 4.86 uses the function Assignable, which computes the boolean value true if loc is assignable and false otherwise, see listing

4.84. Otherwise, the definition

```
Definition FieldUpdateCheck (p:Program) (loc:Location) (st:State.t) : Prop :=
  ∀ n,
  (n < length st@fr@assignables ) →
      (∃ m,
        (m ≤n ∧ m < length st@fr@fresh) ∧
        loc ∈ (ObjSet2LocSet (nth m st@fr@fresh ∅)))
    ∨
      Assignable p st@bl loc (nth n st@fr@assignables (∅,∅)) = true.
```

Listing 4.86: The $\mathcal{S}_{rac3}$ implementation of FieldUpdateCheck.

Listing 4.87 shows the $\mathcal{S}_{rac3}$ implementation of FieldUpdateAction. The difference to the second refinement is the additional update of the back-links data structure, if the updated field is a pivot, in order to keep the back-links in sync with the actual data group structure in the heap. In a first step, we remove all back-links from the data structure that use pivot as pivot, and in a second step, we add back-links to all new pivot-targets.

```
Definition FieldUpdateAction (p:Program) (pivot:Location) (v:Value) (st:State.t) :
                                                                       State.t :=
  if ( isPivot p pivot) then
    st [ fr := st@fr [ assignables :=
                    map (SavePreState p st@bl pivot) st@fr@assignables ]]
       [ bl := SetBacklinks p pivot v (RemoveBacklinks p pivot st )]
  else
    st .
```

Listing 4.87: The $\mathcal{S}_{rac3}$ implementation of FieldUpdateAction.

4.7.9 Proof of the Third Refinement

We present the proof of the third refinement as follows: firstly, we show the correctness of the two interesting frame condition functions presented above. Secondly, we prove the main theorem for this refinement that states that the semantics $\mathcal{S}_{rac2}$ and $\mathcal{S}_{rac3}$ are in fact bisimilar. By this proof, we show that the implementation of the runtime assertion checker is enforcing the semantics of `assignable` clauses.

Correctness Proof of the Frame Condition Implementation

We discuss only the proof of the correctness lemma for FieldUpdateAction since the correctness proofs of the other functions are either not interesting or very similar to proofs already presented in the second refinement.

Lemma 4.30. Correct Field Update Action

The implementation of FieldUpdateAction *in* S_{rac3} *preserves the correspondence relation, after the field has been updated with the new value.*

```
1  Lemma FieldUpdateAction_Correct:
2    ∀ p loc st_rac2 v st_rac2' st_rac3 st_rac3' cn um loc_obj loc_fsig,
3    loc = Heap.InstanceField loc_obj loc_fsig →
4    Heap.typeof st_rac3@h loc_obj = Some (Heap.ObjectObject cn um) →
5    defined_field p cn loc_fsig →
6    assign_compatible p st_rac3@h v (FIELDSIGNATURE.type (loc_fsig)₂) →
7    CorrespondingState p st_rac2 st_rac3 →
8    Rac2.Assignables.FieldUpdateAction p loc v st_rac2 = st_rac2' →
9    Rac3.Assignables.FieldUpdateAction p loc v st_rac3 = st_rac3' →
10   CorrespondingState p
11     st_rac2 '[ h:=Heap.update st_rac2@h loc v]
12     st_rac3 '[ h:=Heap.update st_rac3@h loc v].
```

Proof. The implementation of FieldUpdateAction update the stack of assignable locations and in case of S_{rac3} the back-link data structure. Thus, the only non-trivial goals are to prove that EqualAssignable holds in both states and that the back-link data structure stays correct.

To prove that the two resulting stacks of assignable locations are equal, we show that they contain the same number of elements and that each set in the stack is equal. The earlier is obvious, we do not add or remove elements in the stack. The latter claim is requires a bit more discussion. We need to show that starting from equal stacks of assignable locations, applying the functions SavePreState in both semantics to each element of the stacks results again in equal stacks.

The only difference in the two implementation of SavePreState is the application of the axiomatized function AssignablePivotTargets in S_{rac2} and the implemented function AssignablePivotTargets in S_{rac3}. We have shown in lemma 4.29, that the two functions yield equal sets of assignable pivot targets. Thus, for each element of the stack, SavePreState preserves the equality.

To prove the correctness of the back-link data structure after the update, we apply lemma 4.24. □

Proof of the Bisimulation Property

Theorem 4.31. Correctness of the Third Refinement

If one starts in a state st_{rac2} and performs a step in the semantics to get state st'_{rac2}, and given a state st_{rac3} that corresponds to state st_{rac2}, then there exists a state st'_{rac3} that one gets by applying the same step in the runtime assertion checker and that corresponds to st'_{rac2}.

Moreover, if one can perform a step in the runtime assertion checker from st_{rac3} to st'_{rac3}, and st_{rac2} corresponds to st_{rac3}, then there exists a corresponding st'_{rac2} which one gets by performing the same step in the semantics:

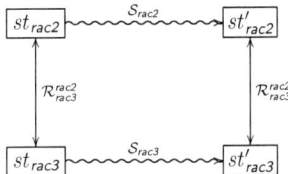

Proof. The proof of the main theorem of the second refinement follows the same reasoning than the proof of theorem 4.5. Thus, we do not show the proof again in details. We perform a mutual induction on the the four inductive definitions of steps. We use the induction hypotheses to reason about the mutual applications of steps, and the correctness lemmas of the $\mathcal{S}_{rac3}$ implementation of the frame condition interface to reason about the application of these functions. □

4.8 Proof of the Main Theorem

We combine the bisimulation relations of the three refinements to prove the main theorem 4.1 on page 126. Fig. 4.9 depicts the approach. We show that if we execute a step in $\mathcal{S}_{sem}$ from state st_{sem} to state st'_{sem}, and given a step st_{rac3} that corresponds to st_{sem}, executing the same step in $\mathcal{S}_{rac3}$ leads to a state st'_{rac3} that corresponds to st'_{sem}. We show the backward direction of the theorem accordingly. We prove the theorem applying the bisimulation relation theorems of all three refinements.

The bisimulation relation $\mathcal{R}^{sem}_{rac3}$ is defined as the conjunction of the bisimulation relations of the three refinements:

$$\mathcal{R}^{sem}_{rac3}(st_{sem}, st_{rac3}) :=$$
$$\exists st_{rac1}, \exists st_{rac2}, \mathcal{R}^{sem}_{rac1}(st_{sem}, st_{rac1}) \land \mathcal{R}^{rac1}_{rac2}(st_{rac1}, st_{rac2}) \land \mathcal{R}^{rac2}_{rac3}(st_{rac2}, st_{rac3})$$

Proof. We only discuss the forward direction of the theorem, the backwards direction is analogous.

We assume that we have two corresponding states st_{sem} and st_{rac3}. Furthermore, a step in $\mathcal{S}_{sem}$ yields the state st'_{sem}. From the definition of $\mathcal{R}^{sem}_{rac3}$ we learn that there exist two states st_{rac1} and st_{rac2} such that the correspondence relations of the refinements hold. From the forward direction of the bisimulation theorem of the first refinement, we learn

CHAPTER 4. CORRECTNESS PROOF OF THE RAC FOR ASSIGNABLE CLAUSES

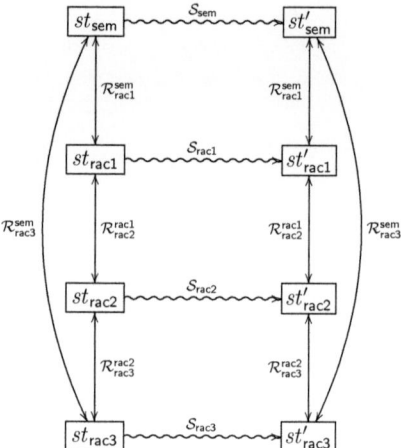

Figure 4.9: The proof concept: by defining the correspondence relation as combination of the relations from the three refinements.

that there exists a state st'_{rac1} that corresponds to st'_{sem} and that we get by executing the step in $\mathcal{S}_{rac1}$. By applying the bisimulation theorem of the second and the third refinement, we get the states st'_{rac2} and st'_{rac3}. Thus, we know by construction that $\mathcal{R}^{sem}_{rac3}(st'_{sem}, st'_{rac3})$ holds.

We also need to be sure that there exist two corresponding states st_{sem} and st_{rac3} to start with. We can easily construct corresponding states to the initial state of a system as described in section 2.6.2 on page 72, by choosing empty or default values for all additional data structures.

Thus, we know for any state in $\mathcal{S}_{sem}$ which is reachable by executing a step from the initial state of the system, that there exists a corresponding state in $\mathcal{S}_{rac3}$ that we can reach by the same sequence of steps form the initial state of $\mathcal{S}_{rac3}$. □

4.9 Summary

In this chapter we proved that the runtime assertion checker for assignable clauses in the presence of dynamic data groups behaves equivalently to the semantics. This is a strong result as showed that a difficult and non-modular task at runtime not only enforces the semantics, but is also precise, that is, does not over-approximate the semantics. Besides, we showed in this chapter that our formalization of JML is well suited to perform complex meta-reasoning on JML's semantics.

Chapter 5

Conclusion

We conclude this thesis by summarizing our achievements, giving a short description of the experiences that we have made during this work, possible and likely future work that build on top of this thesis and a final statement.

5.1 Achievements

We succeeded to formalize an interesting subset of JML in the theorem prover Coq and we have shown its usefulness by proving soundness and completeness of our algorithm to efficiently check frame conditions in JML, which we also presented in this thesis. We accomplished the following in our work.

A Formal Definition of JML Constructs in Coq We formally defined the relevant JML constructs in Coq by deeply embedding the constructs in the theorem prover. We took care to that the semantics of each construct is clearly presented. Thus, our formalization can be used along with the reference manual [49] to unambiguously understand the meaning of JML constructs.

A JML Front-End for Program Verification Our formalization of JML can be used as a front-end of a verification environment such as the Mobius PVE [62]. The formalization provides a well defined interface to access the JML specifications of a given program. Furthermore, it's possible to embed JML annotated Java source code in our formalization in a readable and elegant way, thanks to heavy use of notations. In addition to the formalization in Coq, we provide a Java front-end to automatically translate JML annotated Java files to the corresponding Coq embedding.

A Solid Basis for Meta-Reasoning on JML By the modular structure of our formalization and the emphasis on readability and usability, we provided a solid basis to perform meta-reasoning on the specification language and its tools. We performed several proofs of concepts to ensure that the formalization is suited for meta-reasoning. With the formalized syntactic rewritings from the full form of JML constructs to their more basic form as described in [42] and the proof of the runtime assertion checker, there are already two interesting applications of meta-reasoning on JML, that use our formalization as basis.

An Efficient Algorithm to Check Frame Conditions at Runtime We presented an algorithm to check `assignable` clauses in the presence of static and dynamic data groups. Our algorithm performs well, in particular, on recursive data structures with large and deeply nested dynamic data groups by introducing the concept of lazy unfolding of data groups. We provide the foundation to close a big gap in the runtime assertion checker of JML. The algorithm has been tested against recursive data structures with a prototypical implementation of a runtime assertion checker as well as an OpenJML implementation of the algorithm.

A Machine Checkable Proof of a Runtime Assertion Checker We formally proved the soundness and completeness of our runtime assertion checker for assignable clauses. It is the first proof of a runtime assertion checker. We have made clear that such a proof is necessary to trust in the results of a runtime assertion checker, as the algorithm of the checker significantly differs from a naïve implementation of the semantics. By proving the runtime assertion checker for `assignable` clauses with dynamic data groups, we have proven one of the most difficult constructs for a runtime assertion checker. While the proof is an important contribution on its own, it also serves as an interesting application of our semantics and shows that it's possible to perform complex reasoning with our formalization.

5.2 Experience

Working with Coq We started our work with no prior experience in Coq but with a decent understanding of formal verification and language semantics. Thanks to Bertot's excellent book "Coq'Art: The Calculus of Inductive Constructions" [7] and Giménez' and Castéran's tutorial on (co)inductive types in Coq [35], we managed to quickly get a good understanding of the theorem prover and the underlying logic.

The Bicolano formalization of the Java virtual machine [70], which we used as basis for our formalization, heavily uses the Coq module system [15]. However, the way Bicolano use the module system leads to significant code duplication in order to implement a module type. Nevertheless, we left the module structure unchanged as we intended to take over as much as possible from Bicolano, which otherwise proved to be a very good basis for our formalization. Of course, we properly used the module system for our own parts to avoid these problems. In our technical report about the formalization, we discuss this issue in more details [42, section 4.1.2].

One thing that we *did* rewrite in Bicolano is the way classes and interfaces are formalized. While the two constructs are different abstract data types in the original Bicolano formalization, we combined them into one abstract data type, as they are quite similar for specification purposes, see [49, section 6.1].

While we were working on the formalization of JML, Coq got updated from version 8.0 to 8.3 with significant changes and improvements. We ported our formalization three times to a new version with small and occasional changes to our definitions and proofs. As we were adopting new language concepts and tactics, our sources are not backward compatible and require the currently newest Coq version 8.3.

With more than 14'000 lines of Coq sources (not counting empty lines and comments), our formalization can be considered quite large, which occasionally led to technical problems with Coq. During our work on the formalization, we encountered several minor deficits and two major bugs in Coq that quickly got fixed upon our bug-reports. In one case, we could not reduce the size of the example that triggers the bug, as it was mainly the size of the formalization that led to the bug. Again, the Coq development team was very forthcoming by fixing the bug after we gave them access to our repositories.

Listing 5.1 shows a summary of the lines of code for each file of our formalization, as generated by the tool `coqwc`. We can see that the core part of the formalization of JML takes about 2'500 lines, which is about the same size than the proof of the third refinement alone. Beside the fact that the proof is quite challenging, this is also the case because we did set an emphasis on the clarity of the overall proof structure, but not on a perfectly optimized proof script itself. Thus, the proofs could be made more condensed and user tactics might introduce more automation. While this would be worthwhile in a Coq textbook, it's not the first priority if we are more interested in the result of the proof than the proof scripts themselves. Anyhow, we achieve maintainability of the proofs by decently structuring the proof and outsourcing interesting sub-goals into separate lemmas.

We also had to experience that a machine checked proof is only as good as the model on which we perform reasoning. Concretely, we have had a subtle error in the semantics of assignable clauses, which we carried through all refinements. That is, we performed a machine checked proof that all refinements behave equivalently to the semantics, which itself was not entirely accurate in the first place. This kind of errors can only be found by manual inspection of the semantics and by performing machine checked validation of the semantics by proving desired properties of the JML constructs.

Working with JML JML is a very alive research topic. Many tools based on JML are actively being developed and a lot of novel techniques are being proposed to integrate in JML. In the field of frame conditions, two interesting contributions propose an alternative to the non-modular dynamic data groups as defined in the reference manual. Müller et

```
    spec   proof  comments
// Helpers
     43      35      0 EqBoolAux.v
     51      36     27 ListFunctions.v
     42     136     46 ListHelpers.v
      2      12      0 LogicHelpers.v
     34      19     20 OptionHelpers.v
     33      43      0 PosAux.v
     59       0      0 Prelude.v
    124     296      1 Stack.v
     28       7     81 TaggedList.v
     21      21     23 ZHelpers.v

// Formalization of JML
    952       0    246 JMLProgram.v
    178       0    105 JMLNotations.v
    120       0     19 JMLExpressionNotations.v
      7       0      2 JMLSyntax.v
     56       0      3 JMLNumeric.v
    579     205     85 JMLDomain.v
    719       9    146 JMLSemantics.v

// Operational Semantics
    120      92     35 JMLOpSem.v

// Syntactic Desugaring & Implementation
    132       0    224 JMLFull2Basic.v
   1023      26    438 JMLFull2BasicImpl.v
     50       0     29 JMLProgramPlus.v
   1712     241    364 JMLProgramPlusImpl.v

// Correctness Proof of RAC
    175     616     29 JMLRac.v
    580    1045     25 JMLRac2.v
    626    2615     28 JMLRac3.v
     78     317     16 JMLRac_1_Correct.v
    115     500     16 JMLRac_2_Correct.v
     80     297     16 JMLRac_3_Correct.v

// Total
   7784    6568   2073 total
```

Listing 5.1: An overview of the number of lines of specification, proofs, and comments for each file of the formalization.

al. proposed in [64] to use a hierarchically structured heap and a restrictive programming model to achieve modular frame conditions. Schmitt et al. recently introduced dynamic frames [44] for JML [76] in order to overcome the non-modularity of frame conditions in JML. Even though both proposals pose an interesting alternatives, data groups are still the "official" technology to introduce abstraction in frame conditions in JML, which is supported by most tools to some extend. Furthermore, specifying frame conditions using data groups is very intuitive with little overhead.

When our algorithm to check assignable clauses was ready to be implemented in a JML tool, we were faced with the situation that there are currently many different implementations of JML runtime assertion checkers around. While JML2 [40] is the currently official tool, it is being replaced soon by newer implementations, most notably OpenJML [68], which is based on the OpenJDK [67], and the jml4c tool [41], which is based on the Eclipse Java compiler. Beside these two, there are a handful other tools being developed simultaneously. We decided to go with OpenJML as it's supposed to become the main-stream tool for JML.

While the reference manual is written quite precisely, it was often necessary to check different parts of the manual in order to understand the intended meaning of a construct. Sometimes, reading additional resources like the preliminary design document [46] or papers and reports that concentrate on one specific construct helped a lot to understand the semantics of JML constructs. However, this additional literature is cited in the reference manual.

5.3 Future Work

We see interesting future work along several lines. For the formalization of JML in Coq, we can on the one hand extend the formalized subset, and on the other hand add additional applications from different fields. For the runtime assertion checker, we might want to add support for model fields and introduce more advanced optimizations. In the following, we discuss the most interesting ideas in more detail.

Formalize Additional Constructs In our formalization, we currently ignored constructs that are either rarely used in applications or very similar to handle than already supported ones. Most notably, support for floating point operations could be added based on the formalization of real numbers from the Coq standard library. Another construct that could be added is the \old expressions equipped with a label, see the last to paragraphs of [49, section 12.4.2]. Those \old expressions may refer to a state at a given label rather than the pre-state. This implies that our state model would need to allow access not only to the pre-state of the method, but the states of all labels in the current method body. Thanks to our extendible state model, such a change would be simple to perform without the need of a large-scale refactoring.

Providing Several Semantics for the Same Construct Beside adding support for new constructs, an interesting work would be to add different semantics for existing constructs. Instead of the visible state semantics for object invariants, we can add ownership and alias control for modular object invariants, see [65]. As we already provide the necessary additions on a syntactical level (the universe type modifier), the semantics can be integrated without changing existing data types. We could use the universe type system also to define a modular semantics for frame conditions, as discussed in the last section.

Integrate the Formalization in a Verification Environment Our formalization is suited to be integrated in the Mobius PVE [62]. It would be interesting to evaluate the verification environment, which would generate more convenient proof obligations by using our formalization instead of the JML to first order logic translation that is currently being used.

Extend the Operational Semantics of Java We cover only a very small subset of Java in our operational semantics in order to prove the correctness of the runtime assertion checker. To open the formalization to different applications, we might need to extend this subset, based on the Java language reference and existing formalizations of Java [36, 81, 70, 38].

Support for Model Fields in the Runtime Assertion Checker In a prototypical implementation we already added experimental support for model fields in the runtime assertion checker for `assignable` clauses where we restrict the expressivity of `requires` clauses in order to be able to perform efficient checks. We believe that it's possible to relax these restrictions quite a bit without dramatically tear down efficiency, but more research is necessary to come up with the right solution.

Implement Better Optimizations in the Runtime Assertion Checker With the caches that we introduce per method, we speed up the checks a lot if the same locations get assigned several times in the same method. However, the information in the cache gets lost as soon as the method terminates. We could implement a more clever caching that only invalidates information in the cache if it is actually out of date.

Proof the Correctness of the Optimizations If we introduce a more sophisticated caching to our algorithm to check `assignable` clauses, we would have to prove its correctness as one or more additional refinements. A refinement strategy is very suitable to proof the correctness of optimizations, that is, prove that they behave equivalently to the non-optimized algorithm.

Final Statement

We showed in this thesis that it's possible and worth the effort to formalize a specification language in a theorem prover to perform both meta-reasoning over the specification language and program verification.

We hope that our work will be of good use in the research community and help to motivate others to choose a more formal approach to software verification.

Bibliography

[1] W. Richards Adrion, Martha A. Branstad, and John C. Cherniavsky. Validation, verification, and testing of computer software. *ACM Computer Surveys*, 14:159–192, June 1982.

[2] W. Ahrendt, Th. Baar, B. Beckert, R. Bubel, M. Giese, R. Hähnle, W. Menzel, W. Mostowski, A. Roth, S. Schlager, and P. H. Schmitt. The KeY tool. *Software and System Modeling*, 2004.

[3] Apollo 11 program alarms. See http://www.hq.nasa.gov/office/pao/History/alsj/a11/a11.1201-pa.html.

[4] Virtual AGC and AGS. See http://code.google.com/p/virtualagc/.

[5] M. Barnett, R. Leino, and W. Schulte. The Spec# programming system: An overview. In *Construction and Analysis of Safe, Secure, and Interoperable Smart Devices*, volume 3362 of *Lecture Notes in Computer Science*, pages 49–69. Springer-Verlag, 2005.

[6] B. Beckert, R. Hähnle, and P. H. Schmitt, editors. *Verification of Object-Oriented Software: The KeY Approach*. Number 4334 in Lecture Notes in Computer Science. Springer-Verlag, 2007.

[7] Y. Bertot and P. Castéran. *Interactive Theorem Proving and Program Development. Coq'Art: The Calculus of Inductive Constructions*. Texts in Theoretical Computer Science. Springer-Verlag, 2004.

[8] B. Bruegge and A. A. Dutoit. *Object-Oriented Software Engineering; Conquering Complex and Changing Systems*. Prentice Hall PTR, Upper Saddle River, NJ, USA, 1999.

[9] D. Bruns. Formal semantics for the Java Modeling Language. Master's thesis, Karlsruhe Institut für Technologie, 2009.

[10] L. Burdy, Y. Cheon, D. Cok, M. Ernst, J.R. Kiniry, G.T. Leavens, K.R.M. Leino, and E. Poll. An overview of JML tools and applications. *Journal on Software Tools for Technology Transfer*, 7(3):212–232, 2005.

[11] L. Burdy, M. Huisman, and M. Pavlova. Preliminary design of BML: A behavioral interface specification language for Java bytecode. In *Fundamental Approaches to Software Engineering*, volume 4422 of *Lecture Notes in Computer Science*, pages 215–229. Springer-Verlag, 2007.

[12] N. Cataño and M. Huisman. Chase: A static checker for JML's assignable clause. In *Verification, Model Checking and Abstract Interpretation*, volume 2575 of *Lecture Notes in Computer Science*, pages 26–40. Springer-Verlag, 2003.

[13] Z. Chen. *Java Card technology for Smart Cards: architecture and programmer's guide*. Addison-Wesley Longman Publishing Co., Inc. Boston, MA, USA, 2000.

[14] Y. Cheon. *A Runtime Assertion Checker for the Java Modeling Language*. PhD thesis, Iowa State University, 2003.

[15] J. Chrzaszcz. Implementing modules in the coq system. In D. Basin and B. Wolff, editors, *Theorem Proving in Higher Order Logics*, volume 2758 of *Lecture Notes in Computer Science*, pages 270–286. Springer Berlin / Heidelberg, 2003.

[16] J. Chrzaszcz, M. Huisman, A. Schubert, J. Kiniry, M. Pavlova, and E. Poll. *BML Reference Manual*, December 2008. In Progress. Available from http://bml.mimuw.edu.pl.

[17] Mobius Consortium. Deliverable 3.1: Bytecode specification language and program logic, 2006. Available online from http://jmlcoq.info/mobius/d31.pdf.

[18] Coq development team. The nonterminating Coq wiki - mutual induction, 2010. http://coq.inria.fr/cocorico/Mutual%20Induction.

[19] Coq development team. The Coq proof assistant reference manual V8.3, 2011. http://coq.inria.fr/refman/.

[20] T. Coquand and G. Gerard. The calculus of constructions. *Information and Computation*, 76:95–120, February 1988.

[21] T. Coquand and C. Paulin. Inductively defined types. In *Proceedings of the international conference on Computer logic*, pages 50–66, New York, NY, USA, 1990. Springer-Verlag New York, Inc.

[22] J. Crow, S. Owre, J. Rushby, N. Shankar, and M. Srivas. *A Tutorial Introduction to PVS*, April 1995.

[23] Swiss cyber crime center. See http://www.cybercrime.ch/.

[24] Á. Darvas. *Reasoning About Data Abstraction in Contract Languages*. PhD thesis, ETH Zurich, Switzerland, 2009.

[25] Á. Darvas and P. Müller. Reasoning about method calls in JML specifications. In *Workshop on Formal Techniques for Java Programs*, 2005.

[26] Á. Darvas and P. Müller. Reasoning About Method Calls in Interface Specifications. *Journal of Object Technology (JOT)*, 5(5):59–85, June 2006.

[27] Á. Darvas and P. Müller. Formal encoding of JML level 0 specifications in JIVE. Technical report, ETH Zurich, 2007. Annual Report of the Chair of Software Engineering.

[28] L. de Moura and N. Bjørner. Z3: An efficient SMT solver. In C. Ramakrishnan and J. Rehof, editors, *Tools and Algorithms for the Construction and Analysis of Systems*, volume 4963 of *Lecture Notes in Computer Science*, pages 337–340. Springer Berlin / Heidelberg, 2008.

[29] D. Detlefs, G. Nelson, and J. B. Saxe. Simplify: a theorem prover for program checking. *Journal of the Association of Computing Machinery*, 52(3):365–473, 2005.

[30] W. Dietl and P. Müller. Universes: Lightweight ownership for JML. *Journal of Object Technology*, 4(8):5–32, October 2005.

[31] Departement of defense cyber crime center. See http://www.dc3.mil/.

[32] ESC/Java2 website. See http://sort.ucd.ie/products/opensource/ESCJava2/.

[33] M. Fähndrich and F. Logozzo. Static contract checking with abstract interpretation. In *Proceedings of the 2010 international conference on Formal verification of object-oriented software*, pages 10–30, Berlin, Heidelberg, 2011. Springer-Verlag.

[34] J.-C. Filliâtre. Why: A multi-language multi-prover verification tool. Research Report 1366, LRI, Université Paris Sud, 2003.

[35] E. Giménez and P. Castéran. *A Tutorial on [Co-]Inductive Types in Coq*, August 2007. Available from http://coq.inria.fr/doc.

[36] J. Gosling, B. Joy, G. Steele, and G. Bracha. *The Java Language Specification, third edition*. The Java Series. Addison-Wesley, 2005.

[37] C. A. R. Hoare. An axiomatic basis for computer programming. *Communications of the ACM*, 12(10):576–580, 1969.

[38] A. Igarashi, B. Pierce, and P. Wadler. Featherweight Java: a minimal core calculus for Java and GJ. *ACM Transactions on Programming Language Systems*, 23(3):396–450, 2001.

[39] B. Jacobs and E. Poll. A logic for the Java Modeling Language JML. In H. Hussmann, editor, *Fundamental Approaches to Software Engineering*, volume 2029 of *Lecture Notes in Computer Science*, pages 284–299. Springer-Verlag, 2001.

[40] JML2 website. See http://sourceforge.net/apps/trac/jmlspecs/wiki/JML2.

[41] jml4c website. See http://www.cs.utep.edu/cheon/download/jml4c/.

[42] A. Kägi, H. Lehner, and P. Müller. A formalization of JML in the Coq proof system. Technical Report 714, ETH Zurich, 2009.

[43] D. A. Karp. *Windows 7 Annoyances*. O'Reilly Media, 2010. See http://www.annoyances.org/.

[44] I. Kassios. Dynamic frames: Support for framing, dependencies and sharing without restrictions. In Jayadev Misra, Tobias Nipkow, and Emil Sekerinski, editors, *Formal Methods*, volume 4085 of *Lecture Notes in Computer Science*, pages 268–283. Springer Berlin / Heidelberg, 2006.

[45] G. T. Leavens. An overview of Larch/C++: Behavioral specifications for C++ modules. Technical report, Department of Computer Science, Iowa State University, 1996.

[46] G. T. Leavens, A. L. Baker, and C. Ruby. Preliminary design of JML: a behavioral interface specification language for Java. *SIGSOFT Software Engineering Notes*, 31(3):1–38, 2006.

[47] G. T. Leavens, Y. Cheon, C. Clifton, C. Ruby, and D. R. Cok. How the design of JML accommodates both runtime assertion checking and formal verification. *Science of Computer Programming*, 55(1–3):185–205, 2005.

[48] G. T. Leavens, D. A. Naumann, and S. Rosenberg. Preliminary definition of core JML. Technical report, Stevens Institute of Technology, 2008.

[49] G. T. Leavens, E. Poll, C. Clifton, Y. Cheon, C. Ruby, D. R. Cok, P. Müller, J. Kiniry, and P. Chalin. *JML Reference Manual*, February 2007. Department of Computer Science, Iowa State University. Available from http://www.jmlspecs.org.

[50] H. Lehner and P. Müller. Efficient runtime assertion checking of assignable clauses with datagroups. In D. Rosenblum and G. Taentzer, editors, *Fundamental Approaches to Software Engineering*, volume 6013 of *Lecture Notes in Computer Science*, pages 338–352. Springer-Verlag, 2010.

[51] K. R. M. Leino, A. Poetzsch-Heffter, and Y. Zhou. Using data groups to specify and check side effects. In *Programming Languages Design and Implementation*, pages 246–257, 2002.

[52] K. Rustan M. Leino. Data groups: Specifying the modification of extended state. In *ACM Conference on Object-Oriented Programming Systems, Languages, and Applications*, pages 144–153, 1998.

[53] X. Leroy. Formal verification of a realistic compiler. *Communications of the ACM*, 2009.

[54] C. Marché and C. Paulin-Mohring. Reasoning about Java programs with aliasing and frame conditions. In *Theorem Proving in Higher-Order Logics*, pages 179–194, 2005.

[55] C. Marché, C. Paulin-Mohring, and X. Urbain. The Krakatoa tool for certification of Java/JavaCard programs annotated with JML annotations. *Journal of Logic and Algebraic Programming*, 58:89–106, 2004.

[56] J. D. McGregor and D. A. Sykes. *A practical guide to testing object-oriented software.* Addison-Wesley Longman Publishing Co., Inc., Boston, MA, USA, 2001.

[57] B. Meyer. Applying "Design by Contract". *IEEE Computer*, 25(10):40–51, 1992.

[58] B. Meyer. *Eiffel: The Language.* Prentice Hall, 1992.

[59] B. Meyer, I. Ciupa, A. Leitner, and L. Liu. Automatic testing of object-oriented software. In *SOFSEM 2007: Theory and Practice of Computer Science*, volume 4362 of *Lecture Notes in Computer Science*, pages 114–129. Springer Berlin / Heidelberg, 2007.

[60] J. Meyer and A. Poetzsch-Heffter. An architecture for interactive program provers. In *Proceedings of the 6th International Conference on Tools and Algorithms for Construction and Analysis of Systems*, pages 63–77, London, UK, 2000. Springer-Verlag.

[61] R. Milner. *Communication and Concurrency.* Prentice Hall, 1989. ISBN 0-13-114984-9 (Hard) 0-13-115007-3 (Pbk).

[62] The mobius program verification environment. See http://kind.ucd.ie/products/opensource/Mobius/.

[63] P. Müller and A. Poetzsch-Heffter. Universes: A type system for controlling representation exposure. In A. Poetzsch-Heffter and J. Meyer, editors, *Programming Languages and Fundamentals of Programming*, pages 131–140. Fernuniversität Hagen, 1999. Technical Report 263, Available from sct.inf.ethz.ch/publications.

[64] P. Müller, A. Poetzsch-Heffter, and G. T. Leavens. Modular specification of frame properties in JML. *Concurrency and Computation: Practice and Experience*, 15:117–154, 2003.

[65] P. Müller, A. Poetzsch-Heffter, and G. T. Leavens. Modular invariants for layered object structures. *Science of Computer Programming*, 62:253–286, 2006.

[66] T. Nipkow, L. C. Paulson, and M. Wenzel. *Isabelle/HOL. A Proof Assistant for Higher-Order Logic.* Springer-Verlag, 2002.

[67] OpenJDK website. See http://openjdk.java.net/.

[68] OpenJML website. See http://sourceforge.net/apps/trac/jmlspecs/wiki/OpenJml.

[69] D. Park. Concurrency and automata on infinite sequences. In *Proceedings of the 5th GI-Conference on Theoretical Computer Science*, pages 167–183, London, UK, 1981. Springer-Verlag.

[70] D. Pichardie. Bicolano – Byte Code Language in Coq. Summary appears in [17], 2006.

[71] B. C. Pierce, C. Casinghino, M. Greenberg, V. Sjoberg, and B. Yorgey. *Software Foundations*. Distributed electronically, 2011.

[72] A. Platzer. An object-oriented dynamic logic with updates. Master's thesis, University of Karlsruhe, Department of Computer Science. Institute for Logic, Complexity and Deduction Systems, September 2004. http://i12www.ira.uka.de/%7Ekey/doc/2004/odlMasterThesis.pdf.

[73] A. Poetzsch-Heffter. Specification and verification of object-oriented programs. Habilitation thesis, Technical University of Munich, 1997.

[74] A. D. Raghavan and G. T. Leavens. Desugaring JML method specifications. Technical Report TR #00-03e, Department of Computer Science, Iowa State University, 2000. Current revision from May 2005.

[75] A. Rudich, Á. Darvas, and P. Müller. Checking well-formedness of pure-method specifications. In J. Cuellar and T. Maibaum, editors, *Formal Methods*, volume 5014 of *Lecture Notes in Computer Science*, pages 68–83. Springer-Verlag, 2008.

[76] P. H. Schmitt, M. Ulbrich, and B. Weiß. Dynamic frames in Java dynamic logic. In *Proceedings of the 2010 international conference on Formal verification of object-oriented software*, pages 138–152, Berlin, Heidelberg, 2011. Springer-Verlag.

[77] M. H. Sørensen and P. Urzyczyn. *Lectures on the Curry-Howard Isomorphism*. Elsevier, 2006.

[78] F. Spoto and E. Poll. Static analysis for JML's assignable clauses. In G. Ghelli, editor, *ACM Workshop on Foundations of Object-Oriented Languages*. ACM Press, January 2003. Available at www.sci.univr.it/~spoto/papers.html.

[79] J. van den Berg and B. Jacobs. The LOOP compiler for Java and JML. In *Proceedings of the 7th International Conference on Tools and Algorithms for the Construction and Analysis of Systems*, pages 299–312, London, UK, 2001. Springer-Verlag.

[80] J. van den Berg, E. Poll, and B. Jacobs. First steps in formalising JML: Exceptions in predicates. In *Formal Techniques for Java Programs. Proceedings of the ECOOP'00 Workshop. Techn. Rep., Fernuniversitat*, 2000.

[81] D. von Oheimb. *Analyzing Java in Isabelle/HOL: Formalization, Type Safety and Hoare Logic*. PhD thesis, Technische Universität München, 2001.

[82] D. R. Wallace and R. U. Fujii. Software verification and validation: An overview. *IEEE Software*, 6:10–17, 1989.

[83] C. Ye. Improving JML's assignable clause analysis. Technical report, Iowa State University, 2006.

[84] D. Zimmerman and R. Nagmoti. JMLUnit: The next generation. In Bernhard Beckert and Claude March, editors, *Formal Verification of Object-Oriented Software*, volume 6528 of *Lecture Notes in Computer Science*, pages 183–197. Springer Berlin / Heidelberg, 2011.

i want morebooks!

Buy your books fast and straightforward online - at one of world's fastest growing online book stores! Environmentally sound due to Print-on-Demand technologies.

Buy your books online at
www.get-morebooks.com

Kaufen Sie Ihre Bücher schnell und unkompliziert online – auf einer der am schnellsten wachsenden Buchhandelsplattformen weltweit! Dank Print-On-Demand umwelt- und ressourcenschonend produziert.

Bücher schneller online kaufen
www.morebooks.de

 VDM Verlagsservicegesellschaft mbH
Heinrich-Böcking-Str. 6-8   Telefon: +49 681 3720 174   info@vdm-vsg.de
D - 66121 Saarbrücken   Telefax: +49 681 3720 1749 www.vdm-vsg.de

Printed by Books on Demand GmbH, Norderstedt / Germany